THE REALM

OF THE

SPIRIT

FREQUENCY REVELATOR

GLOBAL DESTINY PUBLISHING HOUSE

Copyright © 2019 Frequency Revelator.

All rights reserved. No part of this book may be reproduced, stored in a retrieval system or transmitted in any form or by any means, electronic or mechanical, photographic (photocopying), recording or otherwise, without the written permission of the copyright holder.

The author has made every effort to trace and acknowledge sources, resources and individuals. In the event that any images or information has been incorrectly attributed or credited, the author will be pleased to rectify these omissions at the earliest opportunity.

Scripture quotations are all taken from the Holy Bible, the New King James Version (Authorized Version). First published in 1611. Quoted from the KJV Classic Reference Bible, Copyright © 1983 by the Zondervan Corporation

Published by the Author © Global Destiny Publishing House,

Sandton, South Africa

Website: www.globaldestinypublishers.co.za

Email: frequency.revelator@gmail.com

Phone: 0027622436745/ 0027785416006/0027797921646

Book layout and cover designed by Frequency Revelator

for Global Destiny Publishing House

OTHER 50 BOOKS PUBLISHED BY APOSTLE FREQUENCY REVELATOR:

How to Become a Kingdom Millionaire

Deeper Revelations of the Anointing

The Realm of Power to Raise the Dead

How To Raise The Dead Back To Life

Resurrection Power To Raise The Dead

How to Operate in the Realm of the Miraculous

The Realm of Glory

New Revelations of Faith

Unveiling the Mystery of Miracle Money

The Prophetic Dimension

The Prophetic Move of the Holy Spirit

The Ministry of Angels in the World Today

The Realm of the Spirit: A Divine Revelation of the Supernatural Realm

Throne Room Prayers: The Power of Praying in the Throne Room

7 Dimensions of the Supernatural Realm

Divine Rights and Privileges of a Believer

Keys to Unlocking the Supernatural

The Dynamics of God's Word

7 Supernatural Dimensions of Financial Prosperity

Spiritual Laws and Principles of the Kingdom

Rain of Revelations Daily Devotional Concordance

Practical Demonstrations of the Anointing

Understanding Times And Seasons In God's Calendar

How To Defeat The Spirit Of Witchcraft

The Practice Of God's Presence

21 Ways Of How To Hear God's Voice Clearly

How To Activate And Fully Exercise The Gifts Of The Spirit

The Prophetic Significance Of Gold Dust Silver Stones, Diamonds And Other Precious Stones

Deeper Revelations Of The Five-Fold Ministry

The Anatomy And Physiology Of The Anointing

Understanding Prophetic Dreams And Visions

Deeper Revelations Of The Glory Realm

The Power Of The Apostolic Anointing

The Anointing, The Mantle & The Glory

The Rain Of Fire: How To Operate In The Power Of Deliverance

The Art Of Spiritual Warfare

Understanding The Spiritual Legal Realm

Jehovah Yahweh: Understanding The Different names of God

The Power of Speaking In Tongues

Miracles, Signs And Wonders

The Essence of Worship

The Virtues of Healing Rains

The Realm Of Love

The Revelation Of Jesus Christ

The Second Coming Of Jesus Christ

DEDICATION

This publication remains an exclusive property of Heaven as it has been given birth to by the Holy Ghost in the Throne Room of Heaven. As a product of the fresh breath of God released in the deepest territories of the glory realm, it is geared at propagating Deeper Revelations of God's Word, Divine Presence and Supernatural Power from the Throne Room to the extreme ends of the World. There is a new type of man coming forth on the earth, to which this book is dedicated, who is rising beyond the confines and dictates of the realm of time, to unlock the *supernatural power* from the *Heaven's Power House* and precipitate it upon humanity in the extreme ends of the world; a distinct breed of believers who shall develop an insatiable appetite, perennial hunger and unquenchable thirst to tread on deeper and unexplored territories of the glory realm and engineer the uncharted, undefinable and unrecorded signs and wonders. Therefore, allow me space to officially announce the expiry date of mediocrity in your life for God is about to use you to explode in the demonstration of signs and wonders that will ruffle the feathers of those comfortable with the status quo and dazzle the minds of those who have pitched their tent in the valley of complacency and passivity.

Therefore, this book is dedicated to a new breed of millions of believers across the globe, whom through the revelations encapsulated in these pages, shall be catapulted into the greater depths of the miraculous, to practically demonstrate the viscosity of the power of God through undefinable, uncharted and unrecorded miracles, signs and wonders, to the glory of God! In this "God moment", you are therefore in line to break the World Record of Signs and Wonders, as you walk in the footsteps of the pioneers of the World revival such as Smith Wigglesworth, John G. Lake, Kenneth Hagin, Kathrine Khulman, Maria Woodworth-Etter, Saint Patrick and many others who left an irrefutable legacy and non-erasable mark in the arena of divine exploits. Get ready as God is strategically positioning you to a level of greater power in the realm of the spirit. God is about to explode in the demonstration of unusual signs and wonders that will dazzle the minds of religious charlatans and ruffle the feathers of the sceptics. As you inundate your spirit with Throne room revelations encapsulated in this book, you will explode in the demonstration of signs and wonders like a blast furnace and move in the demonstration of God's power like a man marching over his own yard and like a farmer sent out to the field for a bumper harvest and like a soldier sent out to war for a massacre. As you are about to be launched into an arena of the unfamiliar, welcome to a world in which it is naturally supernatural to demonstrate the power of God and miracles, signs and wonders are the order of the day. Welcome to the arena of divine exploits in which demonstrating the supernatural power of God through miracles, signs and wonders is the norm and raising the dead, raising the lame from wheelchairs, opening the eyes of the blind and healing the sick, is the order of the day!

ACKNOWLEDGEMENTS

First and foremost, I would like to ascribe to God, the Almighty all the glory and honour due to His name, for granting me through His grace, the divine opportunity to unveil the mysteries of the Kingdom and to practically demonstrate His supernatural power in this generation. This insightful, refreshing, profound and biblically sound revelation awakens the believer to the reality of the realm of the Spirit. It is chiefly the Holy Ghost who trained me in matters of operating in the deeper realms of the Spirit, hence it is my passion that the reader will see Him throughout the pages of this book and not any man. This writing appears in its current form due to the influence of several people, hence as a token of appreciation, I would like to offer my sincere thanks to all of them; Dr. Peter Tan of Eagle Vision Ministry for his anointed teachings on the Holy Spirit; Pastor Chris the President of the Believers' Love World International Ministry for his deep revelations on the ministry of the Holy Spirit and Pastor Benny Hinn of the World Healing Centre Church, who have immensely coached me in the direction of moving and operating in the deeper realms of the Holy Spirit and Apostle-Prophet Maphosa the President of the Manifest Sons of God Movement (MSG). These men of God truly made such a tremendous and overwhelming impact in my life, for it was under their tutelage that I developed an insatiable appetite and perennial hunger to explore the spirit world. I would like to express my deepest and most heartfelt gratitude to my most beautiful and adorable wife Delight Nokuthaba Mpofu who is the love of my life, my life coach and business partner, for having supported me in every way in my ministry as a renowned global author. She is indeed such an amazing blessing that I will forever be grateful to have received from God. I owe a special gratitude specifically to one of my best spiritual sons, Paramjeet Singh Makani from the nation of India, who inspires me a lot through the demonstration of undefinable, uncharted and unrecorded miracles, signs and wonders in this very hour.

I would like to extend my gratitude to my ministry partners for creating such a conducive platform and spiritual climate for me to move in greater depths, higher realms and deeper dimensions of the anointing to shake the nations and touch multitudes around the globe. It is for such a reason that

Frequency Revelator

I have been used by God as a vehicle to propagate the new waves of God's anointing to the furthest territories across the globe, to accomplish God's divine plans at such a time as this. My thanks also goes to Author House Publishing (UK) for making my dream of writing a reality and for enabling me to fulfil God's dream for propagating the world with the revelations of God's word. Allow me to extend a hand of appreciation to Great men and women of God all around the world who have been an inspiration to me: Dr Yana Johnson (London), Prophetess Nomsa M. Maida of New Breed ministry, Apostle Chris Lord Hills of the Supernatural Church, Dr Franklin (South Africa) and Prophet Mathew B. Nuek (Malaysia), for being instrumental in creating a conducive spiritual climate for the birthing forth of the revelations which God has laid in my spirit. Words fail to capture the gratitude I have for my own staff at Global Destiny Publishing House (GDP House), who have typified a new type of man coming forth on the earth, rising beyond the confines and dictates of the realm of time, to access higher realms of the Spirit: Further thanks goes to my ministry partners all over the world who have supported me tremendously by demonstrating an unquestionable thirst, perennial hunger and an insatiable appetite to read my books. I command the blessings of the Lord to abundantly marinate every sphere of your life with the rain of the anointing in Jesus Name!

-Apostle Frequency Revelator

Contents

Dedication	6
Acknowledgements	8
Preface: An Introductory Perspective To The Realm Of The Spirit	12
Chapter One: A Divine Revelation Of The Realm Of The Spirit	17
Chapter Two: A Divine Revelation Of Heaven And The Heavenly Realm	55
Chapter Three: Deeper Mysteries And Revelations Of The Spirit Realm	76
Chapter Four: The Divine Revelation Of The Throne Room Of Heaven	115
Chapter Five: The Degrees, Depths And Dimensions Of Operating In The Realm Of The Spirit	139
Chapter Six: The Heavenly Realm Of Music, Rythm And Melody	176
Chapter Seven: Prophetic Instructions On How To Effectively Operate In The Realm Of The Spirit	198
The Author's Profile	207

PREFACE

AN INTRODUCTORY PERSPECTIVE TO THE REALM OF THE SPIRIT

In retrospect to the deep mysteries and revelations encapsulated in this publication, it is of paramount significance to highlight that it is not possible to describe the various areas of the spiritual world in human language without bringing by the use of earth language a percentage of inaccuracy. Neither can anyone who has an encounter or visions of the spiritual world claim to have visited every aspect of that glorious world. The spiritual world consists of more varying aspects of the universe, which explains why upon visitation to the spirit world, many struggle to compose a single descriptive sentence of the spiritual world in human language. This is why Paul described his own experience of the spirit world in prophetic language as *"something inexpressible for man to tell "*. This is because there are multiples of creations of God in various dimensions of the universe that would take eternities to explore in the realm of the spirit.

For this reason many of those who have true spiritual experiences of the spiritual world, whether for a brief time or through extended encounters, bring only a small microscopic view of the spiritual realm. It is thus an error for anyone with those experiences to think that their encounter is inclusive of what the spiritual world is like and start building doctrines or dogma as to what the true spiritual world is like. It is for this reason that there is an urgent need for humanity to develop a comprehensive understanding of the dimensions of the spiritual world in order to put human existence on earth into proper perspective and order. The purpose for the writing of this book is to provide guidance about the spirit world so as to prepare multitudes of believers in the Body of Christ for the spiritual world. It gives glimpses of the realities of the spiritual world and provides those who have spiritual experiences with a scriptural basis by which to interpret and understand their own spiritual experiences.

Frequency Revelator

Let's jump-start our revelation of the spirit realm with reference to the supernatural experiences by one of God's Generals. Roland Bucks of blessed memory was caught up into the third heaven and was brought into the throne room of God. In there, he was given a paper, which contained events that were to occur in a specific period in his life. When he came out of the vision, he still had the paper in his hands. The paper was made of a very different material from any paper on earth and on it contained everything as it was told and written while he was in the vision. He was able to pull from the vision spiritual material and manifest it on earth. Imbued with this revelation, it gets us inquisitive to know more about the behind-the-veil supernatural realm and how we can navigate and manoeuvre our way through the corridors of the spirit realm to cause spiritual things to manifest in the natural realm.

DEFINITION OF THE SPIRIT REALM

A spiritual realm is an environment which has various places in the spirit, just like the physical realm has earth as its place. These places are called "dimensions", and totally vary. The realm of the spirit is not limited to three dimensions like our physical world. Spiritual realms are more complex than our three-dimension world. This makes it hard for our carnal minds to understand. Only a spiritual mind can fully comprehend the depths of the spirit realm. The spiritual aspect of life can be thought of as additional dimensions beyond the three core dimensions of length, height and breadth. The spiritual world is not another world in another place, but additional dimensions to the physical world we observe. The spiritual realms are just as real as the physical world that we can see although these two realms overlap and interact with each other. However, the realm of the spirit cannot be measured by geographical distance but by realms and dimensions. The first dimension is the sky, which we can all see with our naked eyes, then the next one is one where demonic and angelic spirits exist, waging war. The last one, which is the highest, is the realm where God exists. When God created the heavens and the earth in the beginning, as written in Genesis 1:1, it was not only His Throne that He created as has been erroneously presumed by many folks. The word *"heavens"* is a biblical name for the spiritual world that exists side by side, with the physical world. Notice, that word is in plural form which speaks of more than one Heaven. This implies that God created a multi-dimensional universe. We can only see the dimensions of

The Realm Of The Spirit

physical space and time, so we make assumptions that it's all there is, yet the spiritual dimensions consist of many more dimensions of reality beyond what we can see. They are three in totality, hence called Heavens.

Events in our physical world are shaped by activities in the spiritual realm.

The reason why we need to know about spiritual realms, is that the events in our physical world are shaped by activities in the spiritual realm. When we look at the physical world in isolation, we miss much of what is happening in the universe. Knowing about spiritual realms makes us powerful Christians, the same way that the ignorance of it makes us powerless Christians. Another reason is: God operates from the spiritual dimensions of reality, but He also created and sustains the physical world, where human beings dwell. At the beginning of creation, the Bible says the Spirit of God was hovering over the waters (Genesis 1:2). After the creation, the Holy Spirit remained close to the earth. So the closeness of the Spirit of God with Earth, shows the interlinking between the realm of the spirit and the realm of the natural. The Spirit was not in a distant place. The spiritual realms where He operates, hover just over the earth. The spiritual dimensions of reality are not way out at the edge of the universe, they exist in parallel to the physical world in which we live. These two realms of existence interact with each other in ways that we often cannot see, and fail to understand. We should not ignore what is happening in the spiritual realms that surround us, or we will misunderstand much of what happens in the world. Our knowledge of spiritual realms will change how we view the physical realm, which is the world we are in.

The spiritual realm determines what takes places in the natural realm

The spiritual realm is as real as the natural realm. In fact the spiritual realm determines what takes places in the natural realm. Because both realms are interfaced, events in one realm invariably affect the other. This publication therefore addresses all questions and answers relating to the spirit world as it expounds more about the heavenly places and how walking in the heavenly places and functioning in the heavenly places is like, so that we could understand the realm and the depth that God has for us. As we pray and enter into the spirit world it's important for us to understand what the spirit world is like. The truth is that you can never effectively operate in a world you have no clue about. The greatest challenge facing many believers is that the majority of the people do not know what it is like to really be in the depths of the spirit. Many Christians live their lives from the earth's perspective from the earthly perspective rather than from the heavenly perspective yet God's original Master plan for man was for him to permanently live in the supernatural realm. Most Christians are so earth-bound, they spend a considerable amount of time talking about carnal, worldly things. Very few live in the heavenly realm. They are overly conscious of the physical world and a little bit conscious of the spiritual things. On the contrary, it is imperative to move into that realm whereby you are conscious of the spiritual world and you are aware a little bit of the natural world. If you have an idea of what the spirit realm is like, it is possible to function with a high level of efficiency. Hence the purpose of this book is to share some experiences from the spirit realm that could make you desire to spend more time with God in order to want to move into that realm. By unveiling the deep secrets and mysteries of the spirit world, this publication gives humanity an idea of how the spirit world is like, how it functions and operates in relation to the physical world. Though you're in the world, you're not of this world. Therefore, you can't afford to live by the principles of this physical world. True success is spiritual, and it's based on spiritual principles. Become conscious of the spiritual realm, and control things from that realm. When you focus on and function from the realm of the spirit, nothing in this physical world will be able to hinder your success.

One of the laws of the Spirit is that you can only receive at the level of where you are spiritually

However, it is important to note that just reading through this book once intellectually does not mean that you might have got the full sense and understanding of what it conveys. One of the laws of the Spirit is that one can only receive at the level of where one is spiritually; thus, there are some things that you might have missed getting the spiritual understanding of until you re-read this book after receiving some spiritual experiences. It is for this reason that I urge the reader to read this book carefully and prayerfully. My prayer is that those who read this book would be enabled to progress further in their spiritual development both in this physical world and in the spiritual world. That is why this publication dwells more on the deep things in the spirit world and also on the experiential side. The reason for this publication is to bring us to a point where we are more open and

The Realm Of The Spirit

knowledgeable of the things of the spirit world, especially the heavenly realm so that when God begins to manifest and reveal the heavenly things, we can have some scriptures to compare to those things that He has revealed to us in His Word. It is for this reason that in this publication, reference is made to the Bible for all spiritual encounters and experiences. The Bible has some principles and guidelines as to what the spirit world is like. Therefore having looked at all these things of the spirit world from a Biblical perspective, we realize that it's because of what God wants us to be that He gives us different ability to function and to bring Him glory. I recall vividly the day I was caught up to the third heavens, an experience akin to that of Apostle Paul. I remember how the whole room changed and I was taken into glory, beyond the curtain of time. I saw the streets of heaven, the beauty which no language on earth can describe. Even those with the highest academic degrees of linguistic abilities will fail. In fact, I can definitely assure you that there is no language here on earth to describe such beauty. It would be a crime to compare it to this carcass we call earth. As I moved in the streets, seeing angelic beings litter the whole of heavens made me realise how great God is. After the study tour of seeing the beauty of the Heavenly realm, I was ushered back into my room but my body seemed not to have realized that I was no longer in the heavenly realm. The flesh of my body seemed as if was trying to jump off my bones. I tried to stop it physically but could not. The flesh had experienced the glory but the thought of Haven was very enlightening.

CHAPTER ONE

A DIVINE REVELATION OF THE REALM OF THE SPIRIT

It is imperative that we understand how the realm of the spirit operates so that we can learn how to effectively live and operate in that realm. We live in a multi-dimensional universe in which the spiritual dimensions exist in parallel to our three-dimensional physical world. The spiritual realms operate in continuity with the natural world that we observe. Most humans cannot see into the spiritual dimensions, so we can only observe the physical side of existence. Our eyes are calibrated for a physical world and are so attuned to seeing a three-dimensional world that we find anything grander difficult to conceive. The modern world has taught us that the physical world is all that is important, but that's so not true! Our Education system doesn't teach about the spiritual realms; this is because it's something that can't be scientifically observed, and consequently thought of, as surreal. Consequently, we end up imbibing this materialistic understanding of the world, which we were taught in our classrooms. That is why I strongly contend that education is the elimination of spiritual knowledge. The truth is that events in our physical world are shaped by activities in the spiritual realm. When we look at the physical world in isolation, we miss much of what is happening in the universe. The spiritual realms are not limited to three dimensions like our physical world. The Bible does not tell us how many more, but the fact that it is more complex than our three-dimension world means that it is hard for our natural minds to fathom. The spiritual aspect of life can be thought of as additional dimensions beyond the three core dimensions of the earth. The spiritual world is not another world in another place, but additional dimensions to the physical world we observe. It is based on spiritual laws and principles established by God which are completely different from those of the natural world.

The only real and solid things in the spiritual world are those made up of "spiritual substance.

From the material and physical perspective of casual readers of the Word, the spiritual world seems to be *"airy fairy"*, dimension that is not solid to the physical senses. From the perspective of the spiritual world, it is our material world that is not of *"solid substance."* The only real and solid things in the spiritual world are those made up of "spiritual substance." Everything material looks like it is made up of *"vapour"* from the highest spiritual perspective (James 4:14). The whole material world looks like a "mist" that is fragile and about to be blown away. One can understand why it looks so foolish to the spiritual world when humans born to live in the spiritual world, spend their entire lives clinging on the things of the natural realm which are made up of temporal substance and will all soon pass away like mist (2 Corinthians 4:18). To those who live in the highest realms of God's glory, only the spirit of believers are visible as they shone like bright torches through the darkness of this world; for the spiritual is the only true reality in the spiritual world.

The spirit world is a realm that doesn't operate on logic as is the case in our natural world. It is a realm where our natural logic breaks down.

The truth is that the spirit world is complex and difficult to fully comprehend. As we begin to explore this realm, we realise that the spirit world needs a lot of interpretation. Let's refer to 2 Corinthians 12:1-4 where Paul testifies that:

> *"I must boast; there I nothing to be gained by it but I will go on to visions and revelations of the Lord. I know a man in Christ who fourteen years ago was caught up to the third heaven -whether in the body or out or the body I do not know, God knows. And I know that this man was caught up into Paradise -whether in the body or out of the body I do not know, God knows -and he heard things that cannot be told, which man may not utter".*

Paul is of course referring to himself because in verse 7 he wrote that *unless I should be exalted above measure by the abundance of revelations.* So, we know that he is speaking about himself *in the third person* and of the abundance of the revelations that had come into his life. And he articulated a phrase that *he heard things that were inexpressible*. This is because the spirit world is a realm that doesn't operate on logic as is the case in our natural world. The spirit is a realm where our natural logic breaks down. When Paul was catapulted into the highest spiritual realms of Heaven, he was dramatically affected by what he saw to the extent that he could not describe it (2 Corinthians 12:2-4). For a highly schooled man like Paul, educated under the feet of the greatest scholar Gamaliel, it was not possible for him to lack human vocabulary to describe what he saw in the spirit realm. That means the spirit realm was so deep that human language could not articulate it accurately. In the realm of the spirit, human language is limited and only designed to describe the physical world, hence it could not qualify to adequately describe the realities of the spiritual world. Consider what he had to say about the realities of the spirit realm in 1 Corinthians 2:9: *Eye has not seen, nor ear heard, and no human mind has conceived*. This is to tell you that we need spiritual insight and revelation to understand what is happening in the spiritual dimension. It is for this reason that Paul prayed that the *"eyes our hearts may be enlightened"* (Ephesians 1:18).

Man was designed to live in the supernatural realm

Did you know that man was designed to live in the supernatural realm? Prior to the fall, Adam and Eve could see clearly into the spiritual world. Moving from the natural realm into the spiritual realm was tantamount to moving from his living room into the bed room. They were so attuned into the spirit such that they were able to walk with God in the cool of the evenings and speak directly to Him. Likewise, they were able to see the devil, when he came to tempt them. His activity in the spiritual dimension made him appear like a snake from a physical perspective. However, when Adam and Eve sinned, there was a sudden transaction and drastic transition in the realm of the spirit such that their sight was changed hence they could no longer see into the spiritual realms. Paradoxically, the Bible says *their eyes were opened, and they realized they were naked* (Genesis 3:7). This statement is a huge irony because their eyes were opened to the natural world yet closed to the spiritual realms. Previously, when they could see the effulgence of the glory of the Heavenly realms, their observation of the physical world was dimmed, and they did not notice they were naked. But once the light of Heavenly glory was turned off, their view of the physical world was greatly amplified, such that they realised for the first time that they were naked. However, after the death and resurrection of the Lord Jesus Christ, he gained a spiritual body, which enabled him to interact more freely with the spiritual world and those who receive Him are granted the same grace that enables us to interact with the spiritual dimensions in the same way that Adam and Eve did before the fall. We are now able to see the glory of God in totality as we are catapulted to the highest realms of the supernatural.

The spiritual realm is diametrically opposed to the natural realm

The spiritual realm is diametrically opposed to the natural realm such that at times you might get a shock of your life to see in the spirit world things like a spirit going through a wall, a scroll flying about in the sky or something that our natural mind says it cannot be. Let's consider a quintessential example in the book of Zechariah. 5:5 *Then the angel who talked with me came forward and said to me, "Lift up your eyes, and see what this is that goes forth."* He looks and there is a basket flying about. Where on planet earth have you ever heard of such a thing as a flying basket? To make this worse, it says in verse 9 that he raised his eyes and looked and there were 2 women coming with the wind in their wings. And their wings were like the wings of a stork and not like an angel. And they lifted up the basket between earth and heaven. Where on earth have you ever heard of such a thing as women with wind in their wings? Up to Zechariah's time all the manifestation of winged creatures are men. I mean the angels appeared like men but here it says these 2 ladies were flying about and their wings looking like storks. This is a deep spiritual realm where things are divinely coded in symbols. It's in that realm that Paul refers to when he says in I Corinthians 2:14 that *the unspiritual man does not understand the things of the spirit because they're spiritually discerned.* Sometimes you could be so overwhelmed and terrified by what you see in the spirit world that you just walk about in a trance and people wonder what's wrong with you. The experiences in the spirit realm are so deep that they boggle your mind, challenge your status quo, revolutionise your personality and ruffle the feathers of those who are swimming through the shallow streams of spiritual understanding. It is for this reason that we need to develop a Heavenly understanding of the properties of the spirit realm such as distance, time, matter, space, velocity and density and other diverse attributes of the spirit realm discussed below:

The spirit world is a different world altogether and far too many times we are trying to interpret things from the natural point into the spirit.

Sometimes we interpret the spirit realm wrongly some time we interpret correctly. Do you remember that when Paul met Jesus on the way to Damascus and was struck down by the power of God, some said it thundered and some really hear it? At times how the spirit realm is like depends on our interpretation. In the spirit things are not the way they look from your natural eye. Who have thought of picking up the snake by the tail? God did. He says Moses pick up the snake by the tail. Who would have thought that you could get water from the rock? God did. And when we approach the spiritual world and the Holy Spirit with a natural mind the Bible says in I Corinthians. 2 that the natural man does not receive the things of the Spirit of God. If we cannot relate to the Spirit and we interpret a lot of things of the Spirit in a natural way, we will always get it wrong. The spirit world is different with different laws. Let's say you take a rocket and you go into space and you are orbiting in a space station. You are in what I call free fall. When you are in free fall, things are different. You cannot walk the way you walk because you will be floating. And you cannot clean up the things the way you clean here on earth because if you drop something it floats. The spirit world is a different world altogether and far too many times we are trying to interpret things from the natural point into the spirit. We should never do that. We should let go and let the Spirit teach us what it is. If you cannot see into something you have to trust someone who is inside to tell you what the inside looks like. If you send someone to a tunnel and nobody else have been through that tunnel with a searchlight, and all you can hear is that person's voice over the microphone describing all the things on the inside. You got to trust what that person is telling you. You trust the Holy Spirit. You trust Him to tell you things of the spirit realm. And they have to be in line with the Word of God. The reason why God gives us the Word is so that you could double check what is inside and He will show you some things. It will be a common denominator throughout the Word of God.

The Realm Of The Spirit

PERCULIAR PROPERTIES OF THE REALM OF THE SPIRIT

There is no distance in the realm of the spirit

It is worth exploring the divine truth that the realm of the spirit has no distance. Geographical distance is never there in the spirit world. When we talk about geographical distance that also incorporates the distance between the Heavenly realm and the natural realm. The challenge that many believers face is that they are too earthly bound hence they keep thinking the things of the spirit in geographical terms such as here, there, yonder, beyond yet there is no distance with God in the spirit realm. And that's why it's so hard for such people to think that their spirit could be here on earth while at the same time it is operating in Heaven. They keep thinking about Heaven in earthly terms. The truth is that the realm of the spirit has no distance. That means that as you pray and enter the depths of the spirit, some of the things you see and experience could be from another place or another planet or it could be nearby. Remember our spirit can be here and yet there. In the spirit realm it is more in the experiential realm. When your spirit is in the throne room you experience certain things although your spirit is there and here, because in the spiritual realm there is no distance. There is no distance to experiencing the presence of God. Some people say you feel closer to God when you are flying in an airplane. After all you are about 36,000 feet above the earth and in the spirit world there is no distance.

To substantiate this revelation with reference to scriptural evidence, in 2 Kings 5:20-27, we see some statements made by Elisha that give us a clue of the spirit realm in terms of the how and what of the spirit world. It present an account of how Naaman was healed and consequently offered some gifts to Elisha who refused the gifts but Gehazi, Elisha's servant was covetous and went after those gifts. Gehazi said, *"See, my master has spared this Naaman the Syrian, in not accepting from his hand what he brought. As the Lord lives, I will run after him, and get something from him."* So Gehazi followed Naaman. And when Naaman saw someone running after him, he alighted from the chariot to meet him, and said, *"Is all well?"* And he said, *"All is well. My master has sent me to say, "There has just now come to me from the hill country of Ephraim two young men of the sons of the prophets; pray, give them a talent of silver and two festal garments."* And Naaman said, *"Be pleased to accept two talents."* And he urged him, and tied up two talents of silver in two bags, with two festal garments, and laid them upon two of his servants; and they carried them before Gehazi. And when he came to the hill, he took them from their hand, and put them in the house, and he sent the men away, and they departed. He went in, and stood before his master, and Elisha said to him, *"Where have you been Gehazi?"* And he said, *"Your servant went nowhere."* But he said to him:

> **"Did I not go with you in spirit** *when the man turned from his chariot to meet you? Was it a time to accept money and garments, olive orchards and vineyards, sheep and oxen, menservants and maidservants? Therefore the leprosy of Naaman shall cleave to you, and to your descendants for ever."* So he went out from is presence a leper, as white as snow.

Notable in this Biblical account is that Elisha was taken up right at the moment as Gehazi was turning back not as he was going. The moment the man was turning back, Elisha was there in the spirit and he saw the whole thing and heard everything yet they could not see him for he was in the spirit world. In the occult realm, which is a non-Christian realm, they have what you call *astral traveling*. Those who yield themselves to the occult state of spirit realm seem to be able to travel into that realm. They thought that everything in that realm is good not realizing there are also evil spirits out there. But there is a realm that even the unbelievers who yield themselves utterly to the realm of the spirit seem to be able to move into which is a realm of divine transportation in the spirit.

In the realm of the spirit, things are not learnt but revealed

It is worth noting that in the realm of the spirit, things are not learnt but revealed. In other words, in the realm of the spirit, knowledge is neither acquired through diligent study nor memorisation of scripture but through supernatural revelation. Paul says in 2 Corinthians 5: 16 *"Therefore, from now on, we regard no one according to the flesh. Even though we have known Christ according to the flesh, yet we know Him thus no longer."* That tells us that the only true fellowship is in the spirit world. It says that 'from now on' and it is in reference to those who are born of the spirit of God, we will not regard one another in the flesh anymore. But we will look for that spiritual kindredness, that fellowship lies in the spirit realm as we walk like Jesus with God the Father, intimately. It becomes a torture when you walk with those who are still carnal. The truth is that we know each other in the spirit. But how do we know each other in the spirit? There is something that happens in the spirit realm that if a name of someone you don't even know

The Realm Of The Spirit

is mentioned, you instantly know who he is and his closeness of walk with God even though you haven't even heard anybody mention his name but you supernaturally know him in the spirit realm. You might not have met him in the flesh or know how he looks like but through the course of your fellowship with God in the spirit realm in the presence of God, you know that person already in the spirit. This is how people who function in the prophetic realm receive supernatural revelation about the names of people, cities and even regions.

There is a knowing in the spirit realm among those who walk close with God. This is what John spoke about when he said *you have an anointing from the Holy One and you know all things* (1 John 2:20). When you walk close with God you can meet and say to each other, *"I know you!"* Where did we meet? Somewhere in the third heaven. Not in the flesh but in the spirit. When the seven sons of Sceva tried to cast out the demons, the demons cried, *"Jesus, I know. Paul, I know. But who are you?"* The demons didn't know them and it was the end of their ghost-busting business. Demons recognise those who move in the spirit and fellowship with God. They knew Jesus and Paul because they were constantly in the spirit realm and they know all their activities. If you were to visit Heaven on a study tour, there is a consciousness in you that the saints in Heaven know that you are there. It seems the people in Heaven know what happens to us spiritually. They know if you are walking with the Lord or not. They can sense your spiritual development and growth. When anything spiritual is about to happen in your life, they also seem to know it. The awareness of them is as if you are very close to them even if you may be very far from them.

Paul corroborates in 1 Corinthians 13:12 that, *"We shall know as we are known."* In Heaven when you meet one another, you will know everything about that person, even before knowing their name: their character, their gift, their calling, and their inclination. A portion of that Heavenly experience is possible here on earth. At the mount of transfiguration, the three disciples, Peter, James and John had not even met personally Moses and Elijah. How did they know it was Moses and Elijah? Through supernatural revelation. There is something about the spirit realm that many believers have not known yet. Right now, if the Apostle Paul were to come and stand here without mentioning his name, you will know it is Paul. There is something about communion in the spirit realm that when you see someone, you immediately you know everything about him. Just as in the physical realm, you can tell whether someone is sad or happy; you can know if they are troubled or happy by their facial, physical expression. In the earthly sense, the communion of the saints is so powerful. The day will come when we understand this realm and our spirits know how to have communion. You can be there, I can be here and as we spend time with God, our spirits can meet in Heaven. Sometimes people ask me how I know things. I say, "I know because my spirit has been with that person. I know exactly what they are going through." Some of you who are married, you know it, with your loved ones. Something goes on in their life and you know it, you feel it, tangibly. Like twins, you know exactly what is going on. It is a powerful realm of fellowship and communion the church has not tapped on.

There is a higher realm in the spirit of knowing, communion, and experiencing *koinonia* that is powerful. That is the kind of communion of the saints that takes place when we learn to commune with one another. One day, when we get used to our physical body flowing with your spirit, your body can say to your spirit, "*Take me along*," and you are translated across nations without a passport. But make sure you don't lose your faith because you need to get back without your passport too. That is how it is going to take place, through our growth in the Body of Christ, the communion of the saints.

There is no time in the realm of the spirit. The time dimension is not of essence in the realm of the spirit

There is a realm in the throne room of God, which has a very lasting effect and impression on my heart and in my mind. And that is where at the throne room of God and the experience of the throne is such that all time ceases. There is no past there, no future there and no present. All the realm of what we have lived with all of our life doesn't exist in God. The realm of time doesn't exist at God's throne. Imagine time to be like a big circle around the throne of God. Of course it goes far out into the galaxy and into the universe. The whole universe and the whole galaxy revolve around the throne of God. And God's throne is at the centre of the universe. God's throne is at the centre of all His creation. It is just like the spokes of a wheel. Like my hands being stretched forth, right now, like the spokes of a wheel. There is a scientific principle we need to be aware of that is taking place every time something turns. As I go round in a circle with my hands outstretched like the spokes of a wheel, the velocity of my fingertips is greater than the velocity of my head going round. My fingertips have to move a greater distance in the same time than my head. And right in the central point of my body there would be no motion at all. That is why when ice skaters do the ice ballet, they use the scientific principle of motion and control the diameter or radius of the circle that they are turning. For example if their hands are stretched out and they start turning, they will move to a certain "X" amount of velocity. But if they suddenly pull their hands in, it will cause them to move much faster. Then to slow down again, they would stretch out again. All those principles are always there in nature. The very tip of the spoke of the wheel would have to move at a faster rate than where the centre of the wheel is.

God is in the centre of all His creation. All His creation in time exists at the spokes of the wheel. And the nearer you move into God, the more you realize that time stands still. Time exists only in the spokes of the wheel. And that's something strange because we cannot conceive of being timeless. How does God view our creation then? We say that God is the Alpha and Omega. He is the one who was, who is, and who is to come. Now God can see the past. He can see the present and He can see the future as if the whole thing is completed. So, when God looks from His throne, to Him it looks as if everything is in the past tense, like everything has been completed. The Old Testament has a very strange word that the translators have difficulty translating. It is what you call the vowel conjugation. And when it is used in a certain manner, it is God speaking in a past tense. And there are many passages that are familiar to you and I that the translators had put it where God said to Abraham. Our translators said, "God said, 'I would make you a father of many nations.' "That's what our translators in the English version say. But in the Hebrew it actually says I have made you a father of many nations. You and I know that when God was speaking to Abraham at that time he didn't even have a son. And yet God said I have made you a father of many nations.

The New Testament also tries to explain that principle. In Romans 4:117-22, it says, as it is written, *"I have made you the father of many nations"* In the presence of the God whom he believed, who gives life to the dead and calls into existence the things that do not exist. In hope he believes against hope, that he should become a father of many nations; as he had been told, *"So shall your descendants be."* He did not weaken in faith when he consider his own body, which was as good as dead because he was about a hundred years old, or when he considered the barrenness of Sarah's womb. No distrust made him waver concerning the promise of God, but he grew strong in his faith as he gave glory to God, fully convinced that God was able to do what he had promised. That is why his faith was *"reckoned to him as righteousness."* There are several things that are mentioned here. First God lives in a realm where everything is past tense to Him. Abraham was not yet physically a father of many nations. But God sees past, present, future as past. As if it has already taken place. Here is an important key Abraham needed to move into that same realm to bring it to pass. Since the fall of man circumstances and the physical world are not fully obeying God. That is why Paul in Romans 8 tells us the whole world is groaning. If the whole world were functioning perfectly it wouldn't groan. Obviously the groan is caused by forces that are resisting the way God want things to be. Not everything is in God's perfect will yet which is obvious. Otherwise the Lord's Prayer will not be that His will be done on earth as it is in heaven. It is because His will is not being done on earth. So there are a lot of things that are not flowing in God's power and God's will. How do we move circumstances? Definitely not by our own strength. Definitely not by our own power. Human beings have been altering and changing this earth with brute force as much as they can. But even those brute forces have been guided sometimes by the mercy of God through ideas that God gives to adapt this world to be more a habitable world.

In the realm of the spirit, there is no past, present and future everything has been completed. It is all in the past tense

At the throne room of God there is no present, past or future. When your spirit is praying about anything and the moment you cross the line into the throne room something happens to your spirit. What you ask for in the future becomes past. As far as God is concerned it has been done. Time is irrelevant. Our understanding of His view of time is that the past, present and future are one. When we say past, present and future are one I like to make it stronger by saying that everything is past tense to Him. It is as if it is already occurred. I want to touch two things that are peculiar in that realm so that you could flow into that realm and understand how we pray from that realm. *No. 1 in that realm of the heavenly place all things have been completed.* There is nothing that is not finished. When you leave that realm, it is when you experience things that are not completed yet. But in that realm, everything is completed. To God our future and the future of all that is to be done is past tense. When Jesus intercedes for us at the right hand of God He is interceding that plan for us as completed. He is interceding

The Realm Of The Spirit

not because it has not been completed. He sees it as completed and He intercedes for us to enter that realm. It's a powerful realm.

Let me refer to the Scripture to give you an idea of what that realm is. Consider Revelations 5 when no one could open the seal. Testifying of that experience, John says, *one of the elders said to me, "Do not weep. Behold, the Lion of the tribe of Judah, the Root of David, has prevailed to open the scroll and to lose its seven seals.* In verse 6 it says the Lamb came as though it had been slain having seven horns, seven eyes, which the seven spirits of God sent out to all the earth. So, when the Lamb of God opens the seals all those things and the revelations were released. Have you noticed that some of those things which took place in chapter 6, 7 and so forth are in that seal. And a lot of those things have not taken place yet. It was in a book and that book has already completed. It was not written at the time when Jesus the Lamb opens the seals. It was in a book, in the past tense. Its future to us and John the apostle, but it was past tense. It was even written down. But it's not opened to release it to take place on this earth. I want you to consider the fact that in that realm the Heavenly place at the right hand of God at the throne of Jesus everything is completed. There is nothing that has not been completed. It's a different realm that operates at the throne of God.

To cement this revelation with reference to scriptural evidence, let's turn to Ephesians 1:4 *just as He chose us in Him before the foundation of the world, that we should be holy and without blame before Him in love, having predestined us to adoption as sons by Jesus Christ to Himself, according to the good pleasure of His will.* You and I were not even created yet but God has already seen us at His throne. I pray that you open your eyes to understand what the throne room of God is like. Everything of existence or creation is past tense. When it says that He was, He is and He is to come, that in God past, present and future are in Him, what does it mean? Everything is past to Him. Everything is completed. It's all in one book. You have a book that has recorded your life some time ago and therefore which is past tense to you. It's completed in God before there was even an idea of your existence. Before Adam and Eve were created, you were already in the mind of God. In Revelations 13:8 now you begin to have an idea of why Jesus talked about His glory up there in Heaven before the foundation of the world. There is something in that realm that is peculiar to our finite mind on this earth. The Bible records in Revelations 13:8 that *all who dwell on the earth will worship him (that is the anti-Christ), whose names has not been written in the Book of Life of the Lamb slain from the foundation of the world.* Do you notice that it says Jesus was slain from the foundation of the world?

Frequency Revelator

We know that Jesus died on the cross of Calvary around A.D. 27 to A.D. 30. How was He slain before the foundation of the world? He was not slain physically yet but He was already slain before the foundation of the world because in the mind of God in the throne room it's all done, all completed. That is the first thing that we need to understand.

This is to tell you that if you are praying and you cannot see what you are praying for has already been completed, you haven't entered the throne room yet. How can you know that you are in the throne room when you don't know what the throne is like? How can you say that you have been downtown if you didn't see the cars, the people, the traffic lights, the shopping malls, the post office, the hotels and restaurants? When you go downtown and see such places, then you know that you are in that place. It is possible to enter the throne room based on Ephesians. 2:6, that He has raised us up together, and made us sit together in the Heavenly places in Christ Jesus and based on Hebrews 4: 16, Let us therefore come boldly to the throne of grace that we may obtain mercy and find grace to help in time of need. How do you know spiritually you are functioning from the throne room, when you haven't seen the finished work from the point of view of the throne room? When you don't know what is like in the throne room, you have not entered the throne room yet. Remember this if you really prayed through, you would have entered the throne room and seen the end results in the spiritual realm.

The greatest challenge facing many believers is that we are so used to living on this planet earth that our consciousness of time is linear, that future means future, the present means present and the past is past. But in Heaven all present, past and future is past. That is why in Ephesians 1 when he introduces the subject he says *He has blessed us with all spiritual blessings in the heavenly places.* It doesn't say that He is going to bless us but He has already done it. Whatever you are praying for, if it's in the will of God but you can't see the end result and can't see what it will be like, you are not in the throne room yet. You are still somewhere in the Outer Court. But when you reached the throne room, it's done. I don't mean that when you are in throne room that in the physical sense it's done. But you can see it done. Then when you pray you can feel it is done. Then it may take some time before physically it is manifested and done. All prayers that never gain access to the throne room will never be answered. Because Christians don't understand what the throne room is like and how to bring their petitions to God, they are always struggling in the Outer Court and they can never have the picture in

The Realm Of The Spirit

them that it's being done. And all the time they are out there, they are always struggling. Every prayer must be directed to the throne room. That is why Jesus teaches us to pray to the Father in His name by the power of the Holy Spirit. That is why Jesus does not want us to pray to the Holy Spirit or pray to Him. He wants us to direct our petitions right to the Father God's throne. When some people say, "I have entered into the throne room," what they mean is they have experienced the presence of God. But there are other side manifestations beside the presence of God. Sometimes the feeling of the presence of God is subjective. If you are regular in a spirit-filled church and you have got used to the presence of God, you may not feel the difference. But visitors that come in and worship the Lord in the same church, immediately the hairs on their hands would stand up; they would cry from the beginning to the end of the service because the presence is too strong. But if you are constantly in the presence, you may be so used and acclimatized to that presence, you may not feel the difference. Or if it's a manifestation that you have never experienced before and you enter into that realm where the manifestation is going on you will feel the difference and have a sense of the presence of God but it's a subjective feeling. See our ability to feel the presence of God is subjective and it is developed by our private devotional life. The presence of God is always there.

Sometimes I can feel the presence of God when people don't feel anything. If you go to any church service and start criticizing and having hurt feelings, you would never feel the presence of God in any place even though the presence of God is there. Our attitudes can affect us in the presence of God. Or in our plain laziness, we have taken things of God for granted and it affects our feeling of the presence of God. I am saying that one of our senses is to feel the presence of God when we enter the throne of God. But strong feeling is subjective. When you live in the presence of God you are used to a certain level of presence all the time. But there are some other manifestations where you see those things that have been done in the past, even though they would only take place in the future. In the book "*Angels on Assignment,*" it was written that when Roland Buck went to Heaven, God showed him many specific things that would come to pass, among which was the election of Karol Wyotila as Pope John Paul II. Before that event took place, Roland Buck had already seen it happening. This is an example of what it means when you see some things that have been done in the past but will occur in the future. When this happens, you know you have entered that realm. Whatever you are praying about as long as you can't see it, you are not there yet. You got to pray until you see it, which is a journey from the Outer Court into the Holy place and into the Most Holy place. That journey may mean that you got to give thanksgiving and observe the other principles of prayer. Then you got to pray after you see it until you feel it. And you know on your inside you have prayed through. You have released something about those things to God. Sometimes it takes more than one release. Then it will come by itself into the physical manifestation.

The spirit realm functions at different realms of glory.

Did you know that there are different realms, depths and dimensions of glory in the spirit realm? That is why the Bible speaks of moving form glory to glory implying that there are levels in glory through which humanity can transition from lower panes to higher planes of glory. Paul contends in I Corinthians 15: 39-44 that:

For not all flesh is alike, but there is one kind for men, another for animals, another for birds, and another for fish. There are celestial bodies and there are terrestrial bodies; but the glory of the celestial is one, and the glory of the terrestrial is another. There is one glory of the sun, and another glory of the moon, and another glory of the stars; for star differs from star in glory. So is with the resurrection of the dead. What is sown is perishable, what is raised is imperishable. It is sown in dishonour, it is raised in glory. It is sown in weakness, it is raised in power. It is sown a physical body, it is raised a spiritual body. If there is a physical body, there is also a spiritual body.

Mind the words in verse 41 which says that there is one glory of the sun another of the moon, another glory of the stars. Then he says one star differs from another in its various stages of glory. We know that from the natural viewpoint of science that stars have inherent temperatures. There are blue stars, red stars and all the different types of stars in their various states of heat and the light that they bring forth. And that is compared to the glory of God upon our physical body and upon our lives.

The flowers, the trees, the rocks and all the creation of God that is in the heavens have a certain form of glory. From each of these creation there is something that emanate from them to the beholder that causes the one who looks at these things to want to praise God, to want to bless and worship God. And that's the glory of God that is upon the creation in Heavens. There is also a glory of God on this planet earth too. But the terrestrial glory is lesser than the celestial glory that is the Heavenly glory. And each of us is to radiate and to bring forth a particular aspect of God himself. Even among stars as Paul says there are different differing glories. And even among redeemed men there are different created glories that each one of them is destined to bring forth. Some people have high rank of glory in Heaven, while others who on earth seemed mighty to men were assigned to lower planes of glory and usefulness in Heaven. You could be high and mighty on this earth but in Heaven you could be low in the rank of glory. It doesn't mean that God doesn't want you to get into His rank of higher glory. When one leaves this world, he enters into the spiritual plane that corresponds with the spiritual state in which he would have died. And if you did not develop your character in Christ you would have to go to a lower plane and there you continue developing. Those who touched on the higher realm of glory go straight into the higher realm of glory. It is not fame or wealth on this earth that determines your place of glory in heaven. That is why we should not go after the pride of life or the lust of the eyes, the lust of the flesh and the lust of the things of this world. The book of James tells us that if the desire for the things of this earth is still in us then friendship with the world is enmity with God. We need to live our life for eternity.

Words are pictures in the spirit world. In the realm of the spirit, things are created by imagination and thoughts

One characteristic feature of the spirit realm is that it operates on the basis of pictures, images, codes and symbols. In actual fact, every word you say in the spirit comes out in a picture. While in that realm, whatever words that is spoken forms an object. For example, when you mention the word, "book", a book would appear. Literally in the spirit you see a book being formed right in front of you. If you confess *I'm rich*, riches suddenly appear in front of you and are presented to your hands. By the same token, if you declare *I have a house*, a house appears right in front of you. It is like in Heaven you ask God, "I would like extra rooms to my mansion." In an instant it is there. Do you remember that in Genesis 1 God said *let there be light* and instantly it came. This is exactly how the spirit world operates. What you say becomes. It is for this reason that the spirit realm is 100% picture and vision. That is what the prophet Joel spoke about in Acts 2 when he proclaimed that *young man shall see visions and old man shall dream dreams and they shall prophesy*. All these are ways of God working through pictures. This is contrary to the natural world in which we work with words and logic. But in the spirit world it is like every thought is real, every word is real. And you cannot differentiate words and reality. Word is reality. One sister was sharing that one day she confessed, "*I have got this tremendous headache.*" The moment she said, "*headache*" suddenly the picture of a car accident came. And I said it had something to do with an accident. She did not have an accident. Then I began to tap further. The moment she said she did not have the accident immediately the Lord said it was a close person of her who had that accident. From that day that accident occurred and lost this good friend of her, under that depression the headache came.

Do you know that in the realm of the spirit, what you think becomes. When you are thinking of something, there is a creative force that is released. And when you begin to move and experience the spirit realm you realize that the thoughts and the words that flow forth from your life have tremendous creative force. Every time you say a word, you see a picture. But in the spirit realm the picture is the word and the word is the picture. It is just like a person sharing with me about something in their past. While he is sharing I begin to see the picture of what he is sharing about. I begin to see some of those things actually occurring. It is just like if I were having a conversation with a brother and I ask, "How are you? Did you have a good day?" And he says it was a "Busy day but meaningful." The moment he says, "Busy day and meaningful." I begin to see a road. If he keeps talking then the scene starts coming up and I see a lot of other details concerning how his day has been. I am just giving you an example of what that spirit realm is like. If you move more into that sooner or later you can start picking up the person's name, home address, telephone numbers, names of siblings and other minute details about that person.

In the realm of the spirit, things are created by vision

In the realm of the spirit, visualisation is such a powerful creative force by which things are brought into existence. The words produce the pictures and the words are the pictures. In Kenneth Hagin's book, *I Believe in Visions* in his first vision, he said that he was given a scroll. He read the prophecy from the scroll. Every time he read one line he would see the action come. When he prophesies famine he sees the famine. When he prophesied war he saw the war. That's what the spirit realm is like. This is the same principle by which God too Abraham to see the vision of the stars and sky and then told him that his descendants shall be as many as stars. In a like manner God

The Realm Of The Spirit

took Moses to a high mountain and caused him to see the land of Canaan in its fullness and said as far as you can see, you have it. Elijah also told Elisha that if you can only see me when I'm taken up, it is yours. All these people tapped into that realm where things become reality with visualisation. It is of paramount importance to highlight the divine truth that imagination or visualisation has such a strong magnetic force that has an ability to rain the power of God in any particular situation. In a practical sense, before you could speak the word of God in any situation, it is important that you start by harnessing the power of God though your imagination. This is because there is power in thoughts, visualisation and imagination. The greater truth is that if we want to delve or plunge into a perennial pool of miracles, we have to act like God. Acting like God means thinking as God thinks and seeing as God sees. Therefore, if you want to see an avalanche of the power of God, think what you want to see happen in the natural realm. Imagination goes hand in hand with visualisation. Once you are able to tap into the realm of the spirit to see what you want to do, then it will be easy to manifest it in the physical. One of the powerful ways through which God performs miracles is that He first thinks what He wants to see. As He thinks it, it happens in the physical realm. This is the exact pattern by which He created and moulded the physical world.

Unfortunately, some people do not see the results of power displayed in their lives because they are quick to speak when in actual fact God's vision has not yet fully grown in their spirits. Therefore, when they speak their spirit is empty, hence there are no results of power manifested. Before God declared that, *"Let there be light"*, the Bible says *the spirit of God was hovering over the surface of the deep* (Genesis 1:2). In other words, He had an imagination of the exact picture and prototype of the world He wanted to create before He could speak it into existence. The act of the Spirit hovering upon the surface of the deep gives a revelation of Gods imagination of the exact world He wanted to create. In a way, He was incubating thoughts, habituating ideas of how He would go about doing it and when His imagination was fully conceived, God spoke the world into existence. This tells me that God Himself has an imagination. God has an analytical part to His nature. We were made like Him. We have an imagination because we were made like Him. Before God said anything, or any Word, I want you to see what God was doing through His Spirit. God was hovering over the surface of the deep. Note that darkness was on the face of the deep and not on the face of the earth. There was no earth yet. Therefore, word *"face of deep"* here does not refer to the surface of the earth because the earth was not yet existent then. Instead, it refers to one of the subterranean chambers under the earth where the waters were kept. The Greek word is *elhom*. So, as God was hovering over the surface of the deep, He started forming the image of the earth. God was not wasting His time. There was a purpose for the scripture to record this. The word *hovering* in the Hebrew is the word *brooding*. It is the same word that would have been used to describe the chicken that hatches on the egg. When God was conceiving the image of the creation, the Spirit of God was hovering to birth it forth. And finally God saw everything. Before the first to the sixth day happened, He already saw the whole of creation inside of Him. And when it was all formed nicely He just had to say what He wanted. He said what He wanted and all was made.

It is scripturally evident in Genesis 1 that every time God creates something, the Bible prefaced it with a statement, *"and God said"*. The Holy Spirit records that for us to let us know that God made the world by His spoken word. And before God spoke those words from His mouth, the words were in God's mind. In the spirit realm, God had conceived how the world would be like. God conceived of a world with light so God says *let there be light*. God conceived of a world with the waters above the earth and the waters underneath the earth. Then God *said let the waters of the earth be separated above the firmament and below the firmament*. God conceived that there would be land. Land was not formed yet but in the spirit realm God saw it. God formed it in the spirit realm and then God said *let the land appear*. And the waters parted and the land came forth. And then God conceived all the plants and the foliage and every time when He said it then it came into being. So, the things which are physical were made of things which are invisible. And unless we realize this truth we will be working to change our circumstances and our life the wrong way.

Sadly, some folks erroneously believe that God created the earth out of nothing and that everything came out of the blue, out of the invisible matter. No! That is not the correct picture because everything He created was already in Him. So, when He spoke, and said *let there be light*, light proceeded from within the depths of His being into manifestation in the natural realm. That is why with an indwelling presence of the Holy Spirit, everything you will ever need in life is in you. Therefore, we follow the same pattern which God used to speak things from within our being into existence. Isn't it amazing that God created all things out of himself? As He called, *light be,* light came forth from the depth of His being into existence. When God said, *Let there be light*, what came forth was the voice of the

The Realm Of The Spirit

almighty penetrating the vastness of His perception in the eternal realm as He spoke into existence that which He had already created within His being. The very essence of His thought life was thrust into existence, and seen when He spoke. Thoughts became words, words became objective reality. All He had to do was to call out of Himself those things which were a part of His glory and they responded. The sound of His voice preceded the visible manifestation of each creative work.

The Bible said *the Holy Spirit will show you things to come.* The language of the Holy Spirit is visions and dreams. *In the last days the Spirit shall fall upon all flesh and they shall have visions and dreams.* A vision is a divine mental commercial of coming attractions. In fact, visions and dreams may be classified as pictures received in your sub-conscious mind or your conscious mind. Sometimes through prophecy the Holy Spirit will give you a picture of yourself that God sees. If you take that picture that God has shown you and you hold it and you meditate on it, before long it comes to pass. So, when you close your eyes the picture that you are seeing right now of your ministry or of your life will be played out in the physical realm exactly as you see it. If you see it with half victory you will have half a victory. People don't realize it but when you close your eyes and you see the spirit realm, that spirit realm is real. It is more real than the physical world. It is because that spirit realm will give birth to the physical world. And that spirit realm needs to be seen clearly. I conceive it over and over again in my spirit and in my imagination. I am the ground and God's word is the seed. And the word is like an image that comes to us. Words are actually images. All of us think in images. When I say *a white horse*, we think of a white horse. So, words are actually images spoken out. And so God speaks His words and we receive. See we are the ground God's word is the seed. And the seed comes onto our heart. The heart area is the imagination area. See there are several Greek words for the word mind. And one of those especially talks about imagination. There is a Greek word *dialogismai* which talks about reasoning. There is another word which is *dianoia* which talks about the area of imagination.

The imagination is a part of your heart area and between your soul and your spirit. Your imagination is a part of your soul that is extended into the spirit world and that touches the spirit world. You see our soul touches our body inside us. So that when my soul wants to go to the right, my body goes. There is some sort of control between my soul and my body. There is a connection between your soul and your spirit. And the connection that links your spirit and your soul is your imagination. It is a part of your soul but yet it is in the part which touches the spirit realm when it moves in the spirit realm. And for your spirit to flow through your soul to your body you have to get that connection renewed and washed and cleansed and be used by God's word. In other words the imagination is the eye of your soul. You soul have eyes. If right now we should all go to be with God and leave our bodies down here, you would still have your eyes. The Holy Spirit sometimes helps us by giving us visions and dreams. Those visions and dreams are to be encoded into your imagination so that through your meditation you could produce it at some time in the future. Sometimes a man of God comes and gives you a prophecy. As far as you can remember write it down. If it is in line with God receive it. Get it encoded into your imagination. And the day you could conceive a clear picture the birth begins to come. You begin to give birth to it. And the giving birth from the imagination area, from the spirit realm comes suddenly. That is just how powerful the imagination is in harnessing the power of God.

In the realm of the spirit, it is possible for one to read people's thoughts

In the realm of the spirit, human thoughts cannot be hidden as it is possible for one to read thoughts. Jesus knew the thoughts of the people around Him. They couldn't hide. In Luke. 6:6. On another Sabbath, when He entered the synagogue and taught, a man was there whose right hand was withered. And the scribes and the Pharisees watched Him, to see whether he would heal on a Sabbath, so that they might find an accusation against him. But He knew their thoughts. How did Jesus know their thoughts? It's because thoughts are laid bare in the spirit realm. In the spirit world you can actually read a person's thought. If that person were to open his mouth and say just one word, that one word becomes a revelation of the entire person's life. That's how powerful the spirit realm is like. The moment a person open the mouth and say anything you see the mind. In the spiritual realm, you are observing a person's soul. The moment their soul open for an utterance their mind is revealed. So, in a sense it is not reading the mind. But it is reading the words that comes out from the soul. That's what the spirit realm is like in terms of the thoughts and in terms of the words.

Logic Breaks Down In the realm of the spirit

The other aspect of the spirit world is that it is very illogical. Logic breaks down in the spirit world. We all like to be logical. We all like to think line upon line. And we are all comfortable with that. In the spirit realm even logic cannot reach. It is for this reason that upon visitation to the throne room of Heaven, Paul described his experience in 2 Corinthians as *inexpressible for man to tell*. Paul was a very logical man. We are not doing away with logic. We just need to understand the different realms of the body, the mind, and the spirit so that we don't confuse those realms. The spirit realm is not a realm of logic; it's a realm of reception. Logic is perception. The spirit realm is a reception. It is like a channel of wisdom from God flowing into you all the time. Everything you know in the spirit realm has to come from God and not from yourself. But in our natural realm we know the effort that we make in trying to understand a revelation from God. Yet when you enter into the spiritual realm it feels like you are plucked into God's wisdom and everything you know is God's knowledge imparted to you. You are just a receiver of the flow of God's wisdom and knowledge.

I found in my experience of the spirit realm that the moment I switch to logic the visions become less. The moment I switch off logic the visions become more. That's the reason I am giving you this point. If you understand both sides like right now as I move strongly into the logical area, the visualizing part diminishes. And if I want to minister in the spirit I must let go the logical part of my being. If I don't let go I cannot minister in the spirit. Which is why now you can understand for a minister to minister both in the spirit and in the teaching side is very difficult to mix both. Because to go into one is to diametrically oppose the other. And it takes quite a balance to get into both. I have chosen to try to get into both realms so that when it comes to teaching we are logical and perceptive. Right now if I am talking about the logical realm the vision just disappeared. But if the anointing is there and I want to move into that spirit realm I have to voluntarily choose to give up that logical part of myself and just open to the spirit of receiving. It is not really a passive state. Passiveness of mind is not what God wants. It is what the devil wants. It is still active but it is active in worship and in tuning to God. It's a totally different realm.

The realm of the spirit is the realm of speed and acceleration. Things happen so fast in the realm of the spirit

Acceleration and speed is one of the spectacular elements and key characteristic features of the realm of the spirit. With respect to urgency, the spirit realm is so different from the natural. In the realm of the spirit, what is said comes to pass instantly and what is conceived in the mind immediately it comes to pass. There is no lag time or waiting period for manifestation. As things are said, thought of, visualised, conceived in the spirit, their manifestation becomes i

nstantaneous. This is contrary to the natural realm whereby things take time to manifest. In the natural world sometimes you tell the mountain to move. Then only slowly does the mountain moves; sometimes it may take a few months, sometimes a few years. It seems like a delayed process in this natural world. When you reach to the natural realm, there is a delay even though what you say comes to pass instantly in the spirit world. We know that what we say in the end does come to pass, but the process of it coming to pass can be quite long. Remember the testimony of how a sister was taken up to Heaven and according to earthly time she was there about one minute but according to Heavenly time she was there for about one hour. That's why it says in God a day is like a thousand years. This implies that God is able to accomplish so many things in the earthly realm within a short time. Things are so slow in the realm of the natural. That's why even in your life if you want things to move faster, engage the spirit realm which is a realm of acceleration. In the spirit you are able to accomplish so many things within a short space of time.

In the realm of the spirit, things happen at the same time they are said

In Heaven, what you need the moment you say and believe it, the moment you ask from God, instantly it is there. Let's say in your Heavenly mansion that you are staying and you have a nice landscape garden. And you say, *"How nice if I could have just that river of water here flowing."* Instantly it comes. We will be very careful with our words in that realm. That's what that realm is like regarding words. There is a new prophetic dimension in the glory whereby things are coming to pass as they are being said. In the glory realm, there is no procrastination, or delays because time is inconsequential. When God declared in an atmosphere of glory, *let there be light,* light came forth instantly. He didn't have to wait. Instead, results came forth as words were declared. In the glory realm, there is no waiting because waiting is a process in time, of which we have dominion over time; we operate outside the time dimension because we were given birth to in the eternal realm which falls outside our time dimension. The reason why some believers experience delays in their lives is because of the absence of glory. The less you are filled with the glory, the longer it takes for you to cast out darkness and experience victory in your life. Real spiritual warfare takes place in the glory because there, the Lord fights for your battles. Outside the glory, you fight your own battles but inside the glory, God fights for you. That's why God said to the children of Israel, "This battle is not yours. You do not have to fight for the battles is yours". This is because in the glory realm, God assumes total ownership of every battle, and since it is not possible for God to lose any fight, your position is to watch as a spectator. But why does the above scripture connotes that the battle not yours? It's because you are operating in the glory which belongs to God. Therefore, any man who touches you touches the glory of God. Demons know very well that they cannot enter Heaven, hence with the coming down of the glory, they leave instantly because they know that the same rules apply. That is why deliverance happens so fast in the glory zone because demons are not permitted to enter, sickness is rendered illegitimate and death is not permitted to reign. That is why there is such a thing as Deliverance glory, meaning conducting deliverance while in the glory zone.

Because we have dominion over time, in the glory realm, you can declare a thing and use your royal prerogative to stipulate the time frame when that thing must come to pass, whether in a day, week or few hours. When the Bible attests that you shall declare a thing and it shall be established for you, it doesn't talk about flippantly declaring empty words in any direction but it talks about declaring things while in the glory realm or in an atmosphere of glory. That's when things happen. That is why those who function in higher realms of glory don't wait for things to happen, instead, they make things happen. This is because in the glory realm, it is possible for you to be instantaneously elevated to the reality of overnight success, whereby prayers are being answered even before you start praying.

Let's look closely at how Ezekiel functioned on the prophetic glory: *So, I prophesied as I was commanded and as I prophesied, there was a noise, and suddenly a rattling and the bones came together bone to bone* (Ezekiel 37:7). The instant Ezekiel prophesied, the noise began and the miracle started the moment the prophecy commenced. This is to tell you that prophecy does not just foretell; it creates that which is being said. It is the tool that brings it to pass. Confessing what you want God to do is different from declaring what He is saying right now while the glory is present. Both Elijah and Elisha walked and lived in the prophetic glory realm and when they spoke, it caused heaven and earth, kings and nations, to react and respond. They prophesied the opening of wombs, rain and drought, provisions, resurrections, and deaths, and the list goes on.

In the realm of the spirit, material things are created by spoken words

It is a divine truth that what you speak has such a tremendous effect on everything that you do. Speech is so powerful that it is recorded that everything was created by it. Speech was one of the first ingredients that created everything else you see and the invisible things you don't see. In the beginning the Creator spoke in Genesis 1: 3, saying *"let there be light"*, and light came forth instantaneously. The truth is that when you speak over the airwaves, you are invading and taking back the space of, *"the Prince of the power of the air"*, and displacing the enemy so that God can rule over the airwaves and bring His purposes to pass. From a scientific point of view, sound waves created by speech are so small that if you were to divide the smallest particles and atoms into some of the smallest forms inside them, at their core you would find vibration waves called *quarks*. From this scientific reality, comes a spiritual truth that sound waves are embedded in everything on earth, including rocks, food, trees and everything ever created. Therefore, these sounds waves can be altered and respond to other sound waves or speech. According to the studies conducted by a Japanese Researcher Masaru Emoto, water particles and other subatomic particles actually respond to sound and even speech or words spoken to them. If this is the case, then every created thing can hear in a sense and respond in some way, as they were first created with the same core ingredients – sound and light. This understanding can revolutionise your life, including the way you pray, minister and operate in the things of God.

The Realm Of The Spirit

In the light of the above, start to speak things you want to see manifested in your life. If you are going for a job interview, say that you are going to have favour with everyone you meet, and you will be successful. If you are sick, start telling your body that it is strong and healthy and that no sickness can survive in such a healthy state. Create your day each morning by speaking what you believe will be created that you will be successful in all that you do, that you are full of energy and this will cause things to shift from the invisible realm to the visible realm and will also take you from normal to supernatural. This is what we call *commanding your morning*. When you command your morning, you give your reality divine assignments and pull success from the spiritual realm into your day.

The spirit realm is the original environment or atmosphere in which the earth was created. The earth was originally created in a Heaven like atmosphere

In the beginning of creation, God said let there be a firmament in the midst of the waters and let it divide the waters from the waters. God made the firmament and divided the waters, which were under the firmament from the waters, which were above the firmament, and it was so. When God first created the earth there was a canopy of waters above the earth and a canopy of waters surrounding the planet earth. In fact scientists have analysed that there is more water than land. The land is there not because we have one third land and two third water. The land is there because the land is all clumped together and pushed up like little mountains and plateaus above the waters. If all the land were a complete circle the water will surround the earth. So, there was just water and no land yet and above it there was a canopy of water. The clouds above the earth water were vapour. And above we do not know what it was like. Probably it was a canopy of glass-like kind of water. Before the flood conditions were like that. The earth was like in an air-conditioned state. If you look up it was like a big shield of glass of clouds or whatever form it was in. It was only in Noah's time the canopy of water was broken down. So today we talk about the ozone layer and the ozone hole. Long ago in Noah's time there was a breaking up of that hydrogen dioxide which was water above the earth. In Noah's time the water that was above there was broken and it came down. For the first time the sunray and radiation came and penetrated the earth. The earth that we know before Noah and after Noah is a different world. Today a rainbow is quite a common occurrence. There was no such thing as a rainbow before Noah. So you can imagine it's a different type of weather condition.

There is no hunger pangs in Heaven. Eating is for impartation, leisure and enjoyment

When God created the Heaven and the earth in Genesis 1 and later created all the animals, every one of those animals was not created to eat. Eating was a mere pleasure and enjoyment. In Heaven if you don't eat for 1000 years you still be fine. In Heaven you don't need food to survive. It is for this reason that we ask believers to fast so that they can align their lives with heavenly life. What we call a *fast* today was originally the normal or daily life of man. The truth is that man was never originally designed to grossly depend on food for survival. Do you realize that when God first created the Garden of Eden and Adam and Eve, they didn't have to eat to survive? Life came directly from God. And when God created Adam and Even they could have lived for 1000 years and they look exactly like the day they were created. We read about Elijah when he was discouraged the angel cook him some special food. And when he partook of it, it lasted for 40 days and 40 nights. He was a biological man like us. His body still would normally need food. Let me tell you when you get into that life, the old life that we are so used to all the laws of sin and death just stop.

Adam partook of sin together with Eve. The very day they eat something happened. That life was cut off. Suddenly they could not see the glory any more. Which is why they discovered they were naked. Before that they were filled with the life of God, which comes out through them and becomes like a glory upon their life. The garment of glory instantly disappeared. Now what happened when Adam and Eve fell? They were cut off from the supply of God's life. So now the plants get to survive. You know what they have is only the germ of life. And if the plants don't think of a way to survive, supply thinks. Only the past 10 to 20 years they discovered that the plants do fear. But they have the germ of life. And to preserve that germ of life the plants look around. It is the same with the animals. They didn't know a thing. I presume there was a lion walking half way while Adam and Eve were about to eat the fruit. Imagine if Adam and Eve felt naked what the lion felt like. I wonder what the lion felt while walking half way and suddenly the glory departed. The whole animal and plant kingdom felt something. Suddenly for the first time the lion felt the pang of hunger because the life was no more feeding that body.

Do you know that the pangs of hunger come as a result of the spirit of death? In Heaven you don't have physical hunger any more. Then for the lion it was also like the plant. Every day he got to look for food to preserve life. For Adam and Eve they are subjected to this carnal world where each day is the preservation of the life that is there. From the time you are conceived as a one cell living creature biologically you need nutrition. God only gives the germ of life. What happened to this world? This is the spirit of death at work. In Heaven there is no death on earth now death exists. Do you know that death comes in many ways and many forms? Hunger is a part of the death process. If Jesus did not come we are still in that stage. And here is where the New Testament truth comes in. There is a form of life that is available for those who are His. He calls that eternal life, the life of God. The life of God can flow once again into us. The eternity can begin in our spirits. So we have in us that spirit life that God gives. In 2 Corinthians. 5:17 Therefore, if anyone is in Christ, he is a new creation; the old has passed away, behold, the new has come.

There is no aging in Heaven.

One of the things of heaven is there is no such thing as death, decay. Everything in Heaven functions from the life of God. Which is why there is no decay because everything that God made functions by God's life. There are no old people there in Heaven. Nothing there shows any sign of aging. You ask, "Are there children there? Yes there are. The little infants that go to Heaven they do grow and they reached what I call perfection and that's it. They remain in perfection. If you were to see your loved ones who had gone there before, if they had died in their old wrinkled bodies, when you go there they are in their prime of their life. There are no sad faces in Heaven. There is neither death nor sorrow. Heaven is full of life. We know that once upon a time God created the earth like Heaven. The things that we so commonly known on this earth will one day fade away. If you were to take a walk in the botanical garden and see all the beauty of the scenery around, yet if you observe closely you can find some flowers that have withered away. Some leaves have passed their point of usefulness to the plant and is now dropping off. You would come across death somewhere along. And we are so used to the fact that when we pick flowers from the garden and put them in a vase in your home, you will only have it last for a short time. Marietta Davis in one of the truths of heaven in the book *"Scenes beyond the Grave,"* speaks about how the children in paradise pick the flowers. And they didn't have to put it in a vase because there is life there. There is no death. Then they brought it to one of the mansions and they just kept the flowers on the ground. And the flowers got embedded in part of the ground in the house and they remain permanently there forever and they never die. Nothing in heaven dies.

The spiritual body is of a youthful appearance. There is no old age. Children and infants entering the spirit world grow to adult maturity but in a far shorter time then they would in earth time. Spiritual maturity can be discerned in the countenance and light of a spiritual body. The spiritual body can also expand or contract but not in the same sense as it does in the physical world. The maximum size however is limited by the level of advancement in the spiritual spheres. One is not necessarily the same height as one was in the physical world. Most of the time through spiritual growth (not always true of all aspects of growth – there are myriads of different areas of spiritual growth in the spiritual realm; each producing different radiance with some aspects producing expansion size of the spiritual body capability), one's being is greater in size (height and proportional wise) but one can still take the form of those of the lower spheres at a height or image that is recognisable and visible to those of the lower spheres. There is a translucence of the spiritual body but it is a solidness and lightness of spiritual substance. Light emanates from the spiritual body.

There is neither death nor decay in Heaven. There is no immortality of the body

Did you know that this physical body is functioning at the level which it was not really designed to do. In the Garden of Eden it was designed never to die. And this physical body was not designed to just exist on mere physical food and oxygen. It was supposed to live on God's life. We will not be able to see the fullness of the immortality that God has for this physical body until Jesus comes. However we do have a foretaste of what God has for the physical body here on this earth. And from time to time God does allow us to experience some of the "immortality of the physical body." And we are going to touch on that realm on the immortality of the physical body that we have a foretaste of. Some people like Enoch walked straight into immortality without seeing death, while others partake of a glimpse of what that body can be like. I Corinthians 15: 45 discusses the resurrection of the physical body. Thus it is written, *"The first man Adam became a living being"; the last Adam became a life-giving spirit."* From there we see that Jesus didn't just restore us back to Adam's state. He restored us even greater than Adam's state. Adam was not seated at the right hand of God. But the second Adam brought us into a position to sit at the right hand of God in Jesus Christ. Jesus brought us to share all the privileges and blessings of the Second Person of the Godhead Jesus Christ. There is a difference between the last Adam Jesus Christ and the first Adam. The last Adam became a life-giving spirit. The first one was only a living being. But the second had abundant life, a life that is God like with the ability to create and to impart.

The opening scripture continues in verse 46-47 *but it is not the spiritual which is first but the physical, and then the spiritual. The first man was from the earth, a man of dust; the second man is from heaven.* Notice his analogy here first Adam, then last Adam. First man second man. Why does he use these phrases? If we look at it in the natural we could look airplanes and we could say this is the first model of the plane. Then I could say this is the last model of the plane. What do I imply? This is the last of that type. Now if I say this is the first of its kind. This is the second type of plane. What does it imply? By using the word second it implies that this is totally different. Like the SAA 737 is different from SAA 747. It's a different type of plane altogether although they are developments from the early stages of the plane. So, in the same way Jesus was the last Adam. The last of that kind, the last of that type of the fallen man or the nature that was there that Jesus became part of when He took upon Himself the form of sinful flesh. But Jesus is bringing forth a new kind of man. In 2 Corinthians. 5:17 it says it's a new species. The word new creation in 2 Corinthians. 5:17 in the Greek it is a new species. It means a new type of man. Something more powerful than what Adam could have imagined. So, it's the second type or kind of man.

As was the man of dust, so are those who are of the dust; and as a man of, so are those who are of heaven. Now doesn't that imply that some of the Heavenly attributes of the body through the Lord Jesus Christ can be tasted, can be experienced on this earth. What a blessed promise. We are more than what Adam was. Paul continues that just as we have borne the image of the man of dust, we shall also bear the image of the man of Heaven. This is a different type of physical body. Let me give some examples, which you will be familiar with. Adam had a perfect physical body. If he had lived 1000 years he would have looked the same as the day that he was born. He wouldn't have aged he wouldn't have grown old so with Eve. But that physical body of Adam cannot go through walls. It was in a different dimension from the physical body that Jesus had when He was raised from the dead. There was a limitation to that physical body that he had. He had all the attributes of eternal life but he did not have the attributes of the heavenly life that was extra special.

In the realm of the spirit, the body has superhuman powers

Did you know that there is no immortality of the body in Heaven? In Hebrews 6:5, Paul speaks of *having tasted the goodness of the word of God and the powers of the age to come*. There are powers of the age to come in reference to the Heavenly realm. We realize that here on this earth we do partake of some powers of the Heavenly realm. These include the power of knowledge, the power of life and all these realms are there permanently in Heaven. But thank God while here on earth we have the divine privilege of partaking of the heavenly realm. Some of these powers are powers of the human body. When Jesus was raised from the dead there was a new type of man or species that He came to bring forth. And Jesus' physical body was flesh and bone. He told His disciples when He appeared to them in His resurrection and He says I am not just a spirit. I am also a physical body. He says for a spirit does not have flesh and bones. And they felt and touched that physical body of Jesus that was resurrected. And that physical body could eat. And we know He ate fish. When the doors were locked and Jesus suddenly appeared with the physical body, He says peace be to you. Then He sat down and He ate with them a meal of fish. And after that He went right through the wall. We could understand how the physical body in a way we could visualize it goes through the wall. But He ate physical fish. We understand His physical body going through the wall but can you imagine fish going through the wall also. He was not eating heavenly food. He was eating physical food that has weight. But when that physical food enters that special body of His, it took on that special quality of going through walls.

When immortality under the power of God comes on this physical body, gravitation laws won't limit it. When Jesus walked on the water in Matthew 14, He was walking on a different law. The laws of gravity limit this physical body of ours. For a moment under the power of God Jesus' body was freed from the gravitational pull and He walked on water in Matthew 14. He must have been in God's presence so much that when God said to go across the lake, Jesus did not hesitate. Jesus must have known something about it because He told His disciples, "You go first, and I'll join you later." But no one knew how He would join them. While the disciples were there rowing hard away because of the contrary wind Jesus just walk across the water. That's a tremendous power that was on His body. Some will say Jesus did that because He was Son of God just to show us what He can do. Well Peter did it too. For a moment of time his body too was on that same power. When he says, "*Lord if that's you, call me come onto the water.*" And Jesus says, "*Come,*" now it's up to him. And he walked on water. He was a mortal man tasting a bit of immortality.

There is no record that Adam and Eve were able to float around. Adam and Eve walked on this earth. But the body that we have from the Lord Jesus Christ when He comes again is a body that could float around. That physical body that we will have in heaven, we won't need wings to fly. We would be able for example to think about going up to the mountain and you got a choice of walking up or floating up. I bring that point to show forth that the second type of man and the second kind of body that God gives is different. It is far superior to Adam's body. It's a new species and we are able to partake of that. Three observations of people breaking those laws on the natural body when their physical body to a certain extend began to take on immortality. Every healing is a type of miraculous working on the physical body. Dr. Sally gave a testimony of her visitation to Heaven. She also went to the same room that Robert Liardon went to where the bodily parts are kept. In Heaven there are bodily parts waiting to be sent to this earth. Just over the last week G.B. Paul was in the hospital for heart condition. His wife came for prayer. I asked for a handkerchief and we prayed over the handkerchief. As I prayed the presence of God came down. And the Lord told me that He would visit him. She took that handkerchief and brought it to the hospital. That night while he was laying in the hospital bed an angel came and looked at his body. And this is what they told me: the angel pulled the zip on his body. Then the angel took out something and put it in the rubbish bag. Then the angel took some bodily parts and put it in. Then he zipped him up again. There are a lot of bodily parts that are in heaven that are uncollected. We need faith for us to tap on them.

Things work differently in Heaven. There are laws that are beyond this natural world. And from time to time God does allow our physical bodies to partake of immortality. And if we are to walk close with God this whole body may be transformed and caught with Him. We taste of the powers of the age to come. There are 3 things I want to share of people who go into that realm beyond the limitations of the physical body. First I call it the *energy and life force in the body*. When a little baby is born the energy that is physically there in that body is tremendous. The cells multiply tremendously. Metabolism rate is very high. In the natural realm as a person grows the metabolism rate decreases. That is why infants put on weight easier unless of course the power of God continues on their life. There are even instances of little babies who have lost a finger and grew a new finger. For adults we know this is impossible, but it's easier for babies than for adults. And that energy force that is there can continue to be replenished from the spirit realm because in the heavenly realm the energy force never decreases.

In Romans. 4:18-20, Abraham believed against hope, that he should become the father of many nations; as he had been told, "So shall your descendants be." He did not weaken in faith when he considered his own body, which was as good as dead because he was about a hundred years old, or when he considered the barrenness of Sarah's womb. No distrust made him waver concerning the promise of God, but he grew strong in his faith as he gave glory to God. We know what happened to Sarah's body. She probably received new parts from Heaven. And their youth were renewed like the eagle. Even though their bodies aged yet they gained strength. So much so that Sarah once again looks beautiful. Then one day Abraham took her to king Abimelech's place. Abimelech took one look at her and whistled. Imagine any person doing it to a 90 year-old woman. Surely she must have looked very young. The energy force of God came into her and her physical body regained strength. The bodily parts were renewed. Instead of drying up, the bodily parts became strengthened like it was new.

In Deuteronomy 34: 7, Moses was a hundred and twenty years old when he died; his eye was not dim. I mean he had super eyes. He didn't need to wear glasses. What the world is telling you by the age of 40 the lubrication in your eyes start drying up. And you need to lubricate it a little bit more. And you find it a bit harder to see. And according to your faith be it unto you. You believe it; you accept it and then it became. And you say now I am old. Maybe your grandma told you that; your grandpa told you that, and you began to expect that would happen to you when you are old. Kenneth E. Hagin speaks about a time he was reading an article in Reader's Digest. And it was talking about how by certain age, certain cells stop to function, and

The Realm Of The Spirit

you will begin to lose part of your memory etc. And he said after he read it sub-consciously he accepted it and he started losing his memory. Until something took a hold of him and he asked, "Who said that? Almighty God didn't say that. Who says you must lose your memory when you are old? God didn't say that. His word didn't say that. But rather its man's word based on natural observation."

Sometimes I grow concerned when I see men of God, as they grow in God they started using glasses and all that. I am not against glasses. I mean use them as you require them. But as a minister I rather live a high standard. The reason being is how I as a minister can tell a blind person to tap on healing when I can't get healing for my own eyes. So, here it says his eyes were not dim and his natural force did not abate. He was strong; he was still climbing mountains when he was old. These are all foretaste of immortality. And if we begin to move further and further into that realm the physical body can be so transformed that it may reach a point like Enoch's body reached it and he completely stopped aging. It's time immortal. For those who could walk in faith higher in God, there is a realm you walk where mortality is changed to immortality. Many people are waiting for that to take place at Jesus' second coming. But now for those who desire God's presence and walk deeper with God, that presence can transform you. It can transform your physical being into the fullness of what immortality is like.

Consider Enoch's life. In Genesis 5:23-24 the Bible records that all the days of Enoch were three hundred and sixty-five years. Enoch walked with God; and he was not, for God took him. Now it didn't just say that God took him. If it just said that God took him it may imply that his body was growing in the normal process. It could mean that as he grew old because of God's blessings on his life God took him like the way he took Elijah. But it says he walked with God and was not for God took him. The word *was not* implies a transition from mortality into immortality. As he walked with God the body that *was* became *was not*. The body that was subjected to the laws on this natural plane suddenly was no more subject to it. It was transformed. And people who walk close with God seem to have a certain degree of that. They are preserved from the law of corruption and decay. Do you know that Jesus Christ on this earth walked so close with God, even though He bore all the sicknesses and diseases for us on the cross, it was more in a legal form and not in the physical form. I mean Jesus couldn't physically in one body take all the sicknesses and diseases of the world. He would have looked like a bloated, putrefying pumpkin. It could not be in the physical sense. Although you could see your sickness on Him by faith, but it was a legal transaction. For all sicknesses came because of a broken law. And Jesus took that legal implication in judgment for the broken law.

The Bible tells us in the book of Acts 2:27 *for thou wilt not abandon my soul to Hades, nor let thy Holy One see corruption.* The moment a physical body dies that physical body begin to decay because there are germs and virus that begin to attack that body. In fact while you are alive your body is being attacked all the time. Except that because of the energy and life force in your body, your body cells kill all the germs and viruses that constantly invade your body. The moment life goes out from your body the body cease to defend itself and it just decay. Sometimes you throw your rubbish in a rubbish bin and it was some meat or chicken or something. But you leave that piece of chicken to decay maggots begin to appear. You ask yourself the question where do the maggots come from? I want you to know that Jesus Christ body never decay. God did not allow His flesh to see corruption. For 3 days and 3 nights that physical body that was kept in a tomb was preserved not by any spices or natural ointments like the Egyptian mummies. But it was preserved by a life force that still remains on that physical body. How then did He take our sicknesses and diseases? It was by legal transaction. When Adam fell into sin all sicknesses and diseases have a right to enter the human race. So when Jesus took death He cancelled that right. And anyone who believes in Him, that right of sickness and disease to enter into your body is cancelled. And based on that right believers can be healed by His stripes. Although Jesus' body was wounded because of the stripes that were inflicted on His back but no diseases, germs, viruses could exist on that body because of the glory of God.

I don't know what it was like with Moses' body. Although we read in chapter 34 there must be a tremendous energy that was on his body. And yet when he died we are told in the book of Jude that Satan wanted that body and God wanted that body. So there was a war over a dead body. Moses' spirit and soul was already with God. In the book of Jude verse 9 But when the archangel Michael, contending with the devil, disputed about the body of Moses, he did not presume to pronounce a reviling judgment upon him, but said, "The Lord rebuke you." Satan and Michael the archangel were wrestling over Moses' body. Why? Let me give the understanding here. That physical body has seen the back part of God's glory, which no man has ever seen. Up to Moses' time all men has only seen a glimpse of His glory. Not even a shadow of His glory but Moses has seen the back part of His glory.

The Realm Of The Spirit

We know what happened to Moses on that day. The very skin cells of his face was so affected it became luminous and shone brightly like a light bulb. Surely there are some special effects that is taking place on that physical body.

What about the law of science? God created all the laws of science. Science cannot create new laws. They can only discover laws established by God. Just like scientists can tell you that all the compounds in the body, water has an interesting property. When water temperature drops it begins to contract. Then up to a certain point when it turns to ice it begin to expand. That is why ice can float on water because when it expands ice becomes lighter than water. Other compounds or elements become solidified and heavier when they are chilled. Scientist can only discover that God made it that way so that when winter comes the fish in the lakes and in the sea can still exist underneath. If God didn't make it that way and winter comes the whole lake would have been frozen and every fish would have died. So God is above all those natural laws. Something happened to Moses' physical body. The bible specially mentioned the skin on his face. Exod. 34: 29 Moses did not know that the skin of his face shone. Something happened to the skin. Something happened I believe to the whole body too. See in God death doesn't exist. In God life only exists and there is no death. And a part of that immortality came on his body.

In Numbers 17, there was a time in regard to the challenge of Aaron's leadership that God said, "*Speak to the people of Israel, and get from them rods, one for each fathers' house, from all their leaders according to their fathers' houses, twelve rods. Write each man's name upon his rod and write Aaron's name upon the rod of Levi. And the rod of the man whom I choose shall sprout*". We know what a rod is. It is just a walking stick. A walking stick even in the natural if you had planted it into the ground it will not produce a tree. These are not fresh rod. These are the rods that they constantly used for tens of years. Imagine planting a walking stick in the ground and it grows. But not only had that in one day had it grown. That's immortality. Plants blossom in God's presence. What God was bringing forth was only a shadow of what was already there when He created the earth. If you look at Genesis 1 carefully the plants were created before the sun was created. And we know in the natural according to biology or botany the plants need sunlight to live in our realm today. But plants originally receive life from the glory of God. When that rod was placed in the presence of God the immortality of God brought back life into that physical rod. We have a foretaste of immortality of the life of

God that was possible. Moses then went into the tent of the testimony; and behold, the rod of Aaron for the house of Levi had spouted and put forth buds, and produced blossoms, and it bore ripe almonds. How could that be? This is immortality. If God's presence is there it will just ripen. That is why in Heaven every fruit tree is constantly producing fruit. Every flowering plant is always flowering because of God's presence. And that immortal life can flow into our physical body. Immortality can come in your organs so that no matter how old you grow your physical heart will still be young. Your physical body can still be young. You can grow in age but your body do not need to age. And your eyes don't need to grow dim. You don't need to lose any one of your teeth. You could have perfection of body depending on how much you tap into No. 1 immortality of the body. We see what I call a glimpse, a taste of the power to come.

In heaven, proximity or closeness to God is not measured by fame

I once asked God in one of my times of fellowship with Him this question, "Lord, who are those who are really close to you today?" And God gave me some names. However I have not met any of them. I want you to know that some of those who are very famous in Christian circles are not amongst those names. That is why when we go to heaven we will be very, very surprised. Human beings judge closeness to God by popularity and the pastor shared with me some of the things this person was sharing five years ago. For example, he said this person was constantly walking and moving with angels. It is common for angels to wake him up and talk to him. That's how close he walked with God. He said he saw two angels and one of the angels had a sword that was drawn and the other had a belt. And on the angel who had a sword drawn out, the sword was called 'Circumcision'. The other angel had the belt, and on that belt were the letters 'Enforcer'. That person is actually a prophet but is unknown to the world. He is known here and there but practically the average Christian does not know him. And he said that God was going to judge His house. He was going to circumcise His church -that means to cut off all the flesh in the church. And if people will not yield to God's circumcision then the second angel will operate and he will enforce it. And what you see for the past five years are some of the things that are happening which are the work of this two major angels. This person does not travel much now. He had never been sick all his life and God was about to take his wife home (they were both very old and elderly).

The Realm Of The Spirit

I am talking about the depths of God and fellowship with the Spirit, where you see angels and talk to God 24 hours all through the day. He had reached that level. One day, he was walking halfway through a tunnel and he was sad. The Lord stood in front of him and said, "Why are you downcast?" Then the light of the Lord shone upon him. As the Lord was talking to him about several things, suddenly the Lord turned 360 degrees and he saw a different face of Jesus. He had a face of sorrow and tears. Then the Lord said to him, "You know me as your Lord, you know me as your Saviour, you know me as your Healer but today I want you to know me as the Man of Sorrows." When he met the Lord, the rest of the journey in the tunnel became easy. He understood the depth of being in the Lord and having the heartbeat of God. I won't tell you his name because you might become his fans. There is a danger when people become fans of men of God that become imbalanced themselves. They are like the carnal Corinthians Christians -"I am for Apollos, I am for Paul etc" When I heard his name, I knew he was one of those who were in the race to be closest to God.

The spirit world is highly populated.

Just as in this natural world you see a lot of people in the cities, the spirit world is also very highly populated. Can you imagine one third of the angels fell and some of them became what you consider wicked spirits in the high places? Then what about those disembodied spirits that came about in Noah's time as the result of the flood. The whole earth was populated in Noah's time before the flood. The half-breed race that was produced through the angels mixing with human flesh died and were disembodied. There are so many of them here on this planet. Then not counting the other two thirds of angels that remained faithful, plus all the Old Testament saints and the New Testament saints for the past 2000 odd years till this day. The spirit world is highly populated. Think about everyone who was born into this world having a guardian angel. Plus all the other types of angels, and you can imagine how crowded things are in the spirit world. We should not surprise when we say there is a hosts of angels surrounding us. It is not just an occasional one angel here, or one angel there. Those who are in the natural world don't understand that the spiritual world is crowded. In fact if there are 5 billion people in this world, there are more than that number of spirit beings right now. Out there in the spirit world, spirit beings are constantly moving to and flow on this earth. We cannot describe all the spirit beings

CHAPTER TWO

A DIVINE REVELATION OF HEAVEN AND THE HEAVENLY REALM

DEFINING THE HEAVENLY PLACES

There is a dimension in the physical realm to which human senses have no access. This is a realm in the spirit, a spiritual sphere which depicts the highest level of concentration of God's glory in the supernatural. It is a spiritual powerhouse where the glory of God flows profusely from the Heavenly places to all other planets. It is in this realm where the highest realms of God's glory radiate from into other places or sections of Heaven. It is a place of unfathomable glory. When we enter into the Heavenly places, we are ushered right into the very manifest presence of God and tap into the unimaginable glory of God. It is the spiritual epicentre of the universe. Paul the apostle unveils the revelation of the Heavenly places in Ephesians 2: 5-6, when he proclaimed that even *when we were dead in trespasses, made us alive together with Christ (by grace you have been saved), and raised us up together, and made us sit together in the heavenly places in Christ Jesus that in the ages to come He might show the exceeding riches of His grace in His kindness toward us in Christ Jesus.* Note that it's not just a Heavenly place but Heavenly places in Christ Jesus. The fact that it says Heavenly places (plural) instead of Heavenly place (Singular) means that this realm consists of many dimensions, realms, and depths. Note that the Heavenly places is not just the atmosphere above the earth nor is it a part of Heaven either. It is a realm of heightened spiritual activity. It's a realm of spiritual action. It is a realm of exercising spiritual authority and power. It is worth noting that then phrase *"Seated together with Christ"* does not speak of seating in the sense of relaxation and occupation of chairs in a literal sense. Instead, it speaks of a position of authority, governance, power. This is where we occupy our offices and rule, reign with Christ, we become part of the decision making body in the Heavenly places, we sit in the boardroom, we govern daily affairs of both Heaven and earth, we engage angels, we determine or influence the destinies of man and we make decisions over cities and towns, territories and nations of the world.

The Realm Of The Spirit

This is to tell you that there is a place in God, a realm where we operate and influence critical decisions governing Heavens and earth.

The Heavenly places is not just a mental accent; it is a tangible realm. It is a realm of reality. That is where our offices are. That where our areas of governance are. That's where we rule, reign, govern with Christ and partake of the fullness of His glory as co-heirs. That's why the word of God says *God makes decision in the counsel of gods* and to us He says *we are gods*. We realise and take up this honour when we are in this realm. It is in this Heavenly realm that we are a committee of partners, heirs, decision makers, we sit in the Boardroom of Heaven, to debate and deliberate on its affairs; we govern kingdom affairs as we are involved in the allocation of blessings and make decisions over God's plan over cities, and towns, territories and regions, nations and the world. To get a picture of how we operate in that realm look at how Abraham, pleaded with God not to destroy Sodom and how Moses pleaded with God not to destroy the Israelites after worshiping a calf in Mount Sinai. In a like manner we engage God over the affairs of the world while in this realm. In this realm not only do we hear God speak but we walk with Him and fully dwell in His presence. When the word of God says *whatever we bind on earth shall be bound in Heaven....*" it is taking about functioning in this realm. In this realm, anything that man declares will begin to align itself according to what he says. It is in this realm where we receive answers to our prayers. When one says I have received a breakthrough, that breakthrough would have streamed from this realm.

Note that our opening scripture in Ephesians 2 is in the past perfect tense. It does not say, *"we shall be seated...."* Instead, it says, *"We are seated..."* expressing the act in present tense. Although our physical bodies are on this earth, our spirits can actually be catapulted to higher realms of the spirit at the right hand of God. God gave me the understanding that my spirit can operate there, while my physical body is down here on earth. From time to time, our spirits have to descend to this earth to fulfil our earthly responsibilities but then rise like a phoenix from the ashes of this earthly crisis to operate in the Heavenly realm. The authority that we have on this earth is proportional to the dimension in which our spirit operates in the Heavenly places. Man was never designed to be a visitor in the spirit dimension but to be a permanent resident of that realm. God never want to shut anyone out of the Most Holy place. God never want to prevent anyone from coming near Him. That is why we should not visit God in Heaven once in a while. Instead, it should be the opposite. According to God's original master plan about humanity, our spirit should operate from the Heavenly realms permanently. It is for this reason that God said in Exodus 19:5 *Now, therefore, if you will indeed obey My voice and keep My covenant, then you shall be a special treasure to Me above all people, for all the earth is Mine. And you shall be to Me a kingdom of priests and a holy nation.* The fact that God wanted every one of His children to be a kingdom of priests and kings means that everyone is welcome to His Throne.

In Ephesians 1: 20-23, Paul says *we are blessed with all spiritual blessings in the Heavenly places.* The word of God does not say that we are going to be blessed. Instead, it says we are blessed, putting everything in past tense. This implies that the blessings have been made available before the foundations of the world and God is waiting to see us enter that realm to possess what rightfully belongs to us. This tells me that the Heavenly places is a realm of blessings. This is where our blessings are domiciled. This revelation explains why some people have not been able to receive their anticipated blessings. It is because they don't function or operate in that realm in which the blessings of God have been freely made available. The truth is that God has already reserved and prepared our blessings in the Heavenly places but it takes our faith to lift our spirit and enter that ream and begin to possess our blessings in Christ. Do you want your car, house, business contact or breakthrough to manifest speedily? Then enter the Heavenly realm! We only receive the Heavenly blessings when we are in the Heavenly places. Then from the Heavenly places, our spirit descends with the Heavenly blessings and these blessings work out on this earth in our physical body. There is a Heavenly places or a Heavenly position that Jesus has. This is a realm which God has reserved for us since this world was made. He wants us to be in seated at His right hand and that represents some blessings and position that He has in store for us all through the ages. Jesus did not just come to save us from sins, he did not just come to bring healing to us, and he did not just come to bring us up to Heaven when we depart from this world. But he actually came to bring us up and share the glories, blessings and all that he has at the right hand of God.

To cement this revelation with reference to further scriptural evidence, Colossians 3: 1-3 says "If *ye then be risen with Christ, seek those things which are above, where Christ seated at the right hand of God.* It is evident that Christ is seated at the right hand of God in Heavenly places. Note that it does say the *right hand side* which talks about a physical location but it says the *right hand* which talks about a spiritual position of authority and power in the

The Realm Of The Spirit

Heavenly realm. The word of God tells us in Mark 16:19 that *after the Lord had spoken to them, He was received up into heaven, and sat down at the right hand of God*. The question you are probably asking yourself is: Where is Jesus? He is at the right hand of God. In fact when Jesus said, *"Father, I desire that they also whom You gave Me may be with Me where I am. That they may behold My glory which You have given Me, for You loved Me before the foundation of the world"* (John 17:2), He was talking about the Heavenly realm from which He wants us to operate. Elijah had such an authority over the natural realm because he always said, *"I stand in the presence of God."* That is why he had such power over the weather and the natural elements because his spirit was not operating down on the earthly realm. His spirit had somehow ascended to the higher realms of the spirit because he walked so close with God. That is why he was able to control the natural realm and determine the destinies of the nations. In a similar fashion, today God wants His church to operate in the Heavenly places so that we are able to influence the earthly realm. It is not true to say that if you are so Heavenly minded, you are of no earthly use. We can be so earthly minded that we are of no Heavenly use. Unless you are in the Heavenly places, you are a worm in this earth, making no real impact in it.

Note that the Bible describes our position as being *far above the level of powers and principalities* (Ephesians 1:21). These principalities and powers are demon forces that have set themselves up in the atmosphere of the earth to try and hinder the flow of God's blessings from coming down to us and to inhibit us from reaching up to the effulgence of His glory. Owing to this spiritual manipulation, at times your spirit can be pulled down by your soul and body to gravitate in a lower plane of life, if you allow it. That is why those who live so much in the flesh can never escape from the gravitational pull of the law of sin and death. But for those who walk in the consciousness of the Spirit in them, their spirit can actually ascend high above that level and enter the highest realms of the Spirit. The reason why God wants us to ascend to higher realms of the spirit is that when our spirit is up there, we can begin to shake the throne of Satan by wrestling with principalities, powers and wicked spirits and subdue them. When Jesus cast out demons from the man with legions, He only spoke to the main one of a higher rank. He did not speak to the other smaller demons of a lower rank. The greatest challenge facing believers is that many are gravitating to the lower plane of life and are fighting demons of lower ranks. A lot of Christians are wrestling with the smaller demons of the lower kind, and yet they are not having victory in their lives because they are not ascending to the Throne. The only way you can overcome these demons is to function from the Heavenly realm (Ephesians 3: 9-10). The only way you can shake the nations of the world is to shake the demon forces governing these nations. But the higher we go, the greater the authority we exercise in Christ (Ephesians 6: 12-14). When we begin to ascend up, the demon powers begin to recognize our authority in God because we are now speaking from the Throne Room of God. That is why the demons knew Paul well enough to scream his name out (Acts 19: 15). On the contrary, they did not know the sons of Sceva because they were not operating from the Throne Room of God.

Paul says in Ephesians 2:1 *And you He made alive, who were dead in trespasses and sins, in which you once walked according to the course of this world, according to the prince of the power of the air, the spirit who now works in the sons of disobedience, among whom also we all once conducted ourselves in the lusts of our flesh, fulfilling the desires of the flesh and of the mind, and were by nature children of wrath, just as the others. But God who is rich in mercy because of His great love with which He loves us.* Based on the scriptural reference above, it is evident that heavenly places is a position that God gives to us because of His great love with which He loved us. It's a place that Jesus has always wanted us to be. It's a place that God has always wanted men to be, in His bosom in the Heavenly places with Him. In John 17:4, Jesus testified, *I have glorified You on the earth. I have finished the work which You have given Me to do. And now, O Father, glorify Me together with Yourself, with the glory which I had with You before the world was.* This means there is a glory that Jesus had before the world was made. And that's the glory that Jesus is returning to and He is praying about. Jesus introduced that glory that He had before the world was made. Then from verse 20, He says *I do not pray for these alone, but also for those who will believe in Me through their word, that they all may be one, as You, Father, are in me, and I in You, that they also may be one in Us,* Now that phrase *"One in Us"* has reference to the heavenly places that He has reserved for us. There is a place in God where you are one in God and God flows absolutely into you and you flow into God. We are already one in Him in a sense when we are born again. But there is a Heavenly realm of oneness in which we partake of the nature of God. We are not omnipresent or omnipotent because those are qualities of God yet, there is a place reserved in the Heavenly places in God's throne at the right hand of God where there is a divine flow of oneness.

DISPELING THE MYTHS & MISCONCEPTIONS ABOUT HEAVENLY PLACES

God has reserved the depths of the presence of God in the heavenly places. There is an aspect of the presence of God that we enter into in the heavenly places in Christ Jesus who is at the right hand of God. But in order for you to accurately catch a revelation of how Heaven and the spirit world is like, we need to start dispelling some myths that have been preached for ages and engraved in the minds of believers. Even is some areas preachers who did not have a revelation of Heavenly places have not taught correctly. This has bred confusion, misunderstanding, misconception and a great deal of relying on assumptions. In this publication however, we open your eyes to see vividly the revelation which God wants you to see pertaining to the Heavenly places:

The Heavenly places are not limited to geographical location or territory.

Heavenly places are not just in the geographical atmosphere above the earth. The fact that the Bible describes it as *heavenly places* doesn't mean that it's a physical place or location. One of the essential properties of the realm of the spirit there is no distance. As a spiritual sphere, it's a realm beyond physical space, matter and distance. Based on this revelation, it is therefore impossible to try and measure the heavenly realm geographically. The spiritual realm is not limited to geographical territory like we limit it. The Spiritual realm consists of many different spheres of light that radiate from all the worlds that God has created and reaches right to the heaven of heavens, the Throne of God. It is brimming with life and activity of all the creations of God in various dimensions, each fulfilling their destiny. All the human activity of the earth in this present generation and in all the history of men combined is only one tiny dot in all the activities of the Spiritual realm.

The Heavenly places are not just the outskirts of heaven.

Heavenly places does not connote to the outer areas of Heaven. The Bible speaks of the outer court, middle court (Holy Place) and the inner court (Holy of Holies). One might be tempted to equate the heavenly places with the outer court which is an error. Why would you want to only partake at the Outer Court? Why do Christians limit themselves and shut themselves out of where God wants them to be? The heavenly places are at the right hand of God and they are a position of grace that Jesus shares with you. In essence, the heavenly places is tantamount to the Holy of Holies in Heaven. God wants us to come into the Most Holy place and not just to a paradise in heaven. The heavenly place is the very blissful place where Jesus sits at the right hand of God. The heavenly place is not in the Outer Court because Jesus did not put His throne in the Outer Court in heaven. It is not in the middle place called the Holy place either. Instead, the heavenly place in Christ is in the Holy of holies above where Jesus sits at the right hand of God. That's where we are welcomed to be.

Heavenly places are not only accessed after death or after saints depart to heaven.

You don't need to pass on so that you can then enter God's throne. Instead, you can enter, operate and parade the streets of heaven while on earth. That's why Paul said though we live in this world, we are not of the world. This simply means that we are of heaven. That's where our offices, thrones are. When we came into this world, we brought heaven with us. We carry heaven in us and we are able to influence this world by the heavenly principles that we abide by. In this last dispensation, there are testimonies of many people have visited heaven and have seen God. I am surprised that people who don't believe that they could be in God's throne. It is even scriptural since the Bible tells us to come boldly to the throne of grace. That means God is extending an invitation to all His people to come to His throne. One of the messages that God told me when I was taken to heaven is to tell His people that they are welcomed to God's throne. God says we are welcome to visit the throne room anytime as He wills. We don't need to wait to pass on so that we can be in heaven. You are welcome to Jesus' throne where He shares His glory with you.

Heavenly places are not just mansions.

Mansions are the fringe benefits in the Outer Court of heaven. But this heavenly place is at the right hand of God. God the Father, the Lord Jesus and Holy Spirit does not have a mansion or a place to stay unlike the saints in heaven who have mansions to live in. The Throne Room is actually God's house. This is where He lives. God's Throne Room is His house. We know all of heaven is His habitation, but the Throne Room is where He lives. In John 14: 1, Jesus said in my Father's house are many mansions. Heaven is

The Realm Of The Spirit

God's house. You never read anywhere in the Bible where it says that Jesus has a mansion or the Father has a special place where He goes in to retire from time to time or do whatever things He wants. The Throne Room is where He resides. It is His living room, bedroom and working place, where He permanently dwelt.

Heavenly places is not paradise.

It is worth noting that although paradise is the most blissful realm of Heaven, we don't operate in paradise while we are still on earth. It is not our portion. Instead, we operate in the Most Holy place where Jesus is standing at the right hand side of the Father. Paradise is a section where those who have died in the lord dwells. It is a place of residence for the saints who live in heaven. It is a section or portion of heaven but it is not heaven. ***Heavenly places is not just a section of heaven or a spiritual dimension***. It is a realm of realms, a dimension of dimensions, and a place of places. It is inexhaustible. The fact that it says heavenly places (plural) instead of heavenly place (Singular) means that this realm consists of many dimensions, many realms, many sections, demarcations, and many levels. That's people who move in that ream operate in different levels, places and depths and experience different realms of glory.

Heavenly places in not just a place where angels, spirit beings and departed saints live.

It is a place where even the human beings are permitted to travail, operate, function and continuously and consciously register their presence from the earthly realm. In actual fact walking in the spirit means operating in the heavenly places. Paul instructed us to walk in the spirit. Being in the spirit means walking, moving, travelling, living and parading in the heavenly places. What a privilege! The spirit world is no longer a mystery to us anymore. The veil has been lifted up. You can make heavenly places just like your common room. You can visit heavenly places more frequent that you visit a shopping mall. We can reach the depths in God where our spirits are lifted up to enter a ream in God where we begin to influence the activities of heaven and earth. From God's perspective, heaven alone is not complete. On the other hand the earth is also not compete on its own. These two realms needs to work in collaboration to achieve God's purpose. This reality is made possible by us entering through that realm and where we bring both heaven and earth together to function as one. When we finally depart for heaven to be with the lord, we will not be surprised by the glory and the beauty of heaven because we would have been operating and living in that realm already while on earth.

UNVEILING THE MYSTERY OF THE SPHERES OF THE HEAVENLY REALM

Heaven is not some ethereal place as some people presume it to be. Some Christians have no idea of what things are like in Heaven. They think about Heaven in earthly terms. The truth is that we need to think about Heaven in Heavenly terms. It must be ingrained in our thinking that the realm of the natural is just but a shadow or a pattern of the realm of the spirit. When God gave Moses a plan and a pattern of the tabernacle, he gave instruction that it be structured in such a way that it had three main sections or demarcations that is *the outer court, the inner court (Holy place) and the most holy place.* By this way, God gave him a glimpse of how Heaven looks like. It was a pattern of things already existing in the spirit world (Heaven). In case you don't understand in Heaven, there is a real Outer Court, a Holy place and the Most Holy place. Of course, it's much bigger and larger than we can imagine. It accommodates millions. So when Jesus Christ rose from the dead, He entered the Most Holy place so that you and I don't have to be in the Outer Court although we can enjoy all the blessings in the Outer Court. We don't have to be just in the Holy place either. We can be in the Most Holy place where He lives. God wants us to learn how to enter the most Holy place to enjoy the fullness of His presence. Heaven is God's House. God does not have an earthly House but the whole Heaven is His house. God doesn't sleep, rest nor slumber. He permanently dwells in the Holy of Holies in Heaven. It is in Heaven that millions of angels, and other spirit beings live to worship God.

THE DIVINE REVELATION OF HEAVEN

The Spiritual Universe consists of many different spheres of light that radiate from all the worlds that God has created and reaches right to the Heaven of Heavens, the Throne of God. It is brimming with life and activity of all the creations of God in various dimensions, each fulfilling their destiny. All the human activity of the earth in this present generation and in all the history of men combined is only one tiny dot in all the activities of the Spiritual Universe. In Heaven, everything moves like music and harmony. There are far more colours and harmony of colours than we can perceive on this earth. Everything is more radiant and full of joy which is the highest and it radiates from the very Throne of God. Consider the following testimony of a sister who God took up to Heaven on a study tour. This sister shared, "God spoke to me in the spirit as I was being translated to heaven. He said, "Enter into my gates with thanksgiving and into my courts with praise." In that very second I saw the pearly gates with many colours. These gates were huge column decorated with sculptures across the top, which arch together in a semicircle over the door to form an opening. Below and in between those gates was one golden door, which fit into those gates. It was filled with beautiful sculptures. I could notice this because I was a sculptress at one time. Around the outside edge of the door where it fit into the arch column and down to the centre of it a brilliant golden, orange and yellow lights were shining through it. When I first came to these gates through a mist, it makes the gates look like they were oyster shells pearls. After observing all these details the doors began to open inward. The immensity of the doors was evident because of the smallest of the figures I saw standing inside the door. When these doors opened the Shekinah glory of God shown in such brilliance. It was like looking at the sun without burning your eyes out.

A DIVINE REVELATION OF THE REALMS AND TYPES OF HEAVENS

It is of paramount significance to unveil the divine truth that contrary to what dozens of folks have been taught, God is not "way up there" faraway from our world, and so is Heaven. When we think of Heaven, we think of it as a distant place where we can only go to, when we die. However, this is short-sightedness which derails our effective operation in the realms f the spirit. Literally, Heaven is far, because it's in the third and end realm, meaning: you have to pass the first and second realm before reaching there, but figuratively, it is just here. That's how God would want us to view it, so that we don't think He is very far from us, because He actually is not!. He said so in Jeremiah 23:23, "Am I only a God nearby," declares the LORD, "and not a God faraway? He is actually Omnipresent, that is to say, present everywhere!

Frequency Revelator

There is a difference between heaven the place of God's abode and heaven on earth. From the first sentence of Genesis right through to the final book of Revelations, God's authoritative Word is clear that there are "heavens"—plural. The Bible opens with "In the beginning God created the Heavens and the earth." Heavens—plural. The Apostle Paul visited the "Third Heaven" and couldn't find words to describe it. The fact that Paul spoke about the third heaven means that there is a first and second heaven. There are many "Heavens" where the presence of God is manifested to a different degree in each sphere. All universal spheres of God have their own Heaven and progress to the Heaven of Heavens where God dwells. The glory of each Heaven is progressively greater with the least glory in the sphere of Heaven nearer the earth and the greatest glory in the sphere of Heaven nearest to the heaven of heavens. Although there are innumerable heavens in each creation of God, all the heavens and creations can be classified into three main categories: the First Heaven containing planetary spheres that belong to the particular solar systems, the Second Heaven containing the celestial spheres which belong to the space between solar systems, and the Third Heaven containing the God-spheres which radiate directly outwards from the Throne of God Himself. The progression of spiritual growth is not just in glory alone but also in dimension until it reaches the dimension of God where all dimensions known to us of time, space, omnipresence, etc. disappear because God is outside of all the dimensions which He has created.

For a human spirit that has just left the mortal body, even the first sphere of light would be a paradise compared to the present physical world. There is no death or decay or any of the earthly imperfections; only love, peace and joy. In heaven, God is able to manifest Himself in any part of the Spiritual Universe without leaving His throne. This manifestation takes a spiritual form with all the glory of God as tailored to the specific glory realm of the place where the revelation of God is unfolded. Angels and spirits in the highest spheres also possess a measure of this ability to project their presence in a spiritual form without leaving their places of abode. This spiritual form is alive with the life of the spirit and responsive to all the thoughts, will and emotion of the originating source. There is no natural comparison to this. Time, space and reality in the spiritual world are not as unbending as their physical counterparts (of time, space and matter). Part of the progress in the Spiritual World is to break free from always thinking in our physical three dimensional ways.

The Realm Of The Spirit

The Fist Heaven

"Let there be lights in the firmament of the heavens to divide the day from the night." (Genesis 1:14).

The 1st Heaven is where stars, sun and moon are. The firmament, earth's atmosphere which is the immediate sky, where the "fowls of the heaven" (Genesis 2:19; 7:3,23; Psalms 8:8, etc.), "the eagles of heaven" (Lamentations 4:19), it is the atmosphere that surrounds the earth. The first heaven consists of the clouds and the atmosphere, the sky and the stars. Psalms 78: 23-23 "Yet He had commanded the clouds above, and opened the doors of heaven, had rained down manna on them to eat, and given the bread of heaven." The atmospheric heavens include the air that we breathe as well as the space that immediately surrounds the earth. The technical term for this is the *"troposphere."* It extends about several miles above the earth. The space above this is called the *"stratosphere."* The Scripture uses the term heaven to describe this area. God declared in Genesis 6:7 that *I will destroy humanity whom I have created from the face of the earth, both humans and beasts, creeping thing and birds of heaven.* Another related scripture describes the birds of the *air*, for they neither sow nor reap nor gather in barns; yet your heavenly Father feeds them (Matthew 6:26). The word translated *"air"* is *ouranos*, the same Greek word that is elsewhere translated *"heaven."* In James 5:18, it says Elijah prayed again, and the *heaven* gave rain, and the earth produced fruit

The second Heaven

For we wrestle not against flesh and blood, but against principalities, against powers, against the rulers of the darkness of this world, against spiritual wickedness in high places (Ephesians 6:12).

This use of the term *heaven* also refers to outer space or the heaven of galaxies. It includes the sun, moon, and stars. Immediately after the tribulation of those days the sun will be darkened, and the moon will not give its light; the stars will fall from *heaven*, and the powers of the *heavens* will be shaken (Matthew 24:29). Do you notice that stars are said to be in heaven yet when you lift up your eyes to heaven, you see the sun, the moon, and the stars, all the host of heaven (Deuteronomy 4:19). The second heaven is where the devil and his hordes of demons were assigned to exist for a while. The Second Heaven is the throne room of God's enemy, the fallen angel

Lucifer, who is called Satan in the New Testament. It is the battleground where Satan's dark forces battle God's forces of light. When the Bible talks about spiritual forces of evil and wickedness in the *heavenly places*, it talks about the demonic thrones and activities of demonic angels operating in this realm. This does not mean that demons live in the same place as God. It simply means that they were allowed to operate in this realm which is by far lower than the throne of God. Ephesians 6:12 teaches us that the second heaven is where the demonic principalities, powers, rulers of darkness and spiritual wickedness in high places exist. The scientific name given to this heaven is the Stratosphere. This is confirmed In Isaiah 14:14, when Satan proclaimed, "I will ascend above the heights of the clouds; I will be like the most High." "Wherein in time past ye walked according to the course of this world, according to the prince of the power of the air, the spirit that now worketh in the children of disobedience." (Ephesians 2:2). Satan is also referred to in the Bible as the prince of the power of the air. The word of God teaches us that the second heaven is the domain of Satan and the fallen angels.

The second Heaven is where angels and demons are. Ever since the devil was defeated, he is only in second heaven sending his demonic forces to the earth. Second heaven, there are voices masquerading as the Holy Spirit. Demons posing as angels of light. There are illusions and imaginations, false revelations and delusions. There is even false prophecy as well. Hence we need a discernment spirit to tap into this realm. The demonic clouds primarily exist in the region of the atmosphere above the earth known Biblically as the second Heaven. Scientists have named this region the Stratosphere. These clouds exist high above the first Heaven. The scientific name given to the first heaven is the Troposphere. It is interesting to note that in a dialogue between Win Worley and a demon during a deliverance session, the demon mentioned that the prayers of the people had shut down the "headquarters" overhead. It is very important to understand that this demonic headquarters exists in the second heaven, or Stratosphere, over our heads. The second Heaven is the headquarters of the demonic powers.

THE THIRD HEAVEN

"The heavens cannot contain [Him]" (1 Kings 8:27).

The Scripture speaks of heavenly spheres beyond that which is visible from the earth. It is called the *Heaven of heavens*. Indeed heaven and the highest heavens belong to the Lord your God, also the earth with all that is in it (Deuteronomy 10:14). The psalmist wrote. Praise Him, you *heaven of heavens* and you waters above the heavens! (Psalm 148:4). Behold, heaven and the heaven of heavens cannot contain you (1 Kings 8:27). Yet Scripture also teaches us that there is a certain geographical place where God resides. It is also designated heaven. Heaven is the Father's house (John 14:2). It is the dwelling place of Jesus Christ, His Son (1 Peter 3:21-22). Heaven is also the city of the living God and the redeemed (Hebrews 12:22-23). Paul wrote that he was "caught up to the third heaven" (2 Corinthians 12:2), the celestial kingdom. The Father, Son and the Holy Spirit dwell in the 3rd Heaven, and also here, due to His the Omni-Presence. After the creation, the Holy Spirit remained close to the earth. At the ascension, the Lord Jesus went up into the air and went behind a cloud, but he was really moving back into the spiritual realm, from which He had come. He dwells there. In Heaven. The point of what we are saying is this: We do have such a high priest, who sat down at the right hand of the throne of the Majesty in heaven (Hebrews 8:1). Stephen knew he was going into the presence of the Lord. But Stephen, full of the Holy Spirit, looked up to heaven and saw the glory of God, and Jesus standing at the right hand of God (Acts 7:55). For Christ has not entered the holy places made with hands, which are copies of the true, but into heaven itself, now to appear in the presence of God for us (Hebrews 9:24).

A DIVINE REVELATION OF PARADISE

WHERE IS PARADISE?

The word *"paradise"* is originally derived from the Greek word *parádeisos*. Paradise is a Heavenly realm where the saints who have departed to be with the Lord in Heaven dwell. It is a very blissful, beautiful, pleasant, or peaceful place assigned for the habitation of departed saints. Jesus said *I come to prepare a place for you. In my father's house there are many mansions.* The mansions which Jesus spoke about in the opening scripture are actually in Paradise. A reading of Luke 11 shows that paradise was once located underground, in a place called Hades. There was a great chasm that separated hell from paradise. But after the death of Jesus Christ on the cross at Calvary, He went down to hades and overthrew the devil and his cohorts and made a public spectacle of them. He then took the keys of hades and liberated those who were in paradise. He brought them out and their bodies were seen walking in Jerusalem and appeared to many in broad day light. As Jesus ascended to Heaven, He went up with the saints to Heaven and they occupied their new location. They are resident in paradise until the second coming of Jesus Christ when He comes for His church.

It is important that you know that Paradise used to be underground, just adjacent to hell but following the resurrection of Jesus Christ from the dead it was relocated to Heaven. So, Paradise is now in Heaven and no longer underground as it used to be. The Bible presents the reality of paradise in Luke 23:43 and 2 Corinthians 12:4. That Paradise is the same Paradise that is now in Heaven. Paradise is God's place of bliss; it's God's place, it's in heaven, it's in God's presence, it's in heaven. So it's the same paradise that Paul was talking about in 2 Corinthians 12:4, when he said that he knew a man who went into paradise. So, it's the same place. From verse 3 of 2 Corinthians chapter 12, *"And I knew such a man, (whether in the body, or out of the body, I cannot tell: God knoweth;) How that he was caught up into paradise and heard unspeakable words, which is not lawful for a man to utter* [2 Corinthians 12:3-4]" So, that paradise and the one in Luke 23:43 are the same. There's one paradise and both of them are the same.

Let's make reference to Paradise in Luke 23:43 and 2 Corinthians 12:4. The first one has to do with a statement made by Jesus and, because of the wrong construction, Luke 23:43 – "And Jesus said unto him, [he is talking about during the crucifixion, there were two thieves crucified with Jesus one on either side, left and right and one of them said to Jesus, remember me] in the 42nd verse, "he said unto Jesus, Lord, remember me when thou comest into the kingdom and Jesus said unto him, Verily I say unto thee, To day shalt thou be with me in paradise. [Luke 23:42-43]" Now, that is the construction that is wrongly presented to us particularly in the King James Version. Jesus didn't say *"today shalt thou be with me in paradise,"* as it shows. What He said was, "I say unto thee today," the punctuation is in the wrong place. *"Verily I say unto thee today, thou shalt be with me in paradise."* That's what He said [repeats Luke 23:43] But what we actually have there is "I say unto you, today shalt thou be with me in paradise." But Jesus didn't go to paradise that day. He went to hell. That's what the Bible teaches. Jesus went to hell. When he died, he went to hell. He couldn't have gone to paradise that day; he went to hell.

The Bible says he had taken our sins upon himself. *"He became sin who knew no sin, that we might be made the righteousness of God in Him"* [2 Corinthians 5:21]. So, our sins were laid on Jesus. He died the death of a sinner and so he went

The Realm Of The Spirit

to hell because he died in our place. So he went to hell to pay the penalty for all the sins committed by humanity. So, he didn't go to paradise that day. The third day, he came out of the grave and the Bible does tell us in Matthew 27: 52-53 that there were those…many saints who slept came out of the grave after His resurrection. When Jesus arose, many arose with him. And sure enough, that thief would have come up with them. And they went with Jesus to heaven. That's what the Bible tells us. And, in fact, many of them that came out of their graves were seen in the city; they appeared to many in the city. So, he really didn't say that the thief will be with him that day in paradise because he didn't go to paradise that day. He went to hell that day and defeated Satan for us; and when he defeated Satan, [on] the third day, he came out of that grave. And when he arose, many of the saints that slept arose together with him and then they went with him to heaven. Praise God!

DOES ANYBODY DWELL IN PARADISE?

The saints who die in the Lord and depart from this earth to Heaven live in the most glamorous, blissful and beautiful place called *Paradise*. In Heaven, Jesus prepared a place for us according to spiritual substances we send up and according to our rewards. Some Christians who are greatly rewarded for their work and faithfulness on earth have huge mansions to live in. Other Christians who do not have that great reward may have a terrace house and some may have an apartment. In Heaven, there are many houses of all shapes, designs and sizes belonging to Christians who are still living on earth. The more we walk with God and do His will the more our houses grow bigger. Depending on the level of our obedience to the Holy Spirit in all matters and was faithfulness, Jesus would keep on adding more and more rooms to our mansion. A man of God who visited Heaven on a study tour testifies that upon his visitation to Heaven, he saw many rooms in his mansion that could accommodate visiting pastors from other cities in Heaven. In his mansion, there was also a room that has a computer. This computer had the records of the church members that God entrusted to him. This pastor would be able to check the records of his church members from his computer in his mansion. There is also another room in his mansion where there is a refreshing waterfall and spring. As he soaks himself in this spring, he would be refreshed in a way that God only knows how to refresh.

WHAT ARE THE SAINTS DOING IN PARADISE?

It is worth exploring the divine truth that so many people understand that in Heaven, angels worship God but have not yet caught a revelation of what the departed saints are doing in paradise. Well, when one dies and goes to Heaven, he would continue serving God in Heaven. Our ministries or divine tasks do not end here on earth although there will be executed in a greater unfathomable dimension in Heaven. It is such an unfathomable experience to learn that when we get to Heaven, we will join angels and continue to worship God in Heaven However, contrary to what multitudes of Christians presume, worship is not the only activity in heaven as heaven is a beehive of spiritual activities. There are many instruction schools, training centres where saints gather to be taught the things of Heaven. Some people who depart to be with the Lord in Heaven serve as teachers, instructors, and worship leaders. Pastors from other cities in Heaven convene to teach others how to serve God in the right way. There are worship centres where people gather to receive training on worship. With celestial bodies, we don't get tired like we do now.

Saints also rest in their places or mansions designated for them in Paradise. The mansions of the various spheres of heaven are "*built*" by techniques far beyond our capacity. In a sense, they are not "*built*" as they are "*grown*". Let me give an example. Being curious about things of science and construction by nature, I was given an understanding of how the mansions were "constructed." The task of "building" mansions is always given to angels and spirits of the higher sphere for those of the lower sphere. A group of them would gather together under the leadership of a spirit of the highest sphere at the place where the mansion is to be "built." They would receive the impartation and energizing life from God and using their will and thoughts project it towards the place where the mansion is to be created. At first the foundation would be laid, then the walls and towards the end the leader would complete the roof and the finishing touches. The spiritual substance would, in a mysterious way, somehow also be taken from the spiritual emanations from the future dweller of the mansion and also from all those involved in its "construction" or more accurately "growing." The completed mansion takes the colour, character and uniqueness of all those involved in its creation. It is the law of the spiritual world that all that one creates or does flows forth with the character and impartation of the creator or doer. As each angel and spirit is unique, there are no two mansions that are alike. Each has its own unique flavour and light. God could just speak or think and everything would just be created in the heavens but it is the joy and pleasure of the Father God that His angels and redeemed spirits take part in this delegated work. Not all spirits are involved in this area, only those that have an interest in architecture and creation of buildings. Other redeemed spirits may be involved in music or worship. The tasks are quite intricately divided with some specialising in heavenly furniture, others in gardens, plants and trees.

A DIVINE REVELATION OF CHILDREN'S PARADISE

It is worth highlighting that coming to this earth from the Heavenly realm is a great dimensional shift. There is the need to develop free will spiritual consciousness in ways that have not developed before. For foetuses or babies or children who have short earthly existence, there is a growth process that still needs to be completed spiritually before the regaining of consciousness of pre-existence. Thus foetuses and babies who died early on earth have to enter children's paradise to grow and learn; including learning about the redemption work of Christ on earth. The advantage they will have in children's paradise is that they will grow much faster than on earth and reach spiritual maturity rapidly. When they are fully grown and matured, some of the knowledge of their pre-existence will begin to come to them. The disadvantage of leaving earth early is that there are some areas of growth which they will miss out on but it will be compensated for in other paths of growth in heaven. The lack of knowledge of pre-existence also happens to fully grown humans who died without the knowledge of God, especially those who are drawn to darkness. There their sense of having existed before is sometimes perverted by dark spirits of the lower realms into the wrong doctrine of reincarnation. For those who grow normally on earth, and who are seekers of God, sometimes the knowledge that they have existed somewhere before comes to their consciousness even while on earth but without the Bible and revelation, they do not understand where this sense is coming from.

Some people have a faint sense that they came from somewhere beyond earth; and somehow they don't really belong to this world, especially when they were young children. For Jesus Christ, when He first came to earth and manifested as a human being, also had to reach a certain age of spiritual maturity before He began to acquire knowledge of who He was and His position in the Godhead. He had to learn the human language the normal way and through the Scriptures and direct revelation from God began to comprehend who He was and is – and the child grew and became strong in spirit, filled with wisdom (Luke 2:40), and Jesus increased in wisdom and stature (Luke 2:52). In a similar way, all of us who live to adulthood on earth need to discover God's plan in our specific lives and grow in wisdom and knowledge. It is a divine requirement that all who come to earth experience the growth process again till we are spiritually matured.

THE CASE OF ABORTED INFANTS IN PARADISE.

Have you ever wondered what happens to infants who gets aborted here on earth? Where do their spirit go after abortion? Well let's refer to a spiritual experience of Marietta Davis who visited heaven and was taken to children paradise for a visit. And in children's paradise there are children who have gone to be with the Lord and sometimes small little infants who have gone to be with the Lord. I am sure you know that there are millions foetus have been aborted and these are human beings. And each on them are carried into heaven where they are schooled and trained and brought up in heaven. A Sister whom God allowed to visit heaven on a study tour testifies about her experience in heaven. When she arrived in heaven, she was taken to paradise by the angel to visit. Listen carefully how she describes this place here:

As we advanced I perceived before me a vast and complicated structure, whose outer walls and towers appeared in a form of marbles that was in appearance delicate as snow. This served as a foundation of a vast canopy like a dome, though it was far too extended to be expressed in earthly architectural terms. What I saw was a dome that was too huge to architecturally be classified as an earthly dome. It was beyond earthly architecture. We drew near this building and I perceived that the dome was suspended over the vast circular plain. This says my guide is a place where all infants from your globe I gathered for the instructions. There, infants are first conducted and then nourished beneath the smile of the guardian angel. Each nursery though somewhat varying is a miniature of this vast temple of instructive manifestation. And each one is a home for the infant spirit to enter there until they attain to higher degrees and enter the paradise of more advance useful existence. For degrees of instructions adapted to a more intellectual conditions. Then the angel says whenever an infant dies on earth, the angel guardian who bears up the spirit to the land of peace, perceive its interior type of mind. And according to its type it is classed with others of like order of intelligence. And as the skilful gardener on earth in one flora division trains the various species of the lily in another department roses, so here angelic wisdom classify the infant spirit. And according to their variety of artistic, scientific, social tendency assign each a home. That's adapted to its unfolding of its interior germs of life into intellectual artistic or industrial harmony.

The Realm Of The Spirit
A Divine Revelation of the Grand Stand

In heaven, there is a part where you can stand with God's permission and see what's going on the earth. There is a stadium in heaven where Christians go and watch the goings-on among Christians on earth. There is a place in heaven where you can stand and see what's happening on earth. That is why it's called the Grand Stand because inhabitants of heaven stand and watch what's going on in the earth. Robert Liardon has reported on this when he went to heaven at the age of eight. You find that mentioned in the book of in Hebrews 12:11 where Paul mentioned we have a cloud of witnesses. *Wherefore seeing we also are compassed about with so great a cloud of witnesses, let us lay aside every weight, and the sin which doth so easily beset us, and let us run with patience the race that is set before us.* In this scripture, Paul uses the image of the Greek Olympiad—the ancient Greek games—as an illustration so we can relate to what he is talking about. In ancient Greece, the athletes who competed in this race wore heavy weights on their legs and arms and armour-like plates on their bodies as they trained and prepared for the Greek games. They did this so their bodies would be accustomed to rigorous discipline and hardship—so they would have the endurance, condition, and stamina they would need in the actual contest.

When it came time for the race or the competition in the actual games, those athletes laid aside all those heavy weights. Without all those weights, it seemed as if their bodies were almost weightless; movement seemed effortless, and physical strength and endurance were mightily increased. The stands were full of cheering spectators who watched the athletes as they ran their various races and competed in their great trials of strength and endurance. Paul uses this imagery of the Greek games as a picture or type of the Christian running the race of life. He's also saying that we are compassed about with a great cloud of witnesses just as the Greek athletes were surrounded by thousands of spectators cheering them on from the stands. In fact, one translation of this verse says, "Wherefore seeing that we are standing on the playing field with a grandstand full of witnesses, let us lay aside the weights that would try to entangle us." I can just imagine that great cloud of witnesses—Paul, Peter, Moses, Abraham—the great patriarchs of old and the whole host of our heavenly family—watching from the grandstands of Heaven. Our loved ones who have gone home to be with the Lord are there in that company, too, cheering us on to victory. When thoughts of defeat are racing through your mind, remember this scripture in Hebrews. Remember that great cloud of witnesses cheering,

Frequency Revelator

"Come on! You can make it. The Word says you are more than a conqueror [Rom. 8:37]!" And be encouraged to run your race with patience and with confidence! Sometimes I just think of that great cloud of witnesses, and it just spurs me on to victory. But in this race, you must also realize that you are going to have to fight the good fight of faith. Refuse to give up on the promises God has given you in His Word! Being strong in faith means that you believe that what God has promised you, He is able to perform (Rom. 4:20–21).

CHAPTER THREE

DEEPER MYSTERIES AND REVELATIONS OF THE SPIRIT REALM

There are things in the spiritual world for which there are no words any earthly language can describe (2 Corinthians 12:4). No earthly language can paint their reality. There are colours in the spectrum of light that are beyond the ability of the physical earth to reproduce. There are colours which contain healings and impartations yet unknown to the earth. There are notes and tones too refined for the sphere of the earth. There are forces and powers not yet available to us nor can they be understood or utilized by us in our present development. The blessings of the Spiritual World constantly flow and vibrate down towards the earth but our physical brain, made from material matter, does not feel their impact impinging upon us and lifting us upwards. As each spirit develops the spiritual organs and senses to receive the frequencies of the higher spiritual realms, then only is it able to receive the relative blessings of the impartations flowing like a river from the Throne of God through the various spiritual spheres to the earth.

The Heavenly Attire And Garments.

All of the spirits in the spiritual realm have garments and clothes covering them but those of the lower and darker spheres appear to be in their naked spiritual body, and those lower still than these dark realms have naked spiritual bodies which are so altered that they appear ugly and do not even look human. The spirits in the highest realms have the brightest garments. The aura or light of these garments emanates from the mind of each spirit being. The aura or light that is emanated forms the spiritual garment for the spirit body. At physical death, spirits are still dominated by the earthly influences of the mind and thus produce the particular earthly fashions of the spiritual garments that clothe their spirit bodies but as the spirit matures and learns control of their mind and the spiritual forces at their disposal, they gain more control of their spiritual garments. The intensity or radiant brightness of their garments is still governed by their growth into higher spheres. In the spiritual world, there are more colours than we can see in the physical realm – not just seven colours of the rainbow and their intermediate states but thousands of ranges of colours. The character, strengths, weaknesses and development of the spirit being are reflected in the colour and brightness of their garments. In the spirit world, every one manifests in full and clear view to all their spiritual qualities and exact development level of their spiritual life in their spiritual body and in their spiritual clothing. Even on the earth, humans whose spirits are pure have a radiant light that shines around them like a garment. This is invisible to the physical earth but is visible to the spiritual world. Those whose hearts are evil have a dark mist that surrounds them. The greater the purity of heart and life, the brighter the light: the greater the evil in the heart, the greater the darkness that surrounds a human. Clothing that is made in the spiritual sphere, has textures and hues taken from the quality of the spiritual state of the wearer. Each particular sphere has its own unique tint of colour according to the occupation, interests, bend of mind, gifting or wisdom and knowledge of its inhabitants.

There are differences of attire and residence in Heaven. For Paul had declared long ago that souls would then differ as one star differ from another as Mars from Mercury, as Saturn from Jupiter, but at every step in heaven you get amazed to see that some who were expected to be low down were high up. You get to know that the highest thrones, the brightest coronets, the richest mansions, are occupied by those who have reprobate fathers or bad mothers, but they had laid hold of God's arm, they had cried for a special mercy, they had conquered 7 devils within and 70 devils without and were washed in the Blood of the Lamb. By so much as their conflict was terrific and awful, their victory was consummate. And they have taken places immeasurably higher than those of good parentage who could hardly help being good. These others have 10 generations of piety to help them. The steps that many have mounted to the highest places in heaven were made out of the cradles of corrupt parentage.

In the glory of God, who I am, what I am, what I wear, whatever saints are wearing in heaven and all the brightness of the mansions surrounding the Throne were only a reflection. Literally you could say His life is in us. It is because of the constant pulsating river of life that keeps flowing out from the throne of God that lights up every life in heaven. Glory and life are one in heaven. To have life is to have glory. To have glory is to have life. Another thing you get to be aware of is that the garments are constantly changing for different purpose. We don't have the same clothing for 10,000 years times 10,000 years in heaven. There are different types of clothing that we wear and they are a reflection of God and what He is doing. On this earth, some people wear clothes that indicate their work and rank. In heaven, the garments are the same with an exception. On this earth, many uniforms are uncomfortable and most prefer to wear casual informal clothes. In heaven all the garments feel casual. They are not uncomfortable at all. In heaven, the two are one. All the clothings are an expression of the different rankings and work of the angels for the different type of work they do. Angels changes clothes. They do not have a wardrobe in a sense like we have on earth but when angels come to the Throne Room on an assignment, they would take away different things with them. Sometimes they take with them swords, sometimes a vase, or different things to send to the people on the earth. And each of these things are powerful impartation of gifts or substances. It is literal in the spirit world although it is only a tangible feeling in your spirit when you receive it. When you receive a gift from God, say a ring, it is God literally giving it to you although in your natural body you may just feel only a heavy impartation of the anointing. In the spirit realm, there are many, many types of gifts God sends to His peoples and the angels are commissioned to send them. As the angels came near the Throne Room to receive the commands of God, their garments are changed instantly and they march out of God's Throne with their commission.

Human Talents

All social life in heaven is graded according to earthly struggle and usefulness as proportion to the use of talents given. Some of the most unknown on earth are most famous in heaven. Many who have been the greatest failures on earth are the greatest. Many who had great talents are living in the back streets of heaven. Hence advancement in life and Spirit of Jesus here on earth determines our state of glory in heaven. Although everyone has a mansion in heaven yet there are so many conditions of our mansion in the things that are inside heaven. There are several facts that I want to bring forth. We know that the teaching of the New Jerusalem, which is the city of God also has to do with our mansion. In other words the principles are the same.

Is it possible to lose our heavenly reward? Yes it is. It is possible that when we are not faithful to that which God called us, and in that way we lose the foundation of something that our life is building in heaven. Some of us think that our life here on earth has no connection with heaven. I mean God has mass-produced mansions and all our mansions look the same. Do you know why each mansion looks different in heaven? The mansions in heaven depend upon the material you send there from here. Didn't Jesus say, "Do not gather treasures on this earth where the rust will destroy and the moth corrupt? But He says to lay your treasures in heaven. We do this by sacrificial giving of our life to serve and love others. Then you get the treasures in heaven. It is important for us to take note that faithfulness to what God has called you determines your heavenly mansion. Therefore if you live and die without fulfilling your ministry your heavenly mansion is in a way not the way it should be. I can only speculate because it is silent here in the Word of God. Perhaps in heaven you would be doing certain work in order to earn some heavenly money or merits to continue building your mansion. But we can say with definite scriptural authority that although Jesus has mansions for us in heaven, the materials and the foundations of those mansions depend on your faithfulness to the destiny in your life the call that God has for you. For the 12 apostles of the Lamb their faithfulness built something bigger besides their own mansions, and so their ministries became enshrined as names. Names not so much as the names are written there just for show. It tells you that the materials from their ministries built the heavenly city.

Callings and ministry offices

God has called each one of us to a destiny and to certain ministry to fulfil. And He has given us mantles in our life to fulfil whatever office He sends us. When you are unfaithful to that office or you don't take upon yourself that mantle somebody else will take it. I can certainly say that the twelfth name of the 12 apostles in heaven is not Judas Iscariot. But it was his at one time. Somebody else took that reward. Kathryn Khulman has said that she was God's third choice. In other words, the earlier two persons who were chosen to carry that anointing that Kathryn Khulman carried, did not fulfil their calling. Subsequently it fell on Kathryn Khulman, and the rest they say, is history. It is a very sober thought to think that when we don't fulfil the call and destiny of our life that which is ours disappears and becomes somebody's. You say its God perfect will for me; it's predestination. Predestination is still governed by free will. It was God's plan that all the Israelites who came out from Egypt enter into the Promised Land. But they refused to go in and the next generation went in. Your ministry that God

The Realm Of The Spirit

has called you to is one that comes from the very throne of God.

And your ministry doesn't just determine your recognition or your function in the body of Christ on this earth. We always think that if I am called to be an evangelist, apostle, pastor, prophet or teacher, my main reward is that we could win souls on this earth and we could do our part in the body of Christ and train others in the body of Christ and bring them to perfection of Christ as in Ephesians 4:11 onwards. But this morning we want you to know that your faithfulness to that also determines the foundations of part of the heavenly city in some form or your mansion which will be a part of the whole heavenly city. It is not just wining souls on earth which one of the most important job on earth we have to win souls. Remember this your heavenly mansion is based on your ministry. By ministry it doesn't mean we all are called to full time but whatever destiny that God has in your life, whatever little thing that God has in your life.

In Ephesians 4, all the fivefold prepare the church for their ministry. If for example your call to is your gift of prophecy. And your only function may be to travel all over the world to preach the gospel like some evangelist. Your only function is within the body of Christ to intercede, to pray and to bring forth the word of prophecy and you didn't do it faithfully. When you go to heaven your heavenly mansion is not really what it should be. Now no one will steal that mansion from you in a sense. But somebody may take that reward from you that belong to the heavenly city. Just like Judas Iscariot's name was taken off and another name was placed there. Some believe it was Matthias and some believe it was Paul. We don't want to speculate. But according to Acts it was Matthias who was chosen to replace Judas Iscariot. There are some foundations of those things that are being built in heaven that depend on your life. When we think about your life and your ministry we only think about that on this earth the number of souls God wants us to bring, the fulfillment of our ministry here on earth. But we forgot to think of the fact that your life is building a material somewhere up there. And that if you fail to do so God will raise someone else to build that material and they will lay the foundation for heaven. We are laying foundations for different parts of heaven. The 12 apostles laid the main thing with the 12 patriarchs. But there are so many other parts of heaven that is being built that depends on your faithfulness and my faithfulness to God's call in our life our talents, our gifting, that came as a gift from God.

The next time you think of not being fully obedient to your destiny remember a part of heaven that you are supposed to be building. We always think of the building here but we forgot that we are building a part of heaven by our faithfulness. And it's affecting that part of heaven. And God will give you a time frame. When that time frame is over and you didn't carry out what you were supposed to do, somebody else ends up building your part. Because God will make sure His heavenly city is completed. That is No. 1 our ministry and call have an effect on the heavenly city; have an effect on our heavenly mansion and what other things that are in heaven we know not of. This is why we need to go in fasting and prayer. The sacrifices you made, the love that you have shown, the choices that you have made, and the self-denial that you have walked in, all these go to build the heavenly parts of heaven. Heaven's glory cannot be bought with money. But they are building on your works in your life.

The other thing that we want to look at in Revelation chapter 21:19-20 the foundations of the wall of the city were adorned with all kinds precious stones. I believe that our heavenly mansion is made from those precious stones too. There are many sets of precious stones that go to building our heavenly mansion. Now those precious stones depend on our life on earth too. That is the 2nd area. Turn to the book of I Corinthians chapter 3. Paul talks about laying a foundation. And we always took it that the foundation as a foundation of the church here on earth. No doubt the church is built on a foundation of the early church. But remember what God is building is not just for this earth; it's for heaven. In verse 9 onwards *For we are God's fellow workers; you are God's field, God's building.* According to the commission of God given to me, like a skilled master builder I laid a foundation, and another man is building upon it. Let each man take care how he builds upon it. For on other foundation can anyone lay that that which is laid, which is Jesus Christ. Now if any one builds on the foundation with gold, silver, precious stones, wood, hay, stubble, each man's work will become manifest; for the Day will disclose it, because it will be revealed with fire, and the fire will test what sort of work each one has done. If the work, which any man has built on the foundation, survives he will receive a reward. If any man's work is burned up, he will suffer loss, though he himself will be saved, but only as through fire. That tells us we are saved by grace. You are saved based on your faith in Jesus Christ but there is no reward. Do you not know that you are the temple of God and the Spirit of God dwells in you? Anyone who defiles the temple of God, God will destroy him.

The Realm Of The Spirit
Prophetic gestures such as Giving

In Heaven, your giving is measured by the percentage of the total wealth that you have. Peter Tan testifies that when he visited Heaven, he was amazed at how big and beautiful one of the mansions was. He pointed to the grandly residence and asked, *"Who live there?"* And the angel replied, the widow who gave 2 mites. He wondered what about the people who gave thousands of dollars but whose percentage is small. That woman gave 100%. And she had this huge mansion. The angel then made this statement about some of those professors of religion who were famous on earth. I asked about them but no one in heaven could tell me anything about them. The reason for this teaching is so that none of us is taken by surprise in heaven. We want to be prepared for heaven. We want to live for heaven

Remember this: in the spirit world, all carnal activities are counted for nothing. They are like straw. I know in the natural these activities may appear tremendous. But in the spirit realm they are like straw. If a Christian live 90 % of his life carnally, that 90 % will be burnt up and there will be little left to show to God. This message must go out, otherwise Christians will find their years have been short changed when they thought they had lived for God just because they followed what men told them. It is not important what men say or do, but what God says. Even a spiritual ministry can become carnal when people begin to do it because they want a name and attention. Let me tell you, when they stand before Jesus Christ, everything that was done will be burned up. Unless their work is born out of the love of God, and born out of the pure moving of the Spirit, it cannot last. What is born of flesh is flesh, and what is born of Spirit is spirit.

Heavenly Mansions

Here is a little account that talks about heavenly mansion and the planes of glories that are there. All social life in heaven is graded according to earthly struggle and usefulness as proportion to use of talents given. Visitors from the heavenly land returning tell us that the state of spiritual development in which we live here is the state in which we arrive there. Although Jesus is in all heaven and His life and presence is enjoyed by every saint and angel not all have equal capacity to partake this glory life. Because of this limited capacity it is impossible for saints just from earth at once to enter into the fullness of all the exceeding glories of heaven. And this is an awesome. It says: It appears that very few walk so close to Christ in selfless worldliness, full hearted devotion to God and in such a constant communion with

Him in the Holy Spirit that when they die they are directly led to mansions highest up in the holy city. See, there are mansions at different planes. If we know these things on earth why don't we do something about it? If we are ignorant of those things then that in a certain way doesn't excuse us. That partly explains why we are not so zealous for the things in heaven. But now that we know we should do something about that. This high exaltation immediately upon entering the world of glory belongs to only to earth's rarest saints. And he mentioned some names here. Perhaps only such as directly enter such realms are the apostle John who was near to Jesus' heart, Mary who sat at Jesus' feet, St. Francis of Assisi and others who daily walked and talked with Jesus. And he talks about how the saints grow from glory to glory.

The Language of Heaven

In the realm of the spirit, communication is via thoughts and spirit impressions. In the spirit realm, one can understand perfectly all the spoken languages of the earth. This understanding is not directly through knowledge of the language itself but rather the meaning and thoughts of the speaker are communicated directly and telepathically. God does not speak in human language even though we seem to hear God in the language that we are conversant with in earthly life. There is no language good enough or great enough for God to express Himself through. All human language created by humans is insufficient for the Creator of all life. When we hear God speak in a human language, it is because our spirits understand it in a manner beyond language and then conveys it to our soul in a language that we have acquired during our earthly life. Spirit to spirit communication is beyond language. It is like deep calling unto deep (1 Corinthians 2:10, 11; Romans 8:26, 27). It is like an impartation of experience and knowledge or like the transfer of data from one computer to another except that this computer illustration lacks the transfer of the full experience and senses involved with the subject matter. One instantly "knows" (the word 'know' is limiting here because it also involves the process of actually experiencing the knowledge) what is communicated. The further one progresses spiritually, one does not need even any earthly language thoughts to communicate; then would pass away the last shreds of the limiting earthly habit of human language.

There is a sense of knowing that is beyond the physical world. When you pick up a flower in heaven and desire to look at it to analyse it, you actually *"seem to become the flower"* and know everything about the flower because you have "experienced being a flower". When you meet another person, and desire to know about the person, you "seem to become the person" and be able to know everything about that person. There is a limitation with sentient spirit beings with free will. This special and supernatural "knowing" is only possible with the free will consent of one another. The apostle Paul is speaking about this realm when he said that we shall know as we are known (1 Corinthians 13:12). This sense of being able to *"become what you want to know"* (without actually becoming the object) is an instantaneous knowledge infusion which includes not only objective knowledge but all subjective and perspective knowledge. Thus everyone understands everyone else perfectly. Spoken language is still used more for the beauty and music in the differences of communication and for special areas of purposeful creations through the working of the Holy Spirit.

The Light in Heaven

In the Spiritual World, the only light that lights up the entire universe is the light of Christ that shines from His throne. This light does not cast any shadows but rather flows right through all living creatures in the spiritual realm. Even the light of the brightest angels is the refraction of the light of Christ. Those who are on the earth spheres do not see the light of Christ all the time because in the spiritual world you need the same equivalent spiritual level to see in that same level of spiritual light. From time to time, the light of Christ would shine according to the needs of individuals in the earth sphere but the visibility of that glorious light has to be diminished according to the level of the individual. However, the presence of Christ is always there without the individual spirit, who is not developed to the higher glory, realising it. This light is also the very means by which all life in every sphere is sustained and nourished. The light of the spiritual world is different from the physical sunlight that the material earth has. It is interpenetrating and shines through the physical realm. Thus when we look at a human being from the spiritual realm, we do not really see the physical body, it appears like a mist or envelope – although this also depends on the spiritual development of the spirit; those who are still earth-bound see the material realm as a solid. The well-developed spirits of the higher spirit realm see right into the spirit and soul of humans.

There are no lights in heaven but God is the source of all light in the whole heavens. The Bible says there are no suns in heaven for the glory of God lights up all of heaven. We read in the Word that angels radiate light and their presence have a shininess about them. In heaven, angels have different degrees of brightness of the glory of God, but the awareness was that all those brightness and shininess of all the creations of God in the heavens -angels, saints and others was only a reflection. The awareness of this fact was very strong. In Genesis 1 when God first made the Heaven and the earth, He said *let there be light* and there was light. And God saw the light that it was good and God divided the light from the darkness. God called the light day and the darkness night. So the evening and morning were the first day. Now day No. 1 there was still no sun created. Day and night doesn't have the same reference that we have today. Day and night in a sense of a division, darkness and light. Remember there was darkness all over the earth. The darkness came because Satan fell. Satan fell long before man was created. Then God said let there be light. The darkness was driven off. You ask, "Why is there still darkness? It is because Satan is still around.

When Jesus said that *you are the light of this world,* He meant it literally, in the very sense of the word. In the spirit world, you could recognize a believer just by looking at them. That is how the angels know us. That's how demons know whether you are of God or not of God. There is a light that flows from our life. When someone has a wrong thought there is darkness in them. In the spirit realm when I look at people's faces or minds, sometimes some of them have little black dots in their heart. Some of them have little black dots in their mind. Some of them have a cloud. I say God is this all the time there. And those represent thoughts, motives and intentions. The more evil a person is the darker their inner parts are. I am not talking about the natural body. I am talking about the soul. You could look into a person's soul. And what Jesus experienced here was quite easy to see in the spirit realm. For these kind of people when they were looking at Jesus with hate, there would have been a darkness and a cloud about them. It would be very observable from the spirit realm. We don't exactly read a person's thought but the moment that person open their mouth and say any word that would become like a channel that you could see into that person's mind.

Visibility And Sight in Heaven

The spiritual world has its own substance and just as the spiritual world is invisible to us, our material world is more or less like a mist to those in the spiritual realm – with the exception of spirits in the lowest earth spheres whose basic character and mind is still very much earth based. When the spirit world looks at this material earth, it primarily sees only the spiritual aspects of the earth (the spirits of humans and the spirit life that sustains the material world). The material world is almost invisible to the spirit realm especially to those of the highest sphere. The material world is only temporary and its "temporariness" is visible (like a mist) to those in the spiritual world. The light of God shines through Christ who sits on the throne in the highest realm and lights up all of the universe and the spiritual spheres around the earth. Those who are highest in spiritual development see Christ in His full glory; while to those in lowest development, His appearance is like the sun shining upon them. Unlike the sun, the spiritual light from Jesus shines through all objects and when a spiritual being radiates with light, it is because the light refracts through the spirit being. All the light of everything in the spiritual world come from Christ at the throne on high. The reason why spirits of the lowest realm cannot perceive or see this light is not because it is not there but rather that their own spiritual blindness has prevented them from seeing this light. Like a blind man born without proper eyes, their spiritual eyes are not yet developed to see the light of Christ which ever shines through all His creation. Thus to them, all is darkness save the light of angelic help which they receive. The light of Christ, which shines to and through all, casts no shadows.

Actions And Reactions (Predestination and Free choice)

In the spiritual world, one can see the ultimate result of each thought and action. They ripple through space and time causing the results that we see in the physical earth. Every human that is born into the earth becomes part of the thoughts, actions, and reactions of the totality of thought and spiritual forces (good or bad) released since the creation of the earth. Not all the evil or suffering in the world is caused directly by first choice of the individual. The majority of it is caused by the ripple effect of the thoughts and decisions of others preceding the individual. Whole communities, cities and countries are gripped by the strongest ripple (more like it building to a tsunami wave) of forces that influence people on the earth. The whole earth looks like an ocean of ripples and waves of forces ebbing and flowing according to each new action and reaction of the human race. Positive or negative forces of influence sweep over entire communities, cities or countries from time to time. Every sin causes more suffering for the entire human race and every righteous thought and loving act releases a power that lifts the whole human race.

Frequency Revelator

In spite of this strong invisible influence that grips every new human born to the earth, there is still the power of free choice given to each one. If the humans by free choice choose to understand the existence of this Spiritual World and yield to the power available through the Holy Spirit, the negative effects of these forces are powerless in their lives. It does not take much to open themselves to the spiritual forces available for their aid. Even the smallest cry for help, the weakest prayer of an unregenerate human releases positive change to the spiritual forces that ebb and flow into their lives. God answers both the prayers of those who love Him and even those who hate Him but cry for His help in their need. Great is the mercy and love of our Father God. Even the slightest inclination of heart towards love and goodness releases a measure of help from the Holy Spirit. Humans who do not open themselves to the power of help from the Spiritual World become weak and susceptible to existing forces preceding them. They are too weak to counter the effect of the negative forces present in the human race. All humans need help from outside themselves. Even those who thought that they had succeeded by their own strength and capacity received help from the spiritual world without them knowing it. There is no possibility of success in the physical world against the tide of forces that ebb and flow against the human race. Without aid from the spiritual world no one can overcome. Those who through heart, thought and action choose to continually reject help from the spiritual world in the end succumb to these forces and are destroyed; eventually losing their physical lives prematurely.

Every human is born with the potential for goodness and greatness (John 1:9). Whether one is well known or unknown, of great visible influence or of little visible influence, everyone is powerful in contributing to the forces that affect the entire human race. An insignificant little life could be very important in the spiritual world because of what the impact that life may have twenty generations later in word, deed or action, etc. Everyone born on to the earth has a powerful world influence. Unfortunately, many do not open themselves to their spiritual destinies. No human lives and leaves this earth without contributing to the tides of forces influencing the whole human race whether positive or negative. Those who do not yield to the forces of goodness and love become destroyed by forces of darkness that are attracted to the darkness they allow in their hearts. All humans are like magnets that constantly (by their free choice of thought and heart) attract to themselves forces of good or bad which work for them or against them. No matter how weak they think they are, by choosing the right thing in their heart of hearts, they release forces of good that would gradually overcome all the power of evil assailing against them. One small loving thought or action can fell a tsunami of evil forces.

Evil spirits are powerless against the love of God. Perfect love casts out fear (1 John 4:18). When a person is influenced to do evil or wrong things, it is because they attract evil spirits to themselves by their own evil desires. To be tempted is not wrong but to entertain the temptation and allow it to produce an evil desire in our lives is wrong. This evil desire attracts evil spirits who then entice us to do evil. The desire is our choice, the enticing is the encouragement received from evil spirits to do evil. Each one is tempted when he is drawn away by his own desires and enticed (James 1:14). Thus it is important never to allow wrong or evil desires to form in our heart – they attract evil spirits to our lives who will cause us to sin. The free choice is still ours. We must stop sin at its temptation stage and not allow it to grow into the desire stage. When our heart is pure and no wrong desires exist, not a single evil spirit can stand in our presence. Angels and all the heavenly hosts are attracted to our lives and encamped around us. A pure heart of love is the greatest asset in the spiritual world. Blessed are the pure in heart for they shall see God (Matthew 5:8).

Spiritual Development in Heaven

It is worth exploring the truth that the human spirit grows or develops from glory to glory as we learn how to commune with the Spirit of God. People who don't live their life for God and just before they die they say, *"Jesus Christ forgive me, I am a sinner, come into my heart,"* they straightaway go to Heaven. Or many backslidden Christians who don't live their life for God and just when they are dying they repent. And those who had little experience in the Christian life being like Jesus in character, attitude, words, deeds, just being like Jesus and those who never suffered for Christ. Heaven is measured from a different perspective from earth. But when we learn that tribulations work character and character equals the precious stones, we learn to value the pressure, the hard times. We learn to stay steady to holding on to Christ come what may. We learn to walk in Christian love although sometimes it is difficult. We learn to be Christ like and the heavenly reward is there. Those who had never suffered for Christ or those who have little experience in the Christian life or little development in their spiritual life are at death ushered into the most remote parts for instructions in one of the lower planes of heaven. Great numbers of mansions and temples of instructions are arranged in ascending grades. Since all heaven is a spiritual realm everything in it is spiritual and has spiritual values. So that's from glory to glory. In short we see that all is from glory to glory, from the lowest plane and mansion until the weakest saint for some time through the ages stand in the highest sphere on higher planes and higher heaven would have obtained from glory to glory.

Now, the phrase from glory to glory is from 2 Corinthians 3 and 4 and it tells us that we are transformed from glory to glory. 2 Corinthians 3:18 and chapter 4 And we all, with unveiled face, beholding the glory of the Lord, are being changed into His likeness from one degree of glory to another; for this comes from the Lord who is the Spirit. Therefore, having this ministry by the mercy of God, we do not lose heart. Basically he is talking about you being like Jesus. This is something different from ministry that we covered. When Paul talks about from glory to glory, he talks about the glory to glory on our inside, in our character and in our spiritual development. We grow from one glory to another state of glory so that right now all our physical eyes are to be suspended and our spiritual eyes are to be opened and we look at one another. We see each one having different states of glory. Some will be shinier than others because of their development of their Christ's likeness in their life. But that is the level of glory in us but in heaven there are many planes of glory. And in each plane there are mansions and schools of instructions. There is a higher plane where there are more mansions with a different degree of everything. And so there are so many planes in heaven. There is a lower plane of glory until it reaches to the highest parts of glory. And here is where the key is. You cannot enter to the plane of glory that is different from the glory on your inside. Let's take from example, this could be plane No. 1, plane No. 2, plane No. 3, plane No. 4, plane No. 5 and the higher the number the greater the glory. If the glory development in your life is at plane No. 2, suppose that if you were to suddenly go home right now, you can only go to plane No. 2. You may be allowed to visit the higher realm but that has to be like Sundar Singh says in his book the "Spiritual World" a clothing is given to you so that you can just go and visit for some time and come back to rest in your plane of glory.

On this earth where you live depends on the amount of finances you have. Whether you live in an expensive bungalow house or an expensive condominium or an average terrace house depends on your finances. Your address on this earth physically depends on the level of your ability to pay for it. And it also depends on your choices. Some people are renewed and they don't mind living in any kind of condition. But in the general natural sense where your address is depends on your financial ability. Now what is your address in heaven? Your address in heaven could be No. 12 Elijah Street, or whatever form of address heaven takes. Do you know that your address in heaven is determined by the glory of Christ's likeness in your life? We always take those things to be accidental. I mean, in our hearts, we may pray, "O God everything is your choice. You choose where I live; as long as I get to heaven, I am happy." God is more organized than that. He lets each one who gets into heaven to move into the plane of his or her development. Just like on this earth in a small little way if your spiritual development is not so great, you may not stand people praying in tongues all the time. Some people cannot stand people talking about Jesus all the time. If you were not used to that level you would be suffering in heaven if God puts you on a highest plane. You will be miserable in heaven. They will be talking about the glory of God and their shining glory will be so bright and yours so dim. God in His mercy takes you and puts you among those at your level.

Supernatural Schools in Heaven

As human spirits permanently enter the various stages of glory, they are placed in schools of instructions where they learn lessons that they should have learned down here on earth. And from time to time you could be promoted from glory to glory in heaven. But the fact is that the best place to learn is down here. Here is where sacrifices can be made. Some times when you bring your tithes to God or when you sacrifice a gift to God, it costs you something. You feel the pain and the greater the pain the greater the suffering. Some times when you wrestle against temptation and you stand steadfast in holiness there is a reward up there in heaven. There is no devil in heaven to fight. There is no temptation to draw us away from God only on this earth. This is why the greatest rewards are made possible while on this earth. In heaven there are no unbelievers to draw you away from God. But on earth when you choose to be holy, you choose to spend time in a prayer meeting rather than on other things, you make choices for God, you got to say no to some things and say yes to other things -that's where the reward is. Thus, the first thing to note is that your ministry affects development in heaven. And if you don't do the part God has chosen for you, He still got to build the New Jerusalem and He will put that mantle on somebody else. So be faithful to the ministry God has called you to.

The second thing to note is that your Christ likeness determines the jewels in your life and the precious stones that will go to build your heavenly mansion and your address in heaven. The third area that we haven't looked at is found in the book of Revelations chapter 21. Let's look at the names of the 12 apostles and the jewels of God. In verse 12 I says, it had a great, high wall, with twelve gates, and at the gates twelve angels, and on the gates the names of the twelve tribes of the sons of Israel were inscribed; now the names of the12 apostles were written on the foundations. But here are the gates. On the 12 gates were the 12 tribes of the children of Israel. The 12 tribes are different from the 12 apostles. Now the 12 apostles were chosen for a ministry. But the 12 tribes couldn't help being there. They are right there and it's something that is fixed for them. And here it is not placed on the foundation but placed on the gates. Gates are places of entrance and exit. You go in and out through the gates. Exits and entrances talk about fellowship in God.

It is important for us to be in the right fellowship. I am not talking about a legal organization. Although legal organizations are an expression of that fellowship, this has nothing to do with salvation. Remember you can be in any place, any church, anywhere on this earth and if you believe in Jesus you are saved. But every fellowship has a different grace and different appointment of God. And based on the fellowship, which the Spirit of God draws us to, being a member of a church is not just determined by our choices. No one comes to God except by the drawing of His Spirit. And pastors of any church should not strive in drawing members from other churches to their own church. We put it this way if God doesn't a person to be part of your church, there is no way you can draw him or her anyway. And at the same time if God wants a person to be a part of the church that you have there is no way a person can run because God will keep drawing him or her back. When God appoints leaders He also appoints people to be under the shepherd of His choice, so that they become responsible to a particular fellowship. Lets refer to John. 17:6 *I have manifested Thy Name to the men whom Thou gavest Me out of the world; Thine they were, and Thou gavest them to Me, and they have kept Thy Word.* Do you know that God gives people to people? God gave men to David. God gives men to men whom He appoints to lead. Turn to Acts chapter 5 verse 14 And more than ever believers were added to the Lord multitudes both of men and women. Then in chapter 6 they multiplied again. Verse 7 And the word of God increases; and the number of the disciples multiplied greatly in Jerusalem, and a great many of the priests were obedient to the faith. Then you look at Paul talking to the elders at Ephesians in chapter 20:28 Take heed to yourselves and to all the flock, in which the Holy Spirit has made you guardians, to feed the church of the Lord which He obtained with His own blood.

All the sheep belong to Jesus. No one has the right to say this is my sheep. It is your sheep in a sense but yet God gives what I call men to people. And He gives responsibilities to those He appoints over a certain fellowship. And being in a tribe is like being in a fellowship. Sometimes being in the right fellowship determines the future of your life. For example the apostle Paul as long as he continued in Jerusalem his ministry could never take off. His ministry only took off when he went with Barnabas to Antioch. Antioch became the centre of his base. Notice all the people who gave him troubles because of his special call. He was called to the Gentiles. Only the church in Antioch is more opened to ministry to the Gentiles than the church in Jerusalem. If Paul tried to base his ministry to the Gentiles in Jerusalem, he would have so much trouble defending himself, so much so he could hardly minister to the Gentiles. But if he bases his ministry in Antioch he could be free to just keep going out because the Christians in Antioch supported him. A great portion of all the troubles he had in going to the Gentiles came from Jerusalem. Even the apostle Peter himself nearly got himself into trouble for going to Cornelius. The moment he came back from a revival meeting in Acts 11 he was called to questioning. That is why God can never use that church to preach to the Gentiles. And Paul had to be pulled out by God into the church in Antioch for his ministry to the Gentiles to take off from there. And when Paul was in Antioch, who came to cause trouble in Antioch? They were Judases from Jerusalem claiming to have authority from the church in Jerusalem. So, here in the third point: sometimes being in the right fellowship with the right people is conducive to the total reward to the whole system. We all have individual rewards for our life. We all have rewards for the ministry that we bring to God. Do you know that there are corporate rewards? For example if your company is doing well in certain things, there is an honour given to you as an individual. You could be the best employee. And so there is an honour given to you from that company for your work performance. Then there is an honour given to you for your team spirit and work character and the extra help that you give to others. That is your character. Then there is an honour that is given to you for your whole team. So your team is rewarded.

The Holy Spirit builds churches into team groups. There is an angel set over every church that has come upon this planet earth. Sometimes there is a reward that God gives to the entire fellowship. Not to just one individual, not just because of reward of character or ministry but there are rewards that God gives to the entire group. This is call being in the right fellowship that brings a certain amount of blessings. Look at I Corinthians. 5: 4-5 In the name of the Lord Jesus Christ, when you are gathered together, along with my spirit is present, with the power of our Lord Jesus, deliver such a one to Satan for the destruction of the flesh that his spirit may be saved in the day of the Lord Jesus. Now what they did is what Matt. 18 commanded. They treat that person as a heathen after the third admonition. First admonition, in a one to one confrontation; second admonition, bringing two to three other witnesses, and finally if the person still do not change, he is brought before the entire church. Then it says in Matt. 18 that person is to be treated as a heathen. In I Corinthians. 5:5 You are to deliver this man to Satan. Now it's not something that you could just simply do. A lot of people try to excommunicate church members out of their own emotional anger that is not from God. But here we are just pointing to a fact that what actually took place was that person was removed from the fellowship. The moment the fellowship was removed Satan came in to claim that person? There is a measure of protection and reward that we get by being in the right fellowship. We cannot take that lightly. Likewise, being in the wrong fellowship can cause destruction. Perhaps there are a whole group of people who are drunkards, who are sinners and they are your good friends. Psalms chapter one tells you do not sit in the seat of the scornful. Don't sit with them. But because your natural ties is stronger than your spiritual growth you went along with them thinking that you could protect them. You can only protect them if you are living in God's perfect will then your umbrella can cover them. If you are not living in God's perfect will you don't get protected and you get destroyed.

Let me give a few examples of that. When Joshua sent the spies into the Promised Land there was only one place that the spies could be saved, and that was by hiding in Rahab's house. And the Israelite spies later promised that Rahab and her household would be saved from the onslaught of Israel if they remain in the house. If they are outside the house they are not our responsibility. But whosoever that is in the house is protected. That's a form of what I call a corporate covering or fellowship covering that God gives. It can be dangerous for it also works in reverse when there is destruction in that fellowship. But it's a tremendous blessing when it works on the positive side. That's being in the right fellowship in God. So here we see the rewards that God gives in heaven for being in a team together with those whom God appoints. When God rewards corporately, He sends people to you with the right team and you bring out the whole blessing as a team together. There

The Realm Of The Spirit

is an individual reward for being having your character transformed. There is an individual reward for your particular ministry that you are faithful to. Then there is a corporate reward that God brings for being part of the team He assigns you to be with. The right fellowship is important.

So, these 3 things that determines heavenly rewards must be viewed with great importance. From the book of Revelations you remember when destruction is about to come on Babylon in the tribulation week, God calls His people, "Come out of her my people." There is a time when judgment falls and God says get out before the destruction falls. Remember Lot and his family. Lot his wife and his 2 daughters were saved. When Lot tried to talk to his two daughters' husbands they looked to him as a mad man. They should have been saved but because they didn't choose to come out with them, when the destruction fell, it fell on them too. Same with the Passover when they put the blood on the lintel of the house if any Israelites were out on the street and they were first born they would die. It doesn't matter whether they were Israelites or not. You must enter a house with the blood.

Being in the right fellowship does have its blessings. It doesn't mean that an organization alone is sufficient. People have taken that in a wrong sense that if you are not inside their organization you don't have the blessings of God. Not to say that. We can have rewards in 3 realms remember. They could be ministries who refused to base it in a church. They are always going around. They don't realize that the local church is where the base is. They will have their reward for their ministry. They will have their reward if they become Christ like. But there is a third reward they may miss out. If they had remained in a fellowship, their third reward could have been even bigger in their blessings on earth and in heaven. Lets not miss out on these rewards where the gates are. What do the gates symbolize? Entrance and the power of multitudes where we say one can chase a thousand and two chase ten thousands. So what is this telling you? You can reach more people on this earth by joining a fellowship. If 5 ministers work individually by themselves and never have contact with one another, and each man to himself, they each could reach only so much. But I tell you if all five of them would come under a fellowship and they work together corporately, they can reach probably 50 times as much or more. Therefore it magnifies the ministry and magnifies the reward. We need to teach and train people this team spirit because people tend to be very individualistic. We need to understand that team spirit and working together can bring tremendous rewards from God. That is why it's the gates. It can reach out to more people.

Frequency Revelator
School of Revelation in Heaven

Even in the heavens, all the creation of God from the lowest spheres to the highest spheres are seeking to know God and to love Him. Every sphere has schools, universities and places of God's manifestation, each learning and seeking to understand our Awesome God. As true knowledge of God is acquired, a glory transformation occurs to those who understand that particular level of knowledge. In billions of earth years, the highest spheres that have pre-existed planet earth are still coming to the knowledge of God. There is so much to know of God that all the languages of humans are incapable of expressing who He really is. Even the word "God" is insufficient to express who He is. He is truly omnipresent, omnipotent and omniscient but when we use the word "person" to refer to God it is an incomplete description because God is beyond time, beyond space, beyond energy and beyond "person." He is the source, the creator and the sustainer of all life – all of our being and existence are in Him. He is the Supreme Being our Father God. Our Lord Jesus Christ is the manifestation of the Supreme Being our Father God in time, space and energy in person simultaneously to all His creations (all of the Spiritual Universe) – so that all His creations can relate to God. Our Lord Jesus Christ and the Supreme Being our Father God are one. The Holy Spirit is the manifestation of the Supreme Being our Father God who "fills," "sustains," and "is" all time, all space and all energy. The Holy Spirit and the Supreme Being our Father God are one. Thus our Lord Jesus Christ and the Holy Spirit are one. We can understand why for eternities, we will be learning and growing in knowing God.

Lakes and Rivers in Heaven

In Heaven there are lakes and rivers. You could choose either to walk on the top of the river or you could go swimming in the river. You have to have a certain realm of God's presence before that takes place. People who walk with God seem to transcend that gravitation law. Long ago there was a story about a flying monk. And this monk was in a Christian monastery. This monk was in a particular church. He was a very devout man. He spent many hours praying. And sometimes when he was in deep prayer his body starts to float. And it happened to Amie McPherson too. She was at a platform preaching. And as she was walking up and down, sometimes she walked right up to the edge of the platform. Everyone thought she was going to fall down. And she would quickly walked back. But there was a time under

The Realm Of The Spirit

eyewitnesses' account that she walked right on the end near the platform and walked back. Everyone was amazed. For as moment of time she was under that anointing. These are all little glimpses of the physical body taking on the power of the immortal body.

Let's look at 2 Kings 2: 16. And the said to him, *"Behold now, there are with your servants fifty strong men; pray, let them go, and seek your master; it may be that the Spirit of the Lord has caught him up and cast him upon some mountain or into some valley."* It seems that this phenomena constantly occur to Elijah. He could be walking in some places and straightaway he is taken, translated in the physical body. Physically transported from one mountain to another. This is why when Elijah told to one of the generals of Ahab, "Tell Ahab I am here," he said, "When I go you will disappear." People who are familiar with Elijah know that he is no ordinary man. This is a man who walked so close with God that he is like an angel. You could see him and then don't see him. We know it happened in the New Testament in Acts chapter 8 to Philip the evangelist. That after he baptized the Ethiopian eunuch Philip was taken off. That's a foretaste of what the body can do. This body is so limited so that when you travel from one country to another you got to get your visas right, you got to get on the plane etc. One of these days as we get so deep into God's presence you're just going to go there in an instance. What I want to bring you to and show you is that it's possible to happen right now and we have glimpses of it. If you walk deep enough it can be a permanent effect and then you get into glory. It happened to David du Plessis. He shared that in his book *"The Spirit Made Me Go"* that they were late for some appointment and he was running with another pastor for a meeting. The pastor ran ahead of him. And he said that as he ran, suddenly he took 2 steps and he was there. This is real he shared it in the book "The Spirit Made Me Go". That's the immortality of our physical body how our body began to break the bonds of this physical life.

Elijah also had it happening in his life in I Kings 19 we are told that after the confrontation and the fire that came down from heaven, Elijah told Ahab to go first because there is a sound of rain. The bible tells us that Elijah ran faster than a horse. If some of these athletes in the Olympics Games read this account in their bibles they would be adding Elijah's secret into their training program. So what was Elijah's secret? *"I stand always in the presence of God."* We saw Samson how he could lift the gates of the city. These are all feats that belong to the other realm. But we need to understand and we need to know. That's why we are teaching this that a glimpse and a touch of that are possible here. If we are opened to it then it may happen. If we are closed to it, it may never happen.

Food In The Spirit Realm

In the spirit realm, one attribute of body immortality is that the body suddenly takes on a new character and it doesn't need to eat and drink. We see a glimpse of that when Moses was with God without food and water for 40 days twice and a third time when he was interceding. We are told that we can't live more than 3 days without water. That is why the rescuers gave up hope in the Highland Tower tragedy (where a block of condominiums collapsed after some soil erosion) after some time when they realize any survivors would have died of starvation. Those who have never fasted for a standard period in fasting don't know what it is like to break free from the laws of this life. But it is possible as we live in God so close that the presence of God so fills you that you go without food. The bible tells us in the book of I Corinthians that food for the bodies and bodies for food and God will destroy both of them. In heaven our internal organs are all different. There is still food in heaven but the food is not for survival. It's for pleasure and for impartation. You don't have to eat in heaven to live. You live by God's life. How lovely when a glimpse of that comes on this earth.

In I Kings 18:46 we are told of a time when Elijah ran before Ahab to the entrance of Jezreel. Now in I Kings 19:5-8 And he lay down and slept under a broom tree; and behold, an angel touched him, and said to him, *"Arise and eat."* And he looked, and behold, there was at his head a cake baked on hot stones and a jar of water. And he ate and drank, and lay down again. And the angel of the Lord came again a second time, and touched him and said, "Arise and eat, else the journey will be too great for you." And he arose, and ate and drank, and went in the strength of that food forty days and forty nights to Horeb, the mount of God. His physical body took on immorality. It existed on heavenly life for 40 days and 40 nights. Some people think fasting is difficult. It depends on the level of the presence of God. When you break into a certain realm of God's presence, it seems like your whole body goes into a state of suspended animation. The physical functions all cease and the spiritual functions takes over.

It happened to Kenneth Hagin one time when God was dealing with his wife because he was constantly traveling. And his wife didn't want him to travel but it was God's will for him to travel. So in the end the Lord dealt with the wife and say look if you are not going to let him travel I am going to take him home. And in one of his sharing as he was praying his heart stopped beating. A pastor was there; he took the pastor's hand and say, "Feel that my heart for it has stopped beating." But he was still moving around and he still could talk. Because the physical body was in a suspended state of animation and the spirit man just came through. I mean a body that live without the heart beating. We are talking about a different realm.

This physical body is just a shell. There is something more powerful than that. When the divine life and immortality start coming to this physical body something takes place beyond our natural. Jesus lived 40 days and 40 nights without food and water. And He was under that special anointing. And you notice that only after that He was hungry. Before that He was not hungry because the physical body for a moment of time took on the immortality. Everything in the natural seems to have a suspended state of animation. This is one of the things that in Noah's time when he took all the animals into the ark and there was more animals than we know today. Some are extinct and many others that we never knew of or heard of. How did he feed all those animals? He doesn't have to because God's presence was there. We know that God's power surpasses our physical life. The physical body can be immortal.

Now the key behind it all in Hebrews. 11:5 *By faith Enoch was taken up so that he should not see death; and he was not found, because God had taken him.* Now, before he was taken he was attested as having pleased God. He was seeking the pleasure of God all the time. He was always in the realm in the presence of God. Heb. 11:6 continue to say that without faith it was impossible to please God. Rom. 4 talks about Abraham and Sarah and they tapped on that renewing power in the physical body through their faith. So, No. 1 by increasing in faith. I was asked a question a few days ago, how do you develop this great tenacity of faith? The answer is this. I have made it a point that either the Word of God works or I die. When you reach that kind of commitment either the Word is true (and you are relying your whole life on the Word) or you die. You rather die if it's not true than to live. And you could live when it's found to be true. When you begin to trust God with that kind of tenacity and you go into the ministry and you say, "If I die of starvation it's because I died trusting you. And it's your duty to continue to supply. If I die I die, if I trust I trust." When you begin to walk with God with that attitude you say, "Either this Word is true or you are serving a dead religion." Either what we are talking about is reality or just some religion that anybody could have. And if its reality I would rather see the Word works in my life and I live. If this Word doesn't work I rather not live. Thank God the Word is true for whosoever has an absolute trust in the word. Faith that's No. 1.

No. 2 Romans. 8:2 for the law of the Spirit of life in Christ Jesus has set me free from the law of sin and death. Sin and death are all those things that operate on the mortal body. If the law of sin and death is broken then your body is no more subject to mortality. What makes something mortal? It is the law of sin and death. And if that same law is cancelled immortality comes. And it's by the law of the Spirit of life. That's the second key. Part of the operation is through prayer as you see in verses 21 and 26. It's the same law operating and working in God's presence. No. 3 verse 11 If the Spirit of Him who raised Jesus from the dead dwells in you, He who raised Christ Jesus from the dead will give life to your mortal bodies also through His Spirit who dwells in you. Turn over to the earlier portion of the book of Rom. 6:4 We were buried therefore with Him by baptism into death, so that Christ was raised from the dead by the glory of the Father, we too might walk in newness of life. No. 1 faith, No. 2 the law of the Spirit of life. No. 3 the glory of the Father. And there are different degrees. Jesus was full of grace and glory. Which is why the glory of God is important. As you tap in that glory, immortality comes into your body. Moses had one glimpse and his body was transformed. The rod of Aaron was in the glory and it blossomed and bore fruit. The glory of God is what we seek after. That will cause immortality to come on this physical body.

Charles and Frances Hunter wrote about Roland Buck in *Angels On Assignment* and his daughter wrote the other book about him in The Man Who Spoke To Angels. He met Gabriel the angel. He met Michael the Archangel and spoke to them. And had visions and conversation with them which are recorded in those books and all of them are very good. But there was one particular thing that happened one night. One of the angels appeared to him with a ladle. In that ladle was a liquid that looks like a golden colored liquid. Then the angel said tonight I have gift from Father God to you. He was a slightly overweight man. After he ate eat that food from heaven, instantly he felt a sound on his physical body. He was wondering what it was. Then he realized that all the fat was burned up. So if after tonight you saw somebody coming here overweight and went back reduced to ordinary weight that may have taken place while they were praying. But of course it was just one special gift the God gave. And he felt stronger and he felt 30 to 40 years younger. All these sound strange to many people.

The Realm Of The Spirit

Once you are aware of the fact that the spirit world is very real, you will find that it is as real as the natural world. There are foods up there. Sometimes God gives you an opportunity to partake of it. And when you partake there is an impartation in spirit, soul and even physical. There is a positive side effect upon your life. I Kings. 19:4-6 But he himself went a day's journey into the wilderness, and came and sat down under a broom tree; and he asked that he might die saying, "It is enough; now, Lord, take away my life; for I am no better than my fathers." And he lay down and slept under a broom tree and behold, an angel touched him and said to him, "Arise and eat." And he looked and behold, there was at his head a cake baked on hot stones and a jar of water. But it was no ordinary cake. This would have been really genuine angel's cake. And there was a jar of water. So he ate and drank and laid down again. Verse 7 the second time the angel said arise and eat because the journey is too great for you. Verse 8 he arose and ate and drank. And he went in the strength of that food for 40 days and 40 nights. These two meals lasted for 40 days and 40 nights. For it scientifically to happen that meal has to have natural and molecular effect on his physical stomach and body. It has to be something physically imparted for him to carry on like that for 40 days and 40 nights. So here are scriptures that tell that there are times God does give us heavenly food. The Israelites tasted manna, which the book of Psalms tells us its angels' food.

Why do they have to eat in the spirit world? The only reason for eating in heaven is impartation as well as pleasure. So that everything we eat impart something into our spirit, soul and body. The pure need for eating in the natural today is mainly to sustain our body, to keep our body in good shape and form. But in the spirit world the spirit food has tremendous impartation value. I heard the testimony of a Christian who went up to heaven and visited some members of her church there. In one home that she visited, she was offered a glass of water to drink, which she found refreshing and soothing. She also ate some fruits offered by her host. Her host in heaven told her that in heaven they eat to remain young looking. The process of eating the heavenly food is part of the system like we have like laying on of hands. Laying on of hands today is besides baptism in the Spirit, healing, deliverance or ordination is also for impartation. We lay hand to impart. In heaven part of the impartation is received through the food itself. Let's refer to Deuteronomy. 2:7 For the Lord your God has blessed you in all the work of your hands; he knows your going through this great wilderness; these forty years the Lord your God has been with you; you have lacked nothing. Then chapter 8 :4 Your clothing did not wear out upon you, and your foot did not swell, these forty years. The book of Psalms records and tells us that there was not a single weak or sick person in their midst for 40 years. How was that possible? The answer was in verse 3 of chapter 8. And he humbled you and let you hunger and fed you with manna, which you did not know, nor did your fathers know; that he might make you know that man does not live by bread alone, but that man lives by everything that proceeds out of the mouth of the Lord. It is connected to the manna in some way. There is a tremendous impartation in that spirit world and that spirit food.

While you are praying the spirit world opens itself to you and suddenly you see the cup filled with liquid in front of you, you rub your eyes and pray and it's still there. Why do you think God shows you a cup? Take it, drink it, something will take place in your life. There will be an impartation. It will not only impart physical changes in your soul, in your physical body. But it will impart sometimes even an actual gift. You could in the spirit world if there is such a tree let say a tree of music. You partake it even though you are a non-musician straight away you can play music. In the spirit world that's how things are imparted. Or if there is a tree call fruit of prophecy. You have never prophesied before, but when you ate it suddenly you prophesy. In the book of Revelation, John saw this huge angel coming down from the heaven above. Revelation. 10:8-11 *Then the voice which I had heard from heaven spoke to me again, saying, "Go, take the scroll which is open in the hand of the angel who is standing on the sea and on the land." So I went to the angel and told him to give me the little scroll; and he said to me, "Take it and eat; it will be biter to your stomach, but sweet as honey in your mouth."* And then I took the little scroll from the hand of the angel and ate it; it was sweet as honey in my mouth, but when I had eaten I my stomach was made bitter. And I was told, "You must again prophesy about the many peoples and nations and tongues and kings." That book was an actual impartation of the Spirit of prophecy. It took place through eating in the spirit world. The same thing also happened to Ezekiel in chapter 12:17-19 "Son of man, eat your bread with quaking, and drink water with trembling and with fearfulness; and say of the people of the land. Thus says the Lord God concerning the inhabitants of Jerusalem in the land of Israel; they shall eat their bread with fearfulness, and drink water in dismay because their land will be stripped of all it contains, on account of the violence of all those who dwell in it.

Now there is here an actual eating. But as he was eating in the natural there was something that took place in the natural. He was shaking as he ate it. Now the Spirit of prophecy was working through the natural substance as well. Now the real spiritual one is in chapter 3 :1-3 "Son of man, eat what is offered to you; eat this scroll, and go, speak to the house of Israel." So I opened my mouth, and he gave me the scroll to eat. And he said to me, "Son of man, eat this scroll that I give you and fill your stomach with it." Then I ate it; and it was in my mouth as sweet as honey. Same like John the apostle. And after that the Lord says you go and you speak. Now these two experiences of Ezekiel come quite close. One is completely similar to John the apostle. The other is Jesus Christ taking the cup and the bread. And saying this bread is my body and this cup is my blood. Now the partaking was like the turning point. When they partake they were his. But when he partook wrongly like Judas it says after that very moment the devil came into him. The apostle Paul mention in the book of Cor. 11 it says that the Lord's Supper is partaken wrongly by some and because of it they died. But if partaken correctly it brings tremendous blessings. That is the reason why Christians practice saying grace. Not only as a thanksgiving to God. But by saying it we could experience the anointing of God on the food. Sanctify it by word and prayer and partake it and have some sort of a impartation also in the spirit world as a release of our faith. In the ways spiritual things are imparted up above.

You will not believe in 10 years' time the person you will become. You could be the most introverted person ever. But through a series of partaking certain type of heavenly food, you could be the most explosive personality. This is something which is quite impossible in the natural. For the heavenly food transform our personality, transform our mind, and transform our being. And I know that something that took place inside. Of course I didn't understand it fully in those days. But through time there have been many more things that have been partaken. You ask, "Can dreams be so real?" Yes, what about Solomon. Remember that it was in a dream that the Lord asked him, "Ask of me what you want." He may have slept let say with an I.Q. of 150. And he woke up with an I,Q. of 400. So something does take place in the spirit realm. In your prayer sometimes you see a light. And you want to run from that light. Even the light that shines can transform us. John G. Lake was fasting for the baptism in the Spirit in his early days. One day as he was praying he felt a ray of light came and shone around him. That one ray of light was what he held to for the rest of his life. The purity of that light has continued to transform his life even onto the late days of his ministry.

Frequency Revelator

In the book *Scenes Beyond The Grave* there was a scene in which they saw Jesus Christ in the children's paradise and all the scene was being reacted. And after that there was a scene of a preacher going out preaching. Then there was this person who did not accept Christ yet. Right at that moment what they saw in all the 5 dimensions including time and the spirit dimension was a ray of light came right down from heaven and came into this man's heart. Something physically was imparted. There was a real light that shone on that person. And there has been many times in my prayers I have seen light sometimes flashes of light. And I have been opened to them. And when I am opened they went out. Not all that we see in the spirit is necessary of God. Satan can also appear as an angel of light. I want to be balanced here not to frighten you but to be balanced. Otherwise people will yield to every funny kind of manifestation without having the Word. If you yield to the spirit realm minus the Word is the most dangerous thing you could ever do. Without the Word there is no protection in the spirit realm. There is no guidance in the spirit realm. It is just like driving a car when everybody has no rules. You can drive on any side of the road and there is no traffic light. It will be a mess. In the spirit world the Word is the protection. As long as you know your conscience is clear, your spirit is right in the sight of God. Usually all those disturbances do not come. And many of those manifestations are from the Lord. And when they are from the Lord we still have to yield to them.

Let me recount an incident from Kenneth Hagin's life. Before Hagin had the vision of the angel. In one of the visions he saw both Jesus and the angel. As he was talking to Jesus he saw the angel next to Jesus. And every time he turned around to look at this angel, the angel opened his mouth like he wanted to talk. But when he looked back at Jesus the angel closed his mouth and did not talk. He did that several times. Then when Jesus had finished talking to him, Jesus said, "The angel here has a message for you." And of course Hagin being like many intellectual said, "Lord if you are here why don't you give me the message. Why must it be him?" So the Lord has to show Hagin all the scriptures that didn't my word say the angel will be ministering to you. Finally Hagin turn to the angel. The moment he turned to the angel. The angel said these words: "I have been wanting to speak to you about your finances." And the angel said, "Some finances are on the way. By the way that man has offered to do all your things here. You are not supposed to give it to him because that is not God's will for you." But there is one funny part. The angel said I have tried to come and tell you before. That means that before the first encounter with the angel, the angel had tried to talk to Hagin. And he mentioned that incident sometime back. And that incident was before this incident when Hagin was living in a trailer. He remember one night that the angel recounted. When he was in his trailer and that night he felt like somebody came into the trailer stood right near to him. You know the feeling like somebody had just entered the room. But this is the statement he gave me. The angel said, "Because you did not open yourself to the spirit world, I could not speak to you." The angel told him, "I have come to talk to you earlier because you didn't open to the spirit I could not speak to you." And between that trailer experience and the time the angel appeared to him next to Jesus, he went into financial difficulty and financial problem. All because he didn't open himself to the ministering spirit who came to minister to him, he ended up with financial problems. Angels are working with us. Jesus is working with us. Holy Spirit is working with us. And we need to be open to all.

I know some Christians are critical spiritually. They say we have Jesus why we need Holy Spirit. We have Holy Spirit why we need angels. There are others who say we have Father God. God doesn't want us to play favourites like that. He wants to learn to relate to God the Father, to Jesus the Son, to the Holy Spirit and to the angels. He wants us to learn all these different relationships. But there is a realm in the spirit where unless we open ourselves to it we cannot move in. And they cannot manifest. But through sharing experiences like that in the spirit we become more familiar with them, we become more aware of them and we become more in a state of realization of the possibility when they do happen. So that when God so chooses we could just go into that realm. Sometimes a spiritual manifestation take a choice involved. You choose to yield you choose not to. Sometimes some of you have the experience when you pray, pray it looks like if you just pray a little more and you stay a little longer you are going to break into something but you stopped. And in the end you are the loser and you loose out on what God has for you. And I have learnt that it is not only important when to pray, what to pray and how to pray is important where to pray. God can be quite strict. If God want to appear to you on a mountain and you are not there He is not going to appear to you. Which is why I can understand when God tells Moses to meet Him on the mountain. If Moses were to meet anywhere else He won't appear. Why many times Jesus had to climb all the way up to the mountain? Why didn't God talk to Him down in the valley? Besides being quietness there are reasons behind God's manifestation.

Why Elijah should go all the way to the mountain in I Kings. 19. Is God only there? No God is everywhere. But God has His workings, His requirements to discipline us, to check our hunger for Him, our desire for which all works out to physical areas of where, how, which everything which becomes our total expression of our seeking for God. If God so chooses to manifest to you and say tonight I want you to be in such and such a prayer meeting. And you are not there you may miss out. We need to be open in the spirit realm where God has a peculiar way, a particular way of manifesting in the spirit world. And that is how the spirit world runs and is like. The first area we have said that there is no geographical barrier. And there are 3 realms of moving into that area where you transcend geographical barrier. The second we said that there are spiritual materials. And there is an impartation when we partake of spiritual substances and spiritual materials that have a tremendous effect on our physical bodies and on our souls.

HEAVENLY SPIRITUAL SUBSTANCES

Did you know that as much as there are natural substances in the physical world, in the spirit realm, there are also spiritual substances? Let's refer to Hebrews. 11:1 *Now faith is the assurance of things hoped for, the conviction of things not seen. Faith is the substance of things hoped for, the evidence of things not seen.* We need to get that into our heart and into our minds that there is such a thing as a spiritual substance. As much as there are natural substances there are spiritual substances. The spirit world has its own material form. Angels have a form. God has a form. We have to see it that there are two different realms of existence. One is the realm of the spirit the other is the realm of the natural. The two worlds don't contact each other directly. Sometime people in their visions make contact with the spirit world. It is because the spirit world has chosen to materialize into a realm of the natural for us to feel its tangibility. The natural cannot move into the spiritual and go backwards. And when the natural becomes spiritualized there is no return path. That is why when Enoch walked with God, he walked into the realm of God and he doesn't reverse back. His being is just transformed into the spiritual realm. The spiritual realm can transform the natural. The spiritual realm can affect and transmute itself into the physical for the physical people to touch and contact it. They are two separate realms altogether. Angels are created beings. When God made the angels He took spiritual substances and He brought it together. When God made man He made man in a different realm with a spiritual ability. What we want to mention here is that there is a substance that is very real.

In the book of Psalms it says that the manna that the Israelites ate was angels' food. It was transformed into a physical world so that physical man can eat it and survive. How long did they survive? 40 years. For 40 years the whole nation of Israel survived on manna from heaven. And that manna provided all the protein, carbohydrates, vitamins and minerals that they needed. It is remarkable that the spiritual substance can become a physical substance and provide everything that the physical world could have provided. They had everything in a manna form. The angels eat this manna too; yes they do. It is called in the book of Psalms angels' food. There are real tree substances in Heaven. Faith is a spiritual substance. Heb. 11:6 And without faith it is impossible to please Him. For whoever would draw near to God must believe that He exists and He rewards those who seek Him. It says that faith is a substance and now it says without faith it is impossible to please Him. Now faith is a spiritual substance. And spiritual substance is faith. I want to use that expression and replace the word faith with spiritual substance in verse 6. And I read it to you and show you how it can sound different. But without spiritual substance it is impossible to please Him. For he who comes to God must believe that He exists in that realm of the spirit and He is a rewarder of those who diligently seek Him. Can you see the impact of that statement now? Without spiritual substance it is impossible to please Him. The first was faith is a spiritual substance. Then we bring it further in verse 6 without the spiritual substance it is impossible to please God. Since it says without faith it is impossible to please God and faith is a spiritual substance. You just replace those words and you find that without spiritual substance it is impossible to please God.

Now faith is not the only spiritual substance. Grace is a spiritual substance. Glory is a spiritual substance. A lot of the giftings of God is impartation of spiritual substance. Everything is spiritual substance from the spirit world. And we have verse 6 without spiritual substance it is impossible to please God. There must be something imparted from God into our life that enables us to please Him, to do that which He wants us to do. Without that spiritual substance nothing can happen that could be pleasing to God. One peculiar characteristic of the spirit world affecting our life is not just by believing something. There must be some real impartation that comes into our life. Everything in the spirit world is the spiritual substance. And everything that we receive from God comes in a form of spiritual substances. If you receive wisdom from God, God imparts some real substances into your spirit. Now I know He could give spiritual substances in measures. And the spirit of God's presence in our life is also a sort of spiritual substances coming into our life. We have to accept the fact that the anointing of God is a spiritual substance. The Holy Spirit is a person but the anointing of God, which comes from the Holy Spirit, and the *dunamis* of God is a spiritual substance.

Attributes As Spiritual Substances

Did you know that the spiritual attributes of wisdom, knowledge, power, authority, love, peace, joy, self-control, meekness, are actually spiritual substances? When Jesus was walking along in Mark. 5 and the power of God was on His life, the woman with the issue of blood touched Him. Jesus felt some substance flowing out from Him to the woman. It is a spiritual substance. And this is an interesting realm in the spirit world: all things that we receive from God whether in the form of an attitude or ability like wisdom, love and joy are spiritual substances. The spiritual attributes of wisdom, knowledge, power, authority, love, peace, joy, self-control, meekness, can be viewed as spiritual substances. The anointing of God is a substance of God. The power of the Holy Spirit is a substance of God. Let me redefine the whole system. Practically everything in the spirit world is a substance. You may have never viewed these attributes as substances before. But I want you to know that they are substances. It's a different question when you talk about how the substance is imparted and what actually happens. You have never thought of humility as a substance. Or meekness as a substance. And yet we know that there are different degrees of humility. Many people don't think of wisdom as a substance. But it is a substance.

All the heavenly garments were made from substances of the spirit realm like righteousness, praise etc. All these were living substances. When we worship God, these are the substances that go from our spirit to God. Jesus told the rich young man in Luke 18: 22 to sell off all he had and to give it to the poor, and he would receive rewards in heaven. The most important thing about giving and doing any good works is not the works itself or what we do. It is the attitude of your heart that determines the reward. When we do it, led by the Spirit, and the heart attitude is right, there is some spiritual force and substance that goes to God from our spirit. In Philippians 4: 18, Paul says to the Philippians that the offerings that they gave to him were a sweet smelling fragrance unto God. They had tangible spiritual substances. When Noah offered an animal sacrifice offering to God after he came out of the Ark, it was the right attitude of Noah's heart that God smelled as a sweet aroma -it was not the smell of the burnt animal sacrifice (which probably did not smell nice at all) that God was referring to. Noah's right heart attitudes gave rise to spiritual substances that went towards God.

In Revelation 14, it says that the white robe garments in heaven are the righteous works of the saints. This means that whatever good works that you do for God, will be your spiritual deposit in heaven. We read in Isaiah 61 about the garments of praise. In Revelation, it mentions about the prayers of the saints going up in heaven. These right attitudes of hearts of the saints as they carry out spiritual works on earth produce substances that make the heavenly mansions, heavenly rewards, heavenly crowns and garments, etc. It is very important that anything you do for God, your attitude of heart must be right when you do it and the intention is out of love for God and the people then the 'freeness' and the 'fullness' of the spiritual substances from your heart will go to God to make up your heavenly rewards. These heavenly garments are not able to produce light itself. They are like the moon to the sun. The brightness and the shininess of the moon is dependent upon the sun. In the same way the brightness of the angels and heavenly garments of the saints are a reflection of the glory of God. I was fully aware that if God were to somehow stop that light that came from the Throne, every angel, plant and heavenly garment would turn black. There would be none of that brightness anymore then.

Impartation of Spiritual Substances

Spiritual substances govern all the various realms of the spirit. Our spiritual growth is due to actual growth of substances in our spirit man. Our spirit man grows in meekness. What do you mean by growth? In the spirit world if you grow spiritually you really grow in your spirit man. That spirit man on your inside actually grows in height and light and power. Now in the physical world you can never grow unless you have input and intake. Now in the spirit world there can be no growth without some impartation from above. There has to be substance received. Some of the

How does impartation of spiritual substances takes place?

Impartation takes places largely through prayer. Every time you spend time in prayer with God there are some spiritual substances that you take in. Prayer in the spirit world is like breathing oxygen. That is why I say prayer in the spirit edifies you. And every time you pray there is an impartation of actual substances coming into your spirit man. That causes your spirit man to grow. And it is important to have those spirit substances in order for our spirit man to grow. Remember my first statement all growth is caused by spiritual substance that comes into our being. It is not just an attitude of mind and we grow. There is an actual impartation or transportation of spiritual substances from God's realm into our spirit man. And in order to grow we need to continue to receive those spiritual substances from God. You never waste time when you spend time with God. Every time you spend time with God whether your mind or your body knows it or not, there is something that has taken place that changes you. You will never even leave a 5 minutes prayer the same. You have taken in extra substances from God. It is not the instant growth that we are looking for. You don't feel it but something is happening. Those of you who have been spending time in prayer, spending time in prayer meeting and in private, every second you spend time in God something has dropped into your spirit. Reading the word is also another realm. You never ever pick up the bible and read it without having some substances imparted into your spirit man. Something always gets into your spirit. And when it gets there it can remain there permanently. Even if you read only one verse before you go out in the morning there is a substance imparted.

General And Specific Substances

In the spirit realm, there are so many types of spiritual substances. Each has its different effect. There are what I call the general substances that come into our spirit through prayer and the word. But there are some specialized substances like the anointing of God. Then there are other substances like wisdom that could be imparted into our life. Sometimes God even gives some people an open vision to see what actually takes place during an impartation of a spiritual substance. God can give a person something to eat that changes them. And that substance can either have a certain influence on the physical body or it can influence a gifting in their life. If we want to be somebody in God there are spiritual substances that we must acquire. It is not just knowledge that you need to acquire. It is a spiritual substance that you need to acquire between who you are now and where you want to be in God. If you understand that realm you will begin to understand what you must do in God.

The Realm Of The Spirit
Spiritual Substances From Angelic Provisions

Did you know that most of the things we receive from heaven through impartation are actually released by angels? Let's refer to I Kings. 19:5-8 *And he lay down and slept under a broom tree; and behold, an angel touched him, and said to him, "Arise and eat." And he looked, and behold there was at his head a cake baked on hot stones and a jar of water, and he ate and drank, and lay down again, and the angel of the Lord came again a second time, and touched him, and said, "Arise and eat else the journey will be too great for you."* And he rose, and ate and drank and went in the strength of that for forty days and forty nights to Horeb the mount of God. That must be some special food that Elijah ate. He ate the food only once and it lasted for 40 days and 40 nights. It would be wonderful to have that kind of food that Elijah ate to distribute to the church members to eat and say now we can all go on a 40 days fast. What was it? It's a spiritual substance that somehow came in a form of food. It can come in any form. Some spiritual substances have different side effects. Some have a greater effect on our soul; some directly have an effect on the spirit, some on our body. According to the effect that God wants in take place in our life, He chooses certain spiritual substances and put them in the physical form. That particular food and spiritual substance have a physical effect. It must have affected Elijah's physical body. How did it affect Elijah?

The first possibility is that it remained in his stomach for 40 days and 40 nights and kept on issuing more and more substances into his physical body to sustain his physical strength like a time release capsule. The second possibility is that it could have dissolved once but it has a powerful long lasting effect. How and what actually takes place is not important. Sometimes different spiritual substances have different effects. Do not be surprised sometime when you walk with God and because of a certain realm of God's presence that you happened to tap upon that you are so spiritually energized that you could be praising God the whole nightlong. There were a few times in my life when there was a certain realm of anointing that hit. And after the meeting I could never get back to sleep. It had an effect on the physical body. A side effect that all you want to do is to praise God all you want to do is to worship God.

There are many types of spiritual substances that can have different effects on our lives. And some spiritual substance would affect people in different dimension and in different realm. I am sure when people laugh and laugh it must have been some spiritual substance that God is giving. And sometimes that spiritual substance God is giving causes a person to weep and cry. But I want to assure you that there is spiritual substance that when you take it has an effect on your life. Pastor Roland Buck had two books about him, *Angels On Assignment* and *The Man Who Talked With Angels*. He speaks about the time when he was conversing with angels and he was obedient to God. Then one day the angel came and visited him with a present from God. The angel gave him something to drink from a ladle and immediately there was a fizzling sound, and his body fat was immediately reduced. He was supernaturally slimmed down! Do not be alarmed sometimes when you receive something from God and the side effects are tremendously felt in your physical body.

Prophetic Ministry From Spiritual Substances

Prophetic impartation at times comes from spiritual substances. Let's refer to Revelations. 10:8-11 *then the voice, which I had heard from heaven, spoke to me again saying, "Go, take the scroll which is open in the hand of the angel who is standing on the sea and on the land." So I went to the angel and told him to give me the little scroll; and he said to me, "Take it and eat; it will be bitter to your stomach, but sweet as honey in your mouth."* And I took the little scroll from the hand of the angel and ate it; it was sweet as honey in my mouth, but when I had eaten it my stomach was made bitter. And I was told, "You must again prophesy about the many peoples and nations and tongues and kings." Did John eat something? I believe so. Why did God put it in a form of book? Because somehow what he ate has to do with a prophetic ministry. What he ate was a spiritual substance that will produce prophecies that even John himself will not know of. That would bypass his mind and he would just prophesy into that realm. That is a powerful reception that he received. Now many of us may not have this kind of experience. But I want to encourage you; you don't have to see to receive. Every time you spend time with God, sometimes things happen and the angels just come and drop it into your life, sometimes the Holy Spirit Himself, sometimes God sends it from heaven in different ways. Sometimes it's a ray of light from heaven. There are thousands of ways in which God imparts His substance to us. What I want to encourage you is by telling you that's how it takes place in the spirit world. That there is always an impartation of spiritual substance in our life in every meeting that is ordained of God. That Jesus is moving and working. In every time you spend with God privately there is always an impartation, Sometimes its in different realm. But it can be very real. Just because you don't see it, feel it in an open vision doesn't mean it's not real. Sometimes you could have it even in a dream but it's so real. It has a side effect that is powerful in your body that it says with you.

Spiritual Substances From Dreams

Part of the spiritual substances actually comes through dreams. Let's refer to I Kings. 3:4-5 And the king went to Gibeon to sacrifice there, for that was the great high place; Solomon used to offer a thousand burnt offerings upon the altar. At Gibeon the Lord appeared to Solomon in a dream by night; and God said, Ask what I shall give you." Now notice it all took place when he was asleep; it was all in a dream. Not every dream that we have is from God. Dreams like voices and visions come from 3 different sources. It can come from God. It can come from the devil. It can come from us. If you walk right with God the source from the devil is eliminated. Then you still have 2 realms to deal with. It can come from you. It can come from God. So here is one that came from God. Solomon had a dream. Now you know what a dream is like when you wake up. It's just felt like a dream but this was no ordinary dream. In that dream God said, "Ask whatever you want." Solomon said to God, "Look I am so young and inexperienced; give me wisdom to govern your people and God said I will not only give you wisdom I will give you honor and riches." That very next day he had something different. What happened? An impartation. A substance came into him. It was something so powerful. Although he was quite a wise man but now his wisdom is beyond the normal capacity of a human being. It is said that in his time there was no person who could match his wisdom. Sometimes in a dream you could be dreaming about some person it could be from God coming to give you some special gift. Don't take it and throw. It could be an impartation and after that something could change in your life.

In the book, *Within The Gate* the authoress spoke about this experience in heaven. They partake of the heavenly fruit. And they found something strange about the heavenly fruit. All the heavenly trees were named after different substances. There were for example the tree of wisdom, tree of life etc. They received particular attributes by eating those fruits. They took these fruits and they ate them. And they found that whatever that tree was as they ate it they had received something from that tree. Something spiritual was imparted. And some people have received the impartation of praise as they drank from the river of praise. I believe David received the Spirit of praise and worship. Each one of us up to this day has received some similar substances from God. We receive different substances according to the calling we have from God. God moulds and brings to us different things according to the predestination He has for our life.

There are some substances that have to be received incrementally. Some others can be received in an overnight kind of experience. But Christian life consists primarily in spiritual substances accumulating in our life and becoming a part of our spirit man. If you want prosperity in the spirit world it comes in a substance first. When it's on you it attracts physical prosperity. In the end they will always attribute that prosperity to the Spirit of God. The Spirit of God does all these. There are some special ones that God reserved for those who pressed further. What did the church receive in Acts 4? There was a new boldness that came into their life. Even boldness is a substance that came into them that they never had before. It said they spoke the word of God with boldness. They had a measure of it but it is now greater still. Substances are not only just in power gift in healing. Everything you could ever want in the natural life has to be first received in the spiritual substance. And all those attributes in the spirit world are substances.

The ability to pray is also a spiritual substance. If you can't pray, then there are some substances you don't have. How to get it is a different question. Some anointed Christians could lay hands on you and impart some of it into your life. Primarily it is God who gives that spiritual substance to you to enable you to pray. Some of you who may have that substance may lose that gifting in your life if you don't give to other people. But the more you impart your spiritual substances to others the more is flowed back to you. That's the wonderful characteristic about the spirit world. It is more blessed to give than to receive. Whatever you lack in your Christian life, it is due to a lack of spiritual substances. If you lack certain strength or certain character in your life, it could be that when you grew up you may have missed certain spiritual vitamins. What do you lack in the Spirit? What kind of spiritual sicknesses are you suffering from that have caused your character to be twisted? What spiritual vitamin do you lack that is causing your growth to stop to a certain measure? You need to fill it up. You need to draw from God. Sometimes it is instant; sometimes it is incremental. But get that spiritual substance and your life will be full. There is so much more that we can receive from God. If you understand this revelation, your Christian life will not be the same. When you look at overnight prayer you won't be thinking that you must bear through the night. When I press through God will reward me in the end. No all the time you are receiving something from

The Realm Of The Spirit

God. When you become conscious of what you receive from God it makes the process easier. That there is something imparted from God, there is angels all around who comes with different works in our life. All through your Christian life you are receiving substances from God. Whether the substances come through man or through a prayer meeting or whatever, just open your heart and receive them.

Heavenly Precious Stones

The precious stones represents the foundation of Jesus Christ. The precious stones represent the development of your character. The names in heaven and some of the things in heaven are your ministry. Some people have a ministry but they don't develop their character. Some people have character but they don't develop their ministry. They are both different things although both are connected. Effective ministry depends on character. No. 2 the precious stones that are going to adorn your mansion is your character. I mean on this earth if your character is not like Jesus probably hundreds of people know your life. Do they see Jesus in you or when they look at you do they remember you as a bad tempered person. Or do they remember you as a greedy person. Or do they remember you as something else. Do you know that affects your heavenly mansion? It pays to be like Jesus. I didn't say it is easy to be like Jesus. But it pays to walk like Jesus and have the character of Jesus. In the natural precious stones are formed in a hard process of pressure, heat, and of course chemical components. Precious stones are usually found deep in the earth. Precious stones are formed only under right conditions. Likewise, character comes by tribulation, by going under pressure. When we go under pressure and the character of Christ is not formed in our life you lost some precious stones. The next time you are under pressure, the next time you are under a trial, the next time the heat is turned on you remember it will produce some more jewels for your heavenly mansion. And when you allow that pressure to bring out Christ in your life, the tribulation builds character, builds the things of Jesus in your life until you become like Jesus. Those are the precious stones that go towards making your heavenly mansion. The question we ask of you this day is your mansion adorned with precious stones?

CHAPTER FOUR

THE DIVINE REVELATION OF THE THRONE ROOM OF HEAVEN

What Is A Throne Room?

It must be understood that God the Father, the Lord Jesus and Holy Spirit does not have a mansion or a place to stay unlike the saints in Heaven who have mansions to live in. The Throne Room is God's house. This is where He lives. God's Throne Room is actually His house. We know all of Heaven is His habitation, but the Throne Room is where He lives. In John 14:1, Jesus said in my Father's house are many mansions. Heaven is God's house. You never read anywhere in the Bible where it says that Jesus has a mansion or the Father has a special place where He goes in to retire from time to time or do whatever things He wants. The Throne Room is actually where He resides. It is His living room, office, bedroom and work place, where He permanently dwells. In the Throne Room, God is the source of all light in the whole Heavens. In reality, there is no sun in heaven for the glory of God lights up all of Heaven. We read in the Word that angels radiate light and their presence has shininess about them. In heaven, angels have different degrees of brightness of the glory of God. At the Throne Room, the life of God is in everything. It's because of the constant pulsating river of life that keeps flowing out from the Throne of God that lights up every life in Heaven. Glory and life are one in Heaven. To have life is to have glory. To have glory is to have life. In the Throne Room, angels do not have the same garments but garments are constantly changing for different purposes and there are different types of clothing that are won and they are a reflection of God's glory. In the Throne Room, the past, present and the future disappear. It is a realm where you entered into where everything in the past and everything in the future is just like the present, everything is already done, completed and finished. There is no time. The cloak is not ticking. You do not feel it. And everything that God has spoken from the Throne through the prophets that spoke and what Jesus said while He was on the earth will come to pass and Jesus and the Father need not to lift just

The Realm Of The Spirit

one finger to make the word of God come to pass. The power and impact of the spoken word of God even if it was spoken ages ago is so powerful. It is like looking into infinity. You cannot see the end.

Then within Heaven itself, there are different planes or realms of glory. Within each place is a manifestation of God. It is not like having different planes or degrees of glory and there is a Throne of God for each plane. There is only one plane where the Throne of God is but if you were on the lower plane and you approached God from that lower plane, you would still see God's Throne but the Throne of God you would see and experience would be from that lower plane. It is the same Throne but reflected through, for example, seven degrees of glory and you see the Throne of God differently from the way I see it. Believers could reach to the Throne of God and see different parts of the Throne. Heaven is a bee-hive of activities. Different things are coming to the Throne of God and things are also being issued forth. The Throne Room of God is not static. It's always on the move. It does not stay the same where you imagine you see only the glory of God and the shininess of it all the time. Different things take place at the Throne at different times. Sometimes the manifestation of the glory of God is so powerful in the Throne Room that it feels like one is in a furnace and could not even see the face of God. Paul says in 2 Corinthians 12:1-4:

> *I must boast; there is nothing to be gained by it, but I will go on to visions and revelations of the Lord. I know a man in Christ who fourteen years ago was caught up to the third heaven -whether in the body or out of the body I do not know, God knows. And I know that this man was caught up into Paradise -whether in the body or out of the body I do not know, God knows -and he heard things that that cannot be told, which man may not utter.*

Now, Paul was educated and he would not be short of words as far as the average man is concerned. So you could imagine the impact of what he is saying. This is not an ordinary man who lacks the vocabulary. Paul was brought up at Gamaliel's feet. He is one of the most highly educated people in his days. And for him to make a statement that he has been in the spirit realm, and that when he came back he could not describe what it was like, imagine the impact of that. It was just like a Noble prize scientist who is on the top echelon of intellectual ability coming back from the spirit realm and say I could describe atoms, molecules but I can't describe what is there. It would have the same impact. Paul was above the ordinary in everything that he pursued in God. So there is a spirit realm, which is quite hard to comprehend, and we want to talk about something in that area that could motivate us deeper into that realm.

At the Throne of God, the past, present and the future disappear. It's like a position you enter into where everything in the past and everything in the future is just like the present. There is no time. You do not feel it. And everything that God has spoken from the Throne through the prophets that spoke and what Jesus said while He was on the earth will come to pass. There is an awareness that Jesus and the Father need not to lift one finger to make the word of God come to pass. The power and impact of the spoken Word of God even if it was spoken ages ago is so powerful. You could feel the awesome power of it in heaven and on the Throne seat of Jesus. You know the spoken Word of God has come to pass or would come to pass. There is an awareness that it was done, completed and finished. The consciousness of that power that emanated on the Throne of Jesus that could cause the fulfilment of the spoken Word of God was acute.

The power of the Word that is issued forth like a royal command is such that all Jesus has to do was to sit on the Throne and reign and it would come to pass. Hebrews 1:5-8. There is an authority that flows out from the Throne, a power that seems to compel everything, to conform to its reign. In 1 Corinthians 15: 25-27, 'For He must reign till He has put all enemies under His feet and the last enemy that will be destroyed is death.' For 'He has put all things under His feet.' But when He says 'all things are put under Him,' it is evident that He who put all things under Him is excepted. His being on the Throne puts an intense pressure on all things to come under His feet. Jesus said in Mark 11: 23-24, that if you have faith in your words and do not doubt in your heart, the mountain will be removed when you speak to it. This verse is talking about believing in what you say and when you speak to the mountain and believe it, it will put pressure upon the mountain to be removed. That is what it was like in the Throne Room. The intense and awesome power of Jesus reigning upon the God made me unable to stand it for long.

There is another aspect of the Throne. We tend to think that all the things surround the Throne of God. And there is a glassy sea like crystal before the Throne. It is not quite like that. You could not see what was behind the Throne of God. If I take a chair and sit on it, you could see what is behind the chair and around it. It was like some sort of glory or life flowing out from it. It was like the Throne was connected in infinity. Behind the Throne is infinity. You could see as far as you wanted to see, further than the natural. Yet there was no limit to the life that issued forth from the Throne. It was like looking into infinity. You cannot see the end. I believe there is possibly some other universe that Almighty God has created in His greatness and we are only one small tiny part of the universe. It is like infinity times infinity of the worlds God has created. It was awesome to know how powerful and great our Almighty God is like I was aware that the manifestation of the Throne Room is to different degrees. I could hardly comprehend it. It was like if there was another universe somewhere with a different world, then the Throne Room of God which is linked up to infinity would also be linked to this universe and to many, many other universes. And God is conscious of what is here and what is further out there even to the furthest reaches of the entire universe. Seeing infinity is like putting two mirrors opposite each other and you can see as far as you want to see and there is no end to it. And there are many manifestations of the Throne of God to every universe connected to it in infinity.

VISITATION TO THE THRONE ROOM OF GOD

I want to touch two things that are peculiar in the Throne Room so that you could flow into that realm and understand how we pray from that realm. Firstly, in that realm of the heavenly place all things have been completed. There is nothing that is not finished. When you leave that realm, it is when you experience things that are not completed yet. But in that realm, everything is completed. To God our future and the future of all that is to be done is past tense. When Jesus intercedes for us at the right hand of God He is interceding that plan for us as completed. He is interceding not because it has not been completed. He sees it as completed and He intercedes for us to enter that realm. It's a powerful realm. Let's take note of some things that were mentioned to give you an idea of what that realm is. In the book of Revelations 5 when no one could open that seal. In verse 5 One of the elders said to me, "Do not weep. Behold, the Lion of the tribe of Judah, the Root of David, has prevailed to open the scroll and to loose its seven seals. In verse 6 the Lamb came as though it has been slain having seven horns, seven eyes, which are the seven spirits of God sent out to all the earth. So when the Lamb of God opens the seals all those things and the revelations were released. Have you notice that some of those things took place in chapter 6, chapter 7 etc. are in that seal. And a lot of those things have not taken place yet. It was in a book and that book has already completed. It was not written at the time when Jesus the Lamb opens the seals. It was in a book. It was past tense. Its future to us, future to John the apostle, but it was past tense. It was even written down. But its not opened to release it to take place on this earth. I want you to consider the fact that in that realm the heavenly place at the right hand of God at the throne of Jesus everything is completed. There is nothing that has not been completed. It's a different realm that operates at the throne of God.

Let's refer to Ephesians. 1:4 Just as He chose us in Him before the foundation of the world, that we should be holy and without blame before Him in love, having predestined us to adoption as sons by Jesus Christ to Himself, according to the good pleasure of His will. You and I were not even created yet but God has already seen us at His throne. I pray that you open your eyes to understand what the throne room of God is like. Everything of existence or creation is past tense. When it says that He was, He is and He is to come, that in God past, present and future are in Him, what does it mean? Everything is past to Him. Everything is completed. It's all in one book. You have a book that has recorded your life some time ago and therefore which is past tense to you. It's completed in God before there was even an idea of your existence. Before Adam and Eve were created, you were already in the mind of God.

In Revelations. 13:8 now you begin to have an idea of why Jesus talked about His glory up there in heaven before the foundation of the world. There is something in that realm that is peculiar to our finite mind on this earth. Revelation. 13:8 All who dwell on the earth will worship him (that is the anti-Christ), whose names has not been written in the Book of Life of the Lamb slain from the foundation of the world. Who can be slain from the foundation of the world? We know that Jesus died on the cross of Calvary around A.D. 27 to A.D. 30. How was He slain before the foundation of the world? He was not slain physically yet but He was already slain before the foundation of the world because in the mind of God in the throne room it's all done, all completed. That is the first thing that we need to understand. Why do I share this? Because if you are praying and you cannot see what you are praying for has already been completed, you haven't entered the throne room yet. How can you know that you are in the throne room when you don't know what the throne is like? How can you say that you have been downtown if you didn't see the cars, the people, the traffic lights, the shopping malls, the post office, the hotels and restaurants? When you go downtown and see such places, then you know that you are in that place. It is possible to enter the throne room based on Eph. 2:6, and raised us up

The Realm Of The Spirit

together, and made us sit together in the heavenly places in Christ Jesus and based on Hebrews 4: 16, Let us therefore come boldly to the throne of grace, that we may obtain mercy and find grace to help in time of need. How do you know spiritually you are functioning from the throne room, when you haven't seen the finished work from the point of view of the throne room? When you don't know what is like in the throne room, you have not entered the throne room yet. Remember this if you really prayed through, you would have entered the throne room and seen the end results in the spiritual realm.

We are so used to living on this planet earth that our consciousness of time is linear, that future means future, the present means present and the past is past. But in heaven all present, past and future is past. That is why in Ephesians. 1 when he introduces the subject he says He has blessed us with all spiritual blessings in the heavenly places -not will but has. Whatever you are praying for, if it's in the will of God but you can't see the end result and can't see what it will be like, you are not in the throne room yet. You are still somewhere in the Outer Court. But when you reached the throne room, it's done. I don't mean that when you are in throne room that in the physical sense it's done. But you can see it done. Then when you pray you can feel it is done. Then it may take some time before physically it is manifested and done. Let me make this statement: all prayers that never gain access to the throne room will never be answered. Because Christians don't understand what the throne room is like and how to bring their petitions to God, they are always struggling in the Outer Court and they can never have the picture in them that it's being done. And all the time they are out there, they are always struggling. Every prayer must be directed to the throne room. That is why Jesus teaches us to pray to the Father in His name by the power of the Holy Spirit. That is why Jesus does not want us to pray to the Holy Spirit or pray to Him. He wants us to direct our petitions right to the Father God's throne.

When some people say, "I have entered into the throne room," what they mean is they have experienced the presence of God. But there are other side manifestations beside the presence of God. Sometimes the feeling of the presence of God is subjective. If you are regular in a spirit-filled church and you have got used to the presence of God, you may not feel the difference. But visitors that come in and worship the Lord in the same church, immediately the hairs on their hands would stand up; they would cry from the beginning to the end of the service because the presence is too strong. But if you are constantly in the presence, you may be so used and acclimatized to that presence, you may not feel the difference. Or if it's a manifestation that you have never experienced before and you enter into that realm where the manifestation is going on you will feel the difference and have a sense of the presence of God but it's a subjective feeling. See our ability to feel the presence of God is subjective and it is developed by our private devotional life. The presence of God is always there. Sometimes I can feel the presence of God when people don't feel anything. If you go to any church service and start criticizing and having hurt feelings, you would never feel the presence of God in any place even though the presence of God is there. Our attitudes can affect us in the presence of God. Or in our plain laziness, we have taken things of God for granted and it affects our feeling of the presence of God. I am saying that one of our senses is to feel the presence of God when we enter the throne of God. But strong feeling is subjective. When you live in the presence of God you are used to a certain level of presence all the time.

But there are some other manifestations where you see those things that have been done in the past, even though they would only take place in the future. In the book "Angels on Assignment," it was written that when Roland Buck went to heaven, God showed him many specific things that would come to pass, among which the election of Karol Wyotila as Pope John Paul II was. Before that event took place, Roland Buck had already seen it happening. This is an example of what it means when you see some things that have been done in the past but will occur in the future. When this happens, you know you have entered that realm. Whatever you are praying about as long as you can't see it, you are not there yet. You got to pray until you see it, which is a journey from the Outer Court into the Holy place and into the Most Holy place. That journey may mean that you got to give thanksgiving and observe the other principles of prayer. Then you got to pray after you see it until you feel it. And you know on your inside you have prayed through. You have released something about those things to God. Sometimes it takes more than one release. Then it will come by itself into the physical manifestation.

I need to give the second point because it balances up the first point. Nothing except what is the perfect will of God can exist in the throne room. This means that if you have your own plans, your own ideas that you want God to fulfil you can never enter into the throne room. The throne room is not a place where we come to God just to bless our plan. The throne room is a place where you come to God and ask Him for His plan for you in that area. So, in our first point we say when you pray you need to see it. But in the second point, it checks you. You cannot simply come with your covetousness, with your own personal desire that may be out of line with God's will, and try what I call visualizing because in the throne room is no more visualizing you go beyond that point. Visualizing is exercising your spirit man. But in that realm you die to any of your own vision, you die to all your desires, and you ask God to show you His will and how He sees your present situation from His point. All you have is yieldedness to Him. And you pray until you see not what you want to see and what you want to visualize but what He can see. That is the second important point. No one can make a plan better than God made. All the plans of God on this planet earth until Jesus comes again are in the books of God. He knows all the details of your life, whom you will meet, whom you will marry, what you will do, who your parents are and what name they will give to you, all the faults, all the temptations in your life, all the mistakes you made, and many other things are in that book. It is amazing to know that God has all the knowledge about us. As we go into God's throne, let us seek His knowledge not bringing our knowledge and ask Him to reveal what He really sees in that situation.

I want you to very carefully meditate on these truths that are shared. Here is a marvelous thing. He doesn't allow you to know everything. But as you seek His face and pray He may be in His good pleasure reveal some of those things to your life. Maybe you have many prayer requests and some desires in your life that God could enable you to know what He has written in His book. When you pray from the throne room it is a matter of more yielding first. That is why I never believe in the supermarket request form. I don't believe in just getting a form and filling it and saying, "God this is what I want." If you want to pray in the throne room you get into the throne room first not with a prayer request but with thanksgiving and worship. Then when you are in His presence you began to ask God, "Lord, what is your mind in this area?" Help me to pray. Only the Holy Spirit knows and helps us to pray what is in the mind and the will of God. Praying in tongues helps because when we are praying in tongues the Spirit knows what we ought to pray.

What qualifies one to experience a Throne Room Visitation?

Everything that you desire if you pray constantly and believe God's word and do not let doubt and fear steal it from you, God will answer. Sometimes it takes time for the answer to come but it will come. The most important thing about visitations of God is the timing. It is not just in preparations alone, which is important for we need to have a right heart before God. It is not how holy you are, or spiritual or how much good works you have done for God but it is the fullness of the timing of God that determines the visitation of God upon your life. God has a place and time for it. We need to tell Him, "Lord, it doesn't matter how you manifest or when you do it, we just want to be in the perfect will of God to receive the right things at the right time." If it is not God's time for your visitation and if it happens (which would not) the impact and the effect of that visitation would not be permanent.

Nothing except what is the perfect will of God can exist in the throne room.

This means that if you have your own plans, your own ideas that you want God to fulfil you can never enter into the throne room. The throne room is not a place where we come to God just to bless our plan. The throne room is a place where you come to God and ask Him for His plan for you in that area. So, in our first point we say when you pray you need to see it. But in the second point, it checks you. You cannot simply come with your covetousness, with your own personal desire that may be out of line with God's will, and try what I call visualizing because in the throne room is no more visualizing you go beyond that point. Visualizing is exercising your spirit man. But in that realm you die to any of your own vision, you die to all your desires, and you ask God to show you His will and how He sees your present situation from His point. All you have is yieldedness to Him. And you pray until you see not what you want to see and what you want to visualize but what He can see. That is the second important point. No one can make a plan better than God made. All the plans of God on this planet earth until Jesus comes again are in the books of God. He knows all the details of your life, whom you will meet, whom you will marry, what you will do, who your parents are and what name they will give to you, all the faults, all the temptations in your life, all the mistakes you made, and many other things are in that book. It is amazing to know that God has all the knowledge about us. As we go into God's throne, let us seek His knowledge not bringing our knowledge and ask Him to reveal what He really sees in that situation.

The Realm Of The Spirit

As you seek His face and pray He may be in His good pleasure reveal some of those things to your life. Maybe you have many prayer requests and some desires in your life that God could enable you to know what He has written in His book. When you pray from the throne room it is a matter of more yielding first. That is why I never believe in the **supermarket request form**. I don't believe in just getting a form and filling it and saying, "God this is what I want." If you want to pray in the throne room you get into the throne room first not with a prayer request but with thanksgiving and worship. Then when you are in His presence you began to ask God, "Lord, what is your mind in this area?" Help me to pray. Only the Holy Spirit knows and helps us to pray what is in the mind and the will of God. Praying in tongues helps because when we are praying in tongues the Spirit knows what we ought to pray.

MYSTERIES OF THE THRONE ROOM

There Are Varying Degrees And Realms Of Glory In Heaven.

There are different planes of glory in heaven. Within each place is a manifestation of God. It is not like having different planes or degrees of glory and there is a throne of God for each plane. There is only one plane where the throne of God is but if you were on the lower plane and you approached God from that lower plane, you would still see God's Throne but the Throne of God you would see and experience would be from that lower plane. It is the same Throne but reflected through, for example, seven degrees of glory and you see the Throne of God differently from the way I see it. I was intensely aware that believers could reach to the Throne of God and see different parts of the Throne from what I saw. That was what really astonished me. It is like if we have many layers of glass in different degrees of transparency. Suppose I put a light bulb in front of the different glasses. You could see the light bulb in different degrees according to the different degree of transparency of the glasses. If you were on the lower plane you could still see the light bulb but it is not just a reflection but it is like seeing it in a hologram. In the earth you would see it like a reflection. But in heaven if you approached the Throne on the lower plane, it is like seeing the light is there but you know it is not but from a different plane. Because it has passed the different degrees of glory and you are seeing it from the lowest plane you will see the Throne of God differently. People could approach the Throne at these different levels or planes. When you are at the highest plane, you can begin to understand seeing the Throne from other different planes. So in the Children's paradise, they will also have the manifestation of God's Throne Room too, only at a different level.

The Throne Room Of God Is Not Static.

The Throne Room does not stay the same where you imagine you see only the glory of God and the shininess of it all the time. Different things take place at the Throne at different times. After the experience of sitting with Jesus, I was allowed to stand and watch all those things. When Elijah said, "I stand in the presence of God" I began to understand what he meant. It meant standing in the presence of God and being able just to watch all the activities taking place in heaven. Heaven is a bee-hive of activities. Different things are coming to the Throne of God and things were also being issued forth. Whenever people on earth worshipped God and sing how great is our God and Jesus our King and Commander in Chief, there is a type of glory that reflects His kingship, His authority and power in the kingly sense, and each with its different shades. And if people are singing about the God of love, the Fatherhood of God, then the Throne Room would have a different light that shines out and you could see the soft warm love flowing out from the Throne. God is who we say He is. And what God manifest to us at the Throne is what we see and say of Him on earth. When you know Him as Jehovah Jireh and call Him Jehovah Jireh, He becomes Jehovah Jireh to you. When you call Him Jehovah Shammah, He becomes Jehovah Shammah to you, and you will have the nearness of His gentleness. When you call Him Jehovah Tsidkenu, the Righteousness of God begins to come forth. Whichever attribute you call God by, His manifestation changes accordingly.

The Throne Of God Goes Into The Many Different Manifestations Of Glory According To The Worship Of His People.

Did you know that the Throne of God goes into the many different manifestations of glory? That is why He revealed His Name as I AM that I AM. When you begin to add whatever you perceive to I AM, He begins to manifest accordingly because He is the Alpha and the Omega. Whichever name you use to say and speak about God according to your revelation that is what He is, because it contains all of the Alpha and the Omega you could understand of, even beyond what you can see and think. Revelation 4: 11, "You are worthy to receive glory and honour and power; for you have created all things, and for your pleasure they are and were created." The Lord Jesus appeared as a Lamb of God. This was the Throne Room.

The Realm Of The Spirit

We know Jesus is in the form of a glorified Man. But look, He appears differently in Revelation 5: 6, "And I looked, and behold, in the midst of the throne and of the four living creatures, and in the midst of the elders, stood a Lamb as though it had been slain, having seven horns and seven eyes, which are the seven Spirits of God sent out into all the earth." Notice Jesus was representing something else. He was not just representing man seated on the right hand of God, but He was doing something different now for the destiny of nations and it was a full manifestation that was like a lamb.

In Revelation 5: 12, it describes the worship of the Lamb. Whatever we sing about, the heavens begin to manifest and the glory of the Lord begins to shine forth according the The Great I AM that I AM. Not that we change Him for He changes not, but what we receive from Him according to what you see and say of God. Do not say of God according to your limited mind. Say what the Word says He is and He will be all that He is unto you. Sometimes the manifestation of the glory of God was so powerful in the Throne Room that I felt like I was in a furnace and I could not even see the face of God. The sun is constantly having solar flares all the time and according to scientists, there is an 11 year cycle where more sunspots take place in the sun during these cycles. This is only a small illustration of the fiery things that are constantly taking place at the Throne of God. Hallelujah! Somehow what we do spiritually on the earth, does bring some manifestation from the Throne of God. In heaven, one of the busiest times is when there are various activities going on with the saints on earth. Sunday is not only a very busy day on earth whereby many believers all over the world worship God. It pleases God when there are spiritual activities that go on in the earth.

There are things coming out from the earth to heaven. Those things are substances of our praises, prayers, sacrifices, giving, right attitudes of our hearts described earlier that go up to God in worship.

It is not just a one-way thing upward, but a two way traffic -the rays of light that come upwards to heaven and rays of light going downwards. These rays are substances going up to heaven creating an activity in heaven and the angels of God were bringing the substances of the saints and bringing them to God like real offerings before Him. Oh, the awesomeness of the things of God. One of the most beautiful things that God shared with me on the Throne was He gave me a glimpse of what my work would be in heaven.

It is already so wonderful if you discover what God's will for you on this earth. It was so glorious God doesn't just want us to visit His Throne. He wants the Throne Room to be our home. And I began to realize what He was saying -that we do not go to visit God in heaven once in a while and then we come back to earth to do our earthly duties and responsibilities. But Ephesians 2: 6 says the opposite, "we have been raised up and seated with Christ in the heavenly places." The most wonderful message that God gave was that heaven is our home now. Ephesians 2 is in the past perfect tense. It is not, "we shall be", though our physical bodies are on this earth. Our spirits can actually remain there. God gave me the understanding that my spirit can remain there, while my body can be down here on earth. From time to time our spirits have to descend to this earth to fulfil our earthly responsibilities but we need to go back there.

DIVINE EXPERIENCES IN THE SPIRIT WORLD

Have you ever seen your spirit man? Let me ask another question. Have you ever had an out of body experience? Knowing what the spirit is like and experiencing what the spirit man looks like sometimes takes what I call an out of body experience. This section focuses more on the experiential side of the spiritual world than on the theological side. I want to touch on things that from time to time you may experience and you wonder how to handle it. I will also teach how to grow with the experiences that you are having and how to understand what you have been experiencing.

Out of Body Experiences

The first time I ever saw my spirit man was years back when I was very new in the ministry. I remembered as I was lying down sleeping -it must have been in the middle of the night or early morning -I was in a state of between being awake and being asleep. I was fully aware of what is going on around me. But yet it was like a dream like state. I was conscious of what was happening, unlike in a dream where the consciousness is not that strong. Suddenly I saw around me thousands and thousands of demons. They were so many that all I could see were their faces. In the dream or vision or experience whatever you call it, I felt that I was in a little room and I had to move out of that room. And I found myself coming out of my body and I could consciously feel that my body was still lying there. And a part of me got up which at that time I didn't know was my spirit man. And as I was walking towards a certain direction out of that room, I could feel the spiritual pressure. I did not experience any of the demons touching me.

The Realm Of The Spirit

But all I felt was that spiritual pressure. The spiritual pressure was so intense that I felt that it was very difficult to walk. As I was going about 10 to 15 feet away from my body, in that weak state I felt myself suddenly being pulled back into my body. And I got up. Then I realized that I had experienced my spirit man.

I was a Christian but my spirit man was so weak. I was desperate to deal with that deficiency in my life. I was desperate enough to say, "God here I am. I better find the solution to get more energy in my spirit." This was when God began to teach me the principle of meditation and confession. And I began to build up my spirit. Subsequently about a year later I had a vision of my spirit and it was able to fly. And I know that was good. Recently I had another out of body experience. My spirit man came put of my body and this time it was for about 45 minutes. I spend time praying and fellowshipping with the Lord from about 3 a.m. to 6 a.m. At about 6.15 am on a Sunday, I wanted to take a little rest before going to church. We leave the house normally at about 7.30 am. Knowing that I had been exerting my physical body since I had been praying that long, I just wanted to rest just lying down and take 40 winks. And within a few seconds my spirit left my body. I was not seeking for it for all I wanted was to just let my body rest a while.

My spirit went and visited different people. A lot of people do not know that their spirits sometimes leave their body while they are asleep. I saw the spirits of my children and I also went and prayed for them. When I went and prayed for them I put something like a white substance on them to wear. Then for some reasons I saw the spirits of two of my sisters. Their spirits were in a room upstairs in my house. All through those 45 minutes I knew my body was still lying there. So I knew it was not a dream. Then I approached one of them. It was as if their spirits were there to be blessed and prayed for. One of my sisters was kneeling down in a state of prayer. And as I approached her to pray for her, her spirit looked up. Now her spirit looks exactly like her. As I approached her she looked up and asked me, "Why are you shining?" Then I realized that I was shining. It was when she said that, that I notice myself, otherwise I didn't notice it. Then I notice there was light coming out from every part of me. I was wearing a certain type of clothes, but somehow it was not a robe. It was like a loose kind of pants and there were also shoes. Then there was a fitting garment. The whole garment was very loose and there were no buttons and the whole garment was shining. In the spirit realm in my spirit I felt the energy flowing through. It was like liquid fire going through you all the time. In another incident I saw my spirit was when I went to minister to one of the church members. I was no more in my house. I saw my spirit man putting my hand out as if to receive something, then putting my right hand into that person's spirit in the abdominal area. I saw my spirit hand actually enter that person's spirit. Then my spirit began to lift upwards and as my spirit lifted upwards I saw my spirit man taking a whole bundle of black substance out. Looks like my spirit man was ministering some sort of healing to that person.

When I got back into my body, it was like my spirit was quite far away and then suddenly I heard a sound. It was 7 a.m. and my alarm clock was ringing. In that state I suddenly realized I must get back. I could feel my spirit man going into my body. I was conscious for 45 minutes in what the spirit man was doing. When my spirit man stepped into my body I did not for one second lose consciousness. It was not a dream. I was fully conscious. At that time I wanted my physical body to be recharged and strengthened. This body of ours needs constant care and treatment and recharging in order to do what we want to do in the spirit realm. Even Jesus Christ in the garden of Gethsemane prayed and prayed till His body sweated blood. And the bible says in the gospel of Luke that the angel came and strengthened Him and then He prayed some more. And I could feel the energizing force of the spirit man. Then for the next 29 minutes I was just sitting down in a state of ecstasy enjoying the experience. I wanted to make my physical body yield to that which was within me. And as I consciously yielded I could feel the energy flowing into my body. Then my body started to shake. And every time I am conscious of that my body starts to shake. It seems as if our physical body can only take that much of spiritual power. We cannot take it all at once. We got to take it a bit at a time.

Trickle-Charging the Human Spirit

Sometimes God try to charge our body at the maximum possible. Even those who have never been slain in the power do experience a trickle charge. Sometimes those who have been slain in the power have reached a point where they have full charge. In case some of you think that you are peculiar or strange because you have never been slain in the power while others were slain easily, let me explain. I was in that way myself in the early days of my ministry. In fact for about 10 years I never really knew what being slain in the Spirit was like. I have seen other people slain in the Spirit when I pray but I never knew what it was like. And at the back of my mind I was always

The Realm Of The Spirit

asking, "Why, Lord?" Then it dawned on me that you don't have to be slain to receive the blessing of God; God can trickle-charge you until you are slowly charged up. Part of it also depends on your co-operation in your yielding to God.

Let me talk about trickle charge. Even those who had not been slain under the power have times in their prayer or when others are praying for them or in their own private worship when they feel their body move or shake. Whether it is in a slow motion they feel their body moving or hands wanting to shake and they slowly take control again. Or whether their legs want to shake or the head wants to shake or some part of their being wants to shake. Even though I have never been slain in my early days but sometimes during prayer my hands felt like shaking. Sometimes during prayer I could feel my body involuntarily wanting to move in a certain manner. The strange thing about it was that it was up to me whether to let go or not. It was me and yet not me -I never fully understood that. Then I began to realize that when our spirit man is trickle-charging our physical body there is a vibration taking place. Sometimes it is so great that you feel it in your natural body.

Do you know that all over the world whether they are American or African or Asian that when they pray deep in the spirit and in tongues a lot of people sway although some don't? Who taught them that? Who taught people to pray that way? Now those who pray short hours don't enter into that. But when you enter long hours of prayer all these are happening. And you enter a prayer meeting where Koreans are praying they would be on their knees and their bodies would go up and down -who taught them that? Why must their bodies go up and down? A sceptical professor of theology could easily come and say that it is not necessary to pray that manner. All you have to do is to just look up to God and say, "Gracious Heavenly Father." I know that I don't have to move that much when I pray as long as I mean it with my heart. He could say it is not necessary and the people know that it is not necessary. But why does it still happen? I have been in prayer meetings with Americans, and with Australians and both of them also pray that way. So it is not cultural; it is international. Where did it come from?

Vibrations of the Spirit

This is part of the matter of what I believe. I believe that sometimes when you enter into the strength of prayer there is a strength that comes from the spirit man of each one and there is a wave of the Spirit. And everyone just sense that awesome vibration in their body like a wave going through them so they move in that manner. What is that? That is spiritual music. Music is a vibration of sound waves in harmony. The bible say let all that have breath praise the Lord. How do you expect all that have breath to praise the Lord? Through vibrations. Atoms are moving and oscillating all the time. When spiritual energy contacts the natural world there is a certain vibrations. I know that the occult uses such a term. Occult healers use terms like I sense the vibrations. What they are saying is a fact in the spirit realm. Except that they don't know the truth that there are 2 spirit realms: one evil and one good. How does the spirit of cancer work? Cancer can be caused by exposure to certain types of radiation. Consuming preservatives that break down body cells can also cause cancer. Those are natural causes. We know that cancer can also be caused from deep within a person's soul. There is something within the soul that somehow affects the mutation in their physical body. An evil spirit can also cause cancer. I mean deafness may be caused by accident. But there is deafness that can be caused by a deaf and dumb spirit. Now we are only talking about the evil spirits causing the diseases.

How does the spirit of cancer work? This is what I believe. They will attach themselves to a physical body and cause their own perverted and dark life and vibrations to come into that person. Now when a person is suffering from cancer that is caused by a spirit of cancer, the doctors can look at the cancer and see it but cannot see the spirit. I mean the evil spirit is intangible. How can a spirit being cause something in the natural? I believe what the cancerous spirit does is to attach itself to the physical body; usually right at the part where the cancer is. Then it causes the natural cells to vibrate according to its synchrony or vibrations. Remember Satan is now out of tune; demons are out of tune. But out of tune doesn't mean they don't have vibrations. The earth is out of tune; Paul says the earth is groaning. But what the evil spirit does is channel this disharmonic vibration into a person's body. And slowly the cells that are vibrating in harmony in health and life gets perverted and slowly twisted and begins to respond to the wrong song. The song of the devil starts mutating and cancer results in a tangible form. Try to understand what happens in the spiritual realm. There are vibrations that come from God. Remember we touched on the song of the Lamb, the song that is in every one's heart and in every one's body and soul. There is a song in our soul. When that song dies you die. When that song grieves you become grieved. That song in our life and that vibration that is in harmony with God in our life vibrate into other peoples' lives as we contact them and drive out the disharmony out of their lives.

The Realm Of The Spirit

I received a note from a man in one of my meetings. When I went back to the hotel room and read that note, he says that he was having this pain in his jaw and toothache and yet he came to the meeting. When he came to the meeting he was just claiming God's Word and fighting it off. In that note he made a very strange statement. He says the moment I stepped up at the platform and looked at the congregation every pain in him just disappeared. And I was not even praying for healing. How did that happen? It is because of the vibrations that flow from our spirit man. We all need to understand that the state of our spirit man determines the state of our soul. If your soul is down and discouraged, it is because your spirit man is not functioning properly. Either it lacks food or air. Food is the Word and air is prayer and worship with God. Our soul man can be so occupied with worldly affairs that we neglect the spirit man.

The Holy Spirit Working Through Our Human Spirit

The Holy Spirit works through our human spirit Romans 1:9 For God is my witness, whom I serve with my spirit in the gospel of His Son, that without ceasing I mention you always in my prayers. Paul says that I serve God with my spirit. Understand that every time the Holy Spirit moves He needs your spirit to work through. Why is it that now that the Holy Spirit has come to the planet earth? The Holy Spirit is so powerful and awesome that every disease and sickness cannot stand in His presence. We know that was true in Jesus' life. Why is it that He cannot flow through in such a manner like Jesus' time where every sickness was healed? He lacks a strong spirit to flow through. He lacks a strong human spirit. And the vast majority of people's spirits are every weak compared to Jesus'. The reason why the Holy Spirit could flow through Jesus' life in full measure is because the human spirit of Jesus was perfect and strong. Jesus' spirit when He was born as a child had to be nurtured in the same way like all of us. For 30 years He was developing the strength of the spirit man. Don't underestimate the time you spend privately with God to develop your spirit man. How much God can work through your life is directly proportional to the strength of your spirit man. No matter how powerful the Holy Spirit is, no matter how powerful the call and the gifts that God wants to put in your life, it is directly limited to the strength of your spirit man. That is a very dangerous truth to some for this reason. You can be called by God to be an apostle, prophet, evangelist, pastor, teacher, but if you neglect to make your spirit strong, you will live your entire life and ministry in half measures. You would never quite function in the fullness that God wants you to function in. It is a dangerous thing to neglect our spirit man. Because by doing so we instantly limit God in our life. He is limited to the strength of our spirit man.

In the gospel of Luke it tells us that Jesus and as well as John the Baptist. John is a man like us. But Jesus Himself had to grow just like us. Lk.2:40 And the child grew and became strong, filled with wisdom and the favor of God was upon Him. Jesus had to strengthen His spirit for 30 years getting ready for the Holy Spirit to work through His spirit. Paul says in Rom. 1:9 I serve God with my spirit. It is through our human spirit that the Holy Spirit manifests and people don't realize it. When you sing the song Come Holy Spirit I Need You perhaps 10 people are gathered there when you sing that song. Five of them their spirit men is weak and are only 0.5 volt each. Of the other five, three of them are slightly better than the others having 2 volts each. One of them spend more time with God and he has 5 volts and another one spend plenty of time has 10 volts. So here all of them are praying and singing Come Holy Spirit I Need You. And the Holy Spirit has billions of volts and here He comes to them. Even though He has billions volts, He could only manifest to10 volts. No wonder He is disappointed many times. But sometimes the 10 volts guy was not fully ready so he may open himself to 9 volts of the Holy Spirit's power. The Holy Spirit is limited to the development of our spirit man.

And our spirit man is sensitive fragile just like our physical body. Although the spirit laws can overcome natural laws in our physical body, yet those are exceptional cases. We don't push our bodies too far or we pay a price. Learn to keep the Sabbaths, learn to eat properly, learn the value of physical exercise in order to keep our physical body in good health. I was talking to one of our elders John in spite of his age he still goes for a run. When I was in his house he showed me all his gym equipment that he made himself. Then I said those who have never exercised physically don't know how good it feels. Because they are so used to be at their energy level. Always at their 9 to 5 jobs, and when they come home, they look at the papers. They never know the vibrancy of health because they have never sweated, never exercised. But once you have done it you know the difference. Then you know what you had before was not really full health that you thought. Being in full is not just that you are not sick. There are a lot of people who are not sick but they are not healthy either. They are not full of energy in life.

And it is the same way with our spirit. Our spirit man needs to be nurtured just like Jesus Christ has to nurture that spirit man. And our spirit man can grow until the spirit man equals Holy Spirit. Was there such a person? Yes, Elijah. Elijah started like all of us, a man of light passion. But he never ended that way. He ended so strong in the spirit that looking over at II Kings chapter 2 when Elisha who was his disciple asked for the power, he did not ask for the Holy Spirit. He asked for his spirit. Look and see whether he is asking for the Holy Spirit or his spirit. In II Kg. 2:9 I pray you, let me inherit a double share of your spirit. Then in verse 15 now when the sons of the prophets who were at Jericho saw him over against them, they said, "The spirit of Elijah rests of Elisha." Why your spirit and why not God's Spirit? Is it because of a lack of teaching? Elijah spirit has developed to the extend that it was a very perfected vessel for the Holy Spirit. His spirit became like the Holy Spirit. A perfect channel having his spirit was like having the Holy Spirit. Understand that because of his level that without prayer and without calling on God for an anointing, all he had to do was say if I am a man of God like fire come down. What kind of man is this who can talk like that? It is because his spirit has become so like the Holy Spirit that they are almost indistinguishable. That having his spirit was like having the Holy Spirit. No wonder he did not see death. His spirit was so transformed that God says come home and he was taken to heaven and his physical body was placed in a sort of suspended state of animation. And for thousands of years he had existed in heaven in that glorified state, waiting to come down one day when the anti Christ shows up. And we know when the anti Christ show up, he will be one of the two witnesses. The other one is theologians are still trying to find out who. All scholars agree that Elijah is going to come back. When he comes back according to Revelations 12 he is going to be killed. So we know one thing that the physical body he has is still in his mortal form. Such is the power of the human spirit that it can sustain the physical body. Elijah's spirit was the perfect channel of the Holy Spirit. You find it mentioned again on the Transfiguration on the Mount where he appeared to Jesus.

Senses of the Human Spirit

When the spirit man comes alive there are something that begins to happen. In the book of Acts 19:21 Now after these events Paul resolved in the Spirit to pass through Macedonia and Achaia and go to Jerusalem, saying, "After I have been there, I must also see Rome." Let me describe what it was like the few seconds before my spirit left my body. I had spent about nearly 3 hours with God. As I was lying down on the couch and trying to get some physical rest, I closed my eyes I could feel myself almost entering into a dream. Then it was like I felt a demonic pressure. Almost like my first vision. But this time I never see them. I could feel the spirit of heaviness. I made a mental decision. I purposed in my spirit. See the spirit man is subject to your will. And I purposed in my spirit that I am going to concentrate on the presence of God and just lie down. I am conscious of the fact that in the presence of God the enemy cannot stand. Now there are times God may lead you to take authority. But during this time I just wanted a rest and I couldn't be bothered with demons. And I want the presence that I had when I was spending time with God to overwhelm the enemy. And I just sort of couldn't care less whether the demons wanted to come near or didn't want to come near. Makes no difference to me. I felt my spirit man coming out of my body. It was like somebody strong coming out. Suddenly every demon ran off. This is interesting my spirit man could deal with demons. Our physical body couldn't contact the demons but our spirit man can. There is something in our will that is able to purpose to move into the spirit realm. Purpose to concentrate on the presence of God. And our spirit can arise and affect the things around us. And every time there is a presence of God there is a side effect on the physical body that we need to flow with. I have noticed this, if people don't have trickle charge and never yield to trickle charge they can never be charged at all. You asks, "Why does God not force His way? If God forces His way your batteries will explode. When your spirit man is still in your body and you are yielding to the spirit world, your body sort of begins to move.

Let refer to Ezekiel. 36:26-27 A new heart I will give you, and a new spirit I will put within you; and I will take out of your flesh the heart of stone and give you a heart of flesh. And I will put my Spirit within you, and cause you to walk in my statutes and be careful to observe my ordinance. Everybody knows that there are 2 s there. One is a small s and the other is the big S. God says I will put a new spirit in you and I will put my Spirit in you. one is our human spirit that is reborn and one is the Holy Spirit. But there are not 2 things that are new there, there are 3. What is the other new? A new heart. I will give you a new heart and put a new spirit.

What is that new heart? You see the heart consists of 4 areas. The heart consists of your will, your emotion, your intellect and your conscience. Three of them are in your soul and 1 in your spirit. What is He saying here? And this is what a lot of people are not yielding to. God says I give you a new spirit; I give you a new heart. What is the heart? Some people say the heart is the spirit. But you find that is not true all the time. The heart

The Realm Of The Spirit

consists of 4 avenues of our experience. If you take the concordance and study every word where the word heart occur, many times it is mentioned the heart chooses, the heart wills. So you know that there is one aspect of the heart, it chooses. Then it talks about the heart feeling, feeling things, feeling emotions, grief, sorrow, and joy. So you know that emotions are involved in the heart. Then other places say as a man think in the heart. So you find the heart thinks. Then there is another aspect of the heart that we call the intellect. Then you have the conscience. Now 3 of them are actually found in your soul.

What God is also saying is this: I give you a new soul, a new spirit and I will put my Spirit in you. You say I didn't know that I have got a new soul that needs to be developed. What did the bible say about renewing your mind? Look at Genesis and see what the soul is and how it comes about. Genesis. 2:7 Then the Lord God formed man of dust from the ground, so there is his physical body, his physical was perfect but its dead, there is no life, God formed it by His Word. Now God is going to do something. God is going to breathe His Spirit into them. So as God breathed into him. As the spirit contacted the physical realm and the 2 touched. And man became. The Hebrew word is a living soul. How did the soul come about? The soul comes about when the spirit contacted the physical. Now look at the new birth. What is the new birth? Did God breathe into our life again? God took this physical body that has biological life but its dead spiritually and breathed His life into it on the day we accepted Jesus Christ as Lord and Savior. Ezekiel. 36:26-27 three things, new heart, new spirit and my Spirit. And he gives an emphasis in verse 26 on the heart saying I will take the heart of stone and put a heart of flesh in you. He obviously separated the heart and the human spirit although they are linked together.

So we have one scripture from Genesis.2 and one scripture from Ezek. 36 then we have a scripture from the book of Romans. Romans. 8:5-6 For those who live according to the flesh set their minds on the thing of the flesh, but those who live according to the Spirit set their minds on the things of the Spirit. To set the mind on the flesh is death, but to set the mind on the Spirit is life and peace. Notice there are now suddenly 2 minds in you. The only possible way to be double minded is to have 2 minds. We got an old mind of the flesh and a new mind of the Spirit. And we are to choose. Suddenly with the presence of the Spirit it is easy to choose. The will becomes strong. We got a new heart. Our heart cannot respond. Now it can. Last time you were not conscious of sin. Suddenly now you are very sensitive. What has happened? You got a new heart. It has more powerful sensation and feelings, more powerful ability in thinking and more powerful ability in the will. And the difference is that we must learn to yield to that, to subject ourselves to the new influence of the Spirit in our life. And that is why when Jesus was walking on this earth, everything He did He did it through His spirit man. He knew things by His spirit man because He is perfected.

In the gospel of Luke 2 He prophesied that many hearts will be pierced and He will discern the thoughts and the intents of people heart. Luke. 2:34-35 but we want to actually look at is the gospel of Mark. 2, in Luke. 22 and in many others passages of Luke. It is far more often in Luke that any gospel where you will always find this statement, Jesus knew their thought, Jesus perceived their thought. How did Jesus know? Mark.2 tells us how in verse 8 And immediately Jesus, perceiving in His spirit. His spirit has a supernatural ability to perceive. Every thing He does was through His spirit. When He worked a work of healing it was Jesus Christ's spirit that travail. And every thing that was worked was worked through His spirit. We need to know the 2 enemies of our human spirit. We need to know what has happened in our human spirit and what we actually have. We have within us a new mind which is a part of the new heart. New emotions to feel for God. Do you notice the day you were born again there arose emotions that you never have before? Good emotions for God. They are in the realm of the spirit but yet they affect your natural man. You feel emotional about worshiping God. You cry all the time. You feel emotional about seeing someone in need. You feel emotional about the suffering of mankind. Your emotion is now more sensitive than before. There is some thing happening on our inside. Many Christians know they got a new spirit but they didn't know they got a new heart. But the scriptures tell us that a day will come when God will write the laws in their mind and in their heart.

Although it may look like a prophecy for heaven you look at Hebrews. 8 and 10 where the prophecies are repeated twice. That in that day I will write my laws in their heart and in their mind. And if you research what that day mean. That day refers to the day of the covenant. Hebrews. 8:10 This is the covenant that I will make with the house of Israel after those days, says the Lord; I will put my laws into their minds, and write them on their hearts, and I will be their God, and they shall be my people. Verse 12-13 For I will be merciful toward their iniquities, and I will remember their sins no more. In speaking of a new covenant He treats the first as obsolete. And what is becoming obsolete and growing old is ready to vanish away. In other words after those days refer to those days after the old covenant is finished and a new begin.

But we have always put this scripture for heaven. Why do we do such things like that? Why do people say that one day in heaven we all will be healed? Don't you realize that these are scriptures for us today? In Hebrews. 10 it is repeated again. Verse 16 -17 is what we are talking about. He says in verse 14 For a single offering He has perfected for all time those who are sanctified. Has perfected, past perfect tense. Verse 15 And the Holy Spirit also bears witness to us; for after saying. He is talking about now. In case it doesn't satisfy some I Corinthians. 2:16 says But we have the mind of Christ. The strange thing about the bible is unless we have knowledge we cannot receive. Unless we believe that it is there we cannot experience it. Unless we are told that its there we cannot experience it.

Paul asked in Acts 19 to the Ephesians have you received the Holy Spirit. They said we have not even heard of it. How can you receive what you have not heard? Now you heard this today do you have a new heart? Do you have a new mind? Do you have a new spirit? And you have the Holy Spirit. Inside you resides some thing more powerful than you can imagine. The human spirit that is beginning to affect your soul and it's an aspect of the soul that is rising like never before. God is writing His laws right now He wants to perfect our soul. The only thing reserved until Jesus comes is the new body. But until then and in this life He wants to perfect our soul. It's in this life He wants our soul to conform perfectly to Him. And that's the soul we are talking about that can purpose, that can think the way Jesus think. And we can rise into such height of our awareness, consciousness and achievement that He wants us to rise to.

CHAPTER FIVE

THE DEGREES, DEPTHS AND DIMENSIONS OF OPERATING IN THE REALM OF THE SPIRIT

This section dwells on the degrees of depth in the spirit world and entering the spirit world. We talk about experiencing the spirit world. But what we want to speak about tonight is there are different degrees of experiencing the spirit world. You could be sitting there comfortable in your chair and just pray in tongues. And you would be experiencing the spirit world. There are different degrees that we experience the spirit world. Sometimes some people experience the spirit world with different kind of experiences. Sometimes these experiences raise doubts in the minds of many logical thinking, rational, intellectual Christians. See we are not just talking about experiences in the spirit world. We are talking about degrees, depths of experience .The degree and the depth of your encounter of the spirit world determines the side effect or no side effect on your physical body, or your mind, or your spirit. It depends sometimes upon the type of revelation that you received. It sometimes also depends upon the encounter that you have. praying sometimes they feel that they are caught up and they are just about to move into the realm. But half way through they got fearful. The moment they got fearful they would drop down, not physically but spiritually. They felt themselves getting back into the natural. Does it mean that even when we are experiencing the spirit world we have a degree of controlling its depth, yes we have. How much we enter into the spirit world is still in the jurisdiction of our free will and our openness to the encounter that we have. If we open ourselves more there seems to be a greater depth of experience. If we withhold we experience the same thing but at a lower level of depth.

THE REALM OF AN OPEN VISION

This is a much deeper realm or level of walking in the realm of the spirit. In this realm, both the natural realm and supernatural realms are open or visible such that a person gets to move in both realms of existence at the

The Realm Of The Spirit

same time. In other words, in this realm, both the spirit world and the natural world are open to you. It is a realm beyond trances or manifestations. In a trance, your body has to yield or be unconscious in order for you to have a supernatural experience or see in the spirit world but in an open vision, you are able to see in the spirit world without any accompanying manifestation. In an open vision, you are able to see spiritual subjects in both the realm of the natural and the realm of the spirit concurrently.

Under normal circumstances, there are three dimensions in the realm of visions that is a spiritual vision, a closed vision and an open vision. A spiritual vision is the one experienced when only when the human spirit leaves and enters the realm of the spirit, but the body still remains in the physical realm. A closed vision is the one in which the physical body has to give way in order for one to have a spiritual experience and in some instances you may have to fall into a deep sleep, be unconscious or fall under the power for some time so that the spirit will leave the body and enter the realm of the spirit. But the spiritual experience that I'm talking about in this context is that of an open vision whereby the spirit realm and the natural realm are meshed together as one. It's as if a veil has been opened or lifted off you to enable you to see beyond the realm of senses. It's like moving back into the Garden of Eden the experience of which if God comes, you see Him clearly. In that realm, there are no more spiritual secrets in the supernatural and you begin to openly see spiritual subjects such as angels, demons and other spirit beings. The spirit world is opened to you such that Heaven and Hell are exposed to you as you are catapulted right into the Throne Room in Heaven. This is the realm which Stephen taped into in Acts 7:55-56, when the mob was busy stoning him. It is said that and Heavens were opened and he began to see God sitting on the throne and Jesus standing at His right hand such that he began to publicly announce what was going on in the Heavens despite the beatings. In other words, he was conscious of the people who were stoning him in the physical realm while at the same time watching a movie going on in Heaven. In actual fact, Stephen saw the Lord and had communion with the Lord while he was still conscious of what was happening to him in the physical realm. What a spectacular display of supernatural power! This tells me that you have authority over death. Even death itself cannot dictate how you should behave during the moments of your departure to Heaven.

The realm of open vision transcends the realm of discernment or any spiritual gifts. For example you get to a level where the spirit world is clearly open to you such that if you look into the sky, you could see angels parading the spirit realm in all their splendour and dazzling appearance and if you were looking out at people and a demon came across the room, you also see the demon there. If you look out into the sky you could actually see where the thrones of the demons are and you could actually see angels flying up and down. Under normal circumstances, one would see spiritual subjects like demons and angels through the gift of discernment of spirits but in the case of an open vision, it's as if a movie is brought right in front of your eyes. Through the enablement of the gifts of the spirit, some people see visions in the flash or for a while and then the vision disappear and they are back to their natural sight. But living in an open vision is to see all the time. It is a realm beyond discernment and beyond any gift of the spirit. I am not talking about a short vision that lasts for few minutes. I am talking about living in an open vision; living in all dimensions all the time.

The greater truth is that when you are in an open vision all the time and you look out of the window, you are not sure which is of the physical world and which is not of the spirit world. When you are driving a car then suddenly you see the highway disappearing in front of you and you see something else and you can't drive. You can't even walk normally. As you walk, suddenly there could be this vision of a valley as you turn to the next road. As you turn, you fall into the drain in the natural realm. In that realm it is literally impossible to separate the natural from spiritual. In other words, the spiritual becomes as real as the natural. Therefore, it is not easy to live in that realm all the time because everywhere you keep seeing pictures. It's very hard to differentiate between what is real and what is spirit. No wonder God doesn't let it happen all the time otherwise you cannot live a natural life. If a person starts talking to me and I began to see a picture, that picture is as real as that person. Then as the person is talking, I can see a car coming and I think it's a real car yet I'm seeing it in the spirit. It's not a real car but a visualized car.

Exhilarating as it might sound, the truth is that it's impossible to live a natural life in that realm. Which is why God doesn't permit it all the time otherwise we cannot be human any more. In that realm, it's even very difficult to pay attention to logical conversation. While someone is talking about his house, or where they are from, you are not paying attention to what they are saying. Instead, you are paying attention to the pictures that keep coming out. In this realm, people's thoughts are opened and made plain before you. It makes you uncomfortable in the natural when you move

The Realm Of The Spirit

too much into that realm because what people think, you can sort of see the picture coming out of them. And if a person is demon possessed, you could straightaway tell as there is no way the demon can hide. In fact, the demon looks at you eyeball to eyeball.

In the spirit realm when you mature in the realm of open vision, you cannot avoid the pictures. Say, for instance I were to read Matthew 6:6, as I begin to read it, when the anointing of that realm is there, I would began to see Jesus walking into the synagogue. It would be just like a person is talking about anything, all you see is not that person. You cannot read that person's mind but one clue from that person is enough to tell you all that is on his mind. It's just like a forensic expert or a criminologist. They could go to a place where a crime has been committed. The average human being would say we couldn't tell what the crime is since everything is burned. We can't tell how the crime was committed. But the forensic experts take a few samples here and a few samples there and examine them under a microscope. They come back and say this person died at about midnight. This person died in this manner. They are able to draw some conclusions just from those small samples. This is how it is like in the realm of open vision. What a spectacular and phenomenal display of supernatural power! The good news is that this deeper realm is available for exploration by believers living in this critical end time. It's time that you stop clinging on the snowline and delve into the river of God's glory as there are deeper territories to explore in the realm of the spirit.

There was a time I prayed 48 hours in tongues just to see what it was like. And I just briefly mentioned that after that it was like living in an open vision, where it looks like if you were looking out at people and if a demon came across the room you also see the demon there. Usually some people would see it through the discerning of spirit. And they see it in the flash or for a while and then the vision disappeared and they are back to their natural sight. But living in an open vision is to see all the time. It is a realm beyond discernment, beyond any gift of the spirit. I am not talking about a short vision that lasts for about 5 minutes. I am talking about living in an open vision; living in all 4 dimensions all the time. Most of the time we live in this 3 dimension. This was what it was like. It was very strange to live in that realm. And it didn't just suddenly go off. See we have barely touched the fringe of what God wants. When I saw the benefits of praying in tongues for 8 hours, it stirred my desire to see what happens if you go further. That was when I went for 2 days without sleep and for 48 hours

Frequency Revelator

I just went on in tongues. And you would have to have a big jar of water. You will get pretty thirsty in the natural. But at the end of those 48 hours something snapped. It was like a veil was opened. It was like moving back into the Garden of Eden where if God comes you see God. You look out into the sky you could actually see where the thrones of the demons are. And you could actually see angels flying up and down. It was like living in an open vision. But it slowly began to fade and I realized it has to be maintained. There is a certain realm that is there. It's not easy to live in that realm all the time because everywhere you keep seeing pictures. It's very hard to differentiate between what is real and what is spirit. No wonder God doesn't let it happen al the time otherwise you cannot live a natural life. If a person starts talking to me and I began to see a picture, that picture is as real as that person. Then as the person is talking I see a dog coming and I think it's a real dog. But its not; it's a visualized dog. It's impossible to live a natural life in that realm. Which is why God doesn't permit it all the time. Otherwise we cannot be human any more.

When you are in an open vision all the time you look out of the window you are not sure which is of the physical world and which is not of the physical world. When you are driving a car then suddenly you see the highway disappears in front of you and you see something else and you can't drive. You can't even walk normally. As you walk suddenly there could be this vision of a valley as you turn to the next road. As you turn you fall into the drain in the natural. In that realm it is literally impossible to separate the natural from spiritual. In other words the spiritual becomes as real as the natural. Slowly as I faded off in that condition I was a bit dazed. All you want to do is to just sit down on a chair like a prophet and just prophesy. And it's very difficult to pay attention to logical conversation. For example you know what its like when you talk to people and they are not listening to you. When you are in the spirit realm you will be giving that same impression. While someone is talking about his house, or where they are from, you are not paying attention to what they are saying. You are paying attention to the pictures that keep coming out.

What about thoughts? It makes you uncomfortable in the natural when you move into that realm. What people think you can sort of see the picture coming out of them. And if a person is demon possessed you could straightaway tell it. There is no way the demon can hide. In fact the demon looks at you eyeball to eyeball. Now in the spirit world when you become very strong in that you cannot avoid the pictures. Like if I read chapter

6:6 as I read it when the anointing or that realm is there I would began to see Jesus walking into the synagogue. As I said its very easy to express the spirit realm. It would be just like a person is talking about anything all you see is not that person. You cannot read that person's mind. But one clue from that person is enough to tell you all that is on his mind. It is just like a forensic expert or a criminologist. They could go to a place where a crime has been committed. The average human being would say we couldn't tell what the crime is since every thing is burned. We can't tell how the crime was committed. But the forensic experts take a few samples here and a few samples there and examine them under a microscope. They come back and say this person died at about midnight. This person died in this manner. They are able to draw some conclusions just from those small samples.

THE REALM OF TRANCES

This is an entry level experience and encounter in the realm of the spirit. These are what I call provocations into the spirit realm. They mark the first point of contact with the realm of the spirit. This realm is for people who are learning how to express themselves in the spirit realm, hence it is a realm of manifestations. In the realm of trances, the curtain that separates the natural realm from the spirit realm gets closed so that the person only sees what is in the supernatural. As the spirit rises or soars and leaves the body, and enters into the spirit world, the body becomes unconscious or oblivious of what's going on in the physical realm. That means all the natural senses are suspended or switched off to enable the person to have a concentration on the vision of the supernatural. Such a phenomenon is usually prevalent when then anointing upon is intensely manifested upon a vessel. At this level, as people enter the realm of the spirit for the first time, usually they experience different manifestations, for example some may start trembling hysterically or shaking profusely in their bodies, some fall under the power, some scream uncontrollably, some groan and travail in the spirit and some get to the extent of being totally unconscious. All these manifestations are what characterises the realm of trances. They are a result of contact with the spirit world. That is why it is called a realm of manifestations. Laughing, dancing, singing and travailing in the spirit are also common manifestations that might occur in this realm. It must be expressly understood that certain spiritual exercises and sacrifices such as fasting and prayer are required to necessitate our entry into this realm. This is scenario is evidenced in the Word of God in Acts 10:1-11 whereby, Peter felt hungry and as they were preparing food, he fell into a trance and saw the visions of God.

Frequency Revelator

Do you notice that it says Peter became hungry and in that state, he was catapulted into the realm of trance? This tells me that fasting is what provoked or triggered that manifestation. Fasting is a vitamin for your soul. It propels your spirit into the realm of the spirit much like the rocket boosters and the enormous power that propels a space shuttle into orbit. Once in that realm, you tend to hear God better and you are attuned to the frequency of the Holy Ghost as the power and the presence of God increases upon you and your faith deepens. At that level, your spirit is totally focused on the spirit realm and distractions tend to lose their grip. The reason why we fall into trances is because the nature of the spirit realm is such that it needs to be activated, cultivated, and provoked, hence our physical bodies have to yield to a certain degree so that we can enter that realm. A deeper dimension or depth in prayer can actually trigger entry into this realm. Yielding to the spirit can actually provoke the Holy Ghost to launch us into this realm. It is worth exploring the truth that these spiritual experiences were not for Peter only but are a grace which the Holy Spirit has made available for exploration in the realm of the spirit in these end times. You too can tap into the greater heights in the spirit dimension and experience a trance. It will shape and align your spirit for greater exploits and change your destiny forever. Although it's an entry level experience in the realm of the spirit, it will usher you into the greater depths of the miraculous.

THE REALM OF DIVINE TRANSPORTATION IN THE SPIRIT

This is the most spectacular and peculiar realm in the spirit dimension.
It is a much higher realm than the realm of trances and open vision in that in this realm, not only do you see visions and associate with angels, not only is the spirit world revealed to you but you begin to explore the whole spirit world. It is a realm of exploration and discovery. As an introductory perspective to this revelation, lets refer to a popular scripture in Isaiah 5:8: "They that wait upon Lord shall be renewed of their strength. They shall rise of the wings like eagles, they shall walk and not faint, they shall run and not get tired". In most cases, people who interpret this scripture usually emphasize a lot on the aspect of waiting and they hardly get to catch a revelation of what it says one would be able to do after the waiting process. In essence, this scripture gives a revelation and insight of the dimensions of divine transportation in the realm of the spirit. It provides a foundation and background for understanding how transportation takes place in the realm of the spirit. In essence, when the scripture says those that wait upon the

The Realm Of The Spirit

Lord will walk, run and fly, it's not talking about physical walking, running and flying. God has nothing to do with your physical walking and running since physical exercise profits a little but Godly exercise profits unto all things. Instead, what the scripture is talking about are dimensions of the spirit whereby one walks, runs and flies in the realm of the spirit, not in the natural realm. Based on the revelation from the scripture above, when someone is moving in the realm of divine transportation, it's either he is flying, running or walking in the spirit. This implies that in the Christian journey or race, there are different class of people, that is; there are those who are walking, then there are those who are running and there are those who are flying. The question is, in which category do you belong? I know it might sounds a little bit quizzical or bizarre but you got to experience it. There are different ways and means of Holy Ghost transportation. In the physical realm, there are different modes of transportation such as cars, bikes and planes. As it is in the natural realm, so it is in the spirit realm. It is of paramount importance therefore to highlight at this stage that due to its diverse nature or form, this realm has THREE different dimensions.

THE DIMENSIONS IN THE REALM OF DIVINE TRANSPORTATION

FIRST DIMENSION :

THE DIMENSION OF WALKING IN THE SPIRIT

In a view to unfold the mysteries of divine transportation, Paul admonishes us in Galatians 5: 16-19 that, *I say, walk by the Spirit, and do not gratify the desires of the flesh. For the desires of the flesh are against the Spirit, and the desires of the Spirit are against the flesh; for these are opposed to each other to prevent you from doing what you would. But if you are led by the Spirit you are not under the law.* If you do a cross referencing of scriptures, you would notice that in verse 25 of the same chapter, Paul proceeds to say, If we live by the Spirit, let us also walk by the Spirit. By so doing, he unveils an exciting dimension in the realm of divine transportation. This is a dimension in which your spirit is no more earth-bound or pulled by gravitational force of the law of sin and death. Instead, the spirit begins to soar into the heights of the Heavenly realm. The experience in this dimension is like a leap of faith into the spirit realm. In the natural realm, we start by walking before we could run. The spirit realm is just like the physical realm in comparison. When a person is born and is a little child, they don't know how to walk yet. They learn to walk. They toddle at first, they stumble and fall, but after sometime your child learns to walk. In the spirit realm, it is the same way. When a person's spirit is newly born, they are like spiritual babies. The sad thing is, many people remain spiritual babies for ever. But when our spirit man grows, it grows to the extent where it is not limited by this physical body. I'm not talking about astral travelling or forcibly doing things that are outside of God. I am not talking about desiring it either or purposefully trying to protect yourself. I am talking about fellowshipping with God and yielding to God to the extent that your spirit ascends to the greatest heights of the Heavenly realm. When you pray, suddenly your spirit is there, and you know what is going on in the Heavenly realm.

To cement this divine revelation with reference to further scriptural evidence, the Bible unveils the reality of this dimension in 2 Kings 5, whereby Elisha the prophet healed a man called Naaman from Leprosy. Naaman then offered some gifts to Elisha but he refused. It happened that Gehazi, Elisha's servant was covetous and went after those gifts and collected them from the man. After that he then went in and stood before his master, and Elisha said to him, "Where have you been Gehazi?" And Gehazi said, "Your servant went nowhere." But he said to him, "Did I not go with you in spirit when the man turned from his chariot to meet you? Was it a time to accept money and garments, olive orchards and vineyards, sheep and oxen, menservants and maidservants? Wait a minute here! Do you notice that Elisha says, "Did I not go with you in spirit?" This means that Elisha followed Gehazi in the Spirit. Elisha was taken up right at the moment as Gehazi was turning back not as he was going. The moment the man was turning back, Elisha was there in the spirit and he saw the whole thing and heard the whole conversation except they could not see him for he was in the spirit world. His body was at home but it's only his spirit that followed them. This is what we call an out-of-the-body experience. In the context of the scripture, Elisha says, "Was I not with u when you went?" Since Gehazi and Naaman were not running but walking, this implies that even Elisha's spirit might have walked with them

In the realm of the spirit, there were times when in prayer the Lord can take us into various places, and homes of people, usually for certain purposes and reasons, to pray for them or just to show something and it is through this realm that you get to be enlightened on what happens in the lives of other people behind the scenes. For instance, Kenneth Hagin had an experience where one day he was transported in the spirit and he got into the car with a young girl and a young boy. And he was seated in the car behind them and went with them all the way as they drove into the park committed sin and drove back. All the time Kenneth Hagin was sitting there. This implies that you might be in a certain country and want to go and see how thing are like in another country and you can just go and peep and then come back and on the following day people will be shocked when you call them and update them concerning how things are in that country when in actual fact you have not been physically there for the whole year. I remember the day I was divinely transported in the realm of the spirit to America. I had never been to America before but I was caught up into the spirit such that i went and prayed for people and actually stopped someone who was about to have a medical operation. This is how powerful this dimension is in the area of ministry.

Sometimes it is possible for our spirits to leave our bodies and enter the spirit realm to impart other lives just like in the experience of Paul in Colossians 2: 5 where he was divinely transported to monitor the activities in his churches. He testifies: "For though I am absent in the flesh, yet I am with you in spirit, rejoicing to see your good order and the steadfastness of your faith in Christ." Do you notice that Paul says "My spirit is with you", and it is not just a figure of speech because a figure of speech does not have the quality or the ability to see what is going on. Do you also notice that he says: "I can see you and I can behold what you are doing." This implies that his spirit was divinely transported into the Colossian churches and he could see, understand experience and know what they were going through. There are times when God gave him to know what is happening in the church of Colossae by a supernatural visitation. So there are times in the spirit that you are transported like Paul where you are able to watch in the human level not so high up just like Paul could behold the order of the Colossians. I have heard some people testifying that when they were in trouble they dreamt that the pastor came and prayed for them at night. In reality, the pastor was divinely transported in the spirit and was actually there praying for them although they could not see him in the natural realm.

THE SECOND DIMENSION:

THE DIMENSION OF RUNNING IN THE SPIRIT

Did you know that just like walking, running is another dimension in the realm of the spirit, which is of a level a bit higher than that of walking? The Bible records an incident in 1 Kings 18:41 whereby Elijah declared in the hearing of the masses saying, "I hear the sound of heavy rain". And it happened that as rain was approaching he ran faster than King Ahab although the King was riding on a horse, which was probably the fastest and best fed in the whole of Israel. How possible is it that a man can overtake a horse in the natural realm? The truth is that this was not a physical run but a dimension of the spirit in which Elijah was catapulted into. There is no record in the Bible of Elijah being an athlete yet he physically outran the King's horse which by nature was probably the fastest in the country. How do you explain that phenomenon? This was not a physical run, it was a dimension of transportation in the spirit which Elijah tapped into. This is a realm and dimension in the spirit which Elijah entered and moved into and was carried by the wings of the spirit. I have heard a testimony of two man who were coming from a crusade and on their way home rain caught up with them and the younger one ran faster ahead of the older one leaving him far behind. But then the Holy Spirit caught up with the older man who could not run physically and was instantaneously catapulted into that realm of transportation and began to run extremely faster in the spirit such that he was home in few seconds. The distance of ten miles that could have taken an hour to reach, he actually covered it in seconds. The younger brother was shocked when he found him already home. This is the dimension of running in the spirit which I'm talking about.

The explanation is that when a person is transported in the dimension of running in the spirit, it is just his physical body tagging along with the spirit. But when your spirit is so used to that, the day will come when the revival of God will move so powerfully that people will be transported from different corners of the earth to various places to preach the gospel and then be transported back. But that will be a normal consequence because the spirit would have been travelling a lot. When you are an intercessor and you pray deeply, your spirit can travel into a different realm, into a higher realm, and you do battle with spiritual forces. That is happening all the time. When you have grown in God and your spirit has developed, it is not limited by any earthly boundaries; it moves and travels.

THE THIRD DIMENSION :

THE DIMENSION OF FLYING AND DISAPPEARANCE IN THE SPIRIT

The highest and most profound dimension in the realm of divine transportation is what we call flying or disappearance in the spirit. There is something about the development of our human spirit when it attains

The Realm Of The Spirit

a certain quality and ability. The Bible gives an account of an incident in Acts 8:26-40 whereby, Immediately after baptising the Ethiopian Eunuch in water, Philip was carried by the spirit to Azotus such that the Eunuch saw him no more.

Do you notice that it says, "the eunuch saw him no more?". What do you think happened here? In simpler language, Philip disappeared into the spirit realm. In other words, he was carried by the waves of the wind in the spirit all the way to Azotus. In other words, his physical body was transported along as he flew in the spirit. This is what we call an out-side-the-body experience. But how do you explain this phenomenon? When Philip was transported physically; his body had to take on a different physical quality in order to break the force of gravity . This is something that is physically not possible. So under this dimension , the body takes on a very supernatural quality . There is a realm your body crosses the line of the spirit. If your body doesn't cross that line, it's just subject to the spirit. But when your body crosses that line and enters into the spirit world, it takes on a different quality. This is a migration that takes place in the spirit when the Holy Spirit wants His job to be done with a sense of urgency. This is the quintessence of the realm of divine transportation. Such a realm is going to be popular in this last dispensation as the Holy Ghost wants to accomplish God's work with speed just before the Master closes the curtain shortly at the end of age.

How Is Transportation In This Dimension Possible?

In this type of divine transportation, your physical body has yielded to a certain extent. It has more to do with our relationship between your spirit, soul and body. The challenge is that some of you are not related properly to your physical body. If you are not related properly to your physical body you won't be able to experience all these spectacular divine experiences. You see, you have to have a right relationship with your physical body. To strike a balance, you don't necessarily need to persecute your body but you just have to focus on developing the quality of your spirit and stretching your spiritual capacity so that your spirit is capacitated to carry your body along into the realm of the spirit. When you have developed that greater weight or supernatural mass, it will lift your body up into the atmosphere. So when your physical body knows its place and is much yielded to the realm of the spirit, it can reach a stage where your spirit carries or tags it along. The truth is that the glory of God coming upon you exerts a greater weight of glory on your body that just lifts it off the ground. At that time, your physical body seems to take on a peculiar quality, which was never there in the natural realm. That explains why the size of the blessing which a man can receive is equivalent to the size of his spirit because the larger the spirit, the greater the blessing.

How Does One Enter This Dimension Of The Spirit?

In the occult realm, which is a non-Christian realm, they have what you call astral travelling. Those who yield themselves to the occult state of spirit realm seem to be able to travel into that realm. But there is a realm that even the unbelievers who yield themselves utterly to the realm of the spirit seem to be able to move into. And for the unbelievers and the occult people to do that, they need a certain level of freedom from their body. There are different levels in which our body is related to our soul and our spirit. Let's say this Bible is the body and your human spirit is the hand. Your body can be under the dominion of your mind and your spirit or your body can be dominating your soul and your spirit. The spirit, soul and body are in different types of relationship. It's just like a husband and wife relationship. There are some wives who are dominates their husbands. And there are some husbands that dominate over their wives. There are some who have a perfect relationship of equality and consultation. And you could see many couples have different types and degrees of relationship. In a similar comparison, there is a relation between our spirit, soul and body. And some people have their body and soul control them so much that they are never able to move into the spirit realm whether they are unbelievers or Christians. Even the unbeliever who wants to move into the realm of the spirit and experience astral traveling has a price to pay. They either go on a vegetarian fast or they try to seclude themselves from worldly activities. They give themselves to concentration of what they call meditation in order to enter that realm. The principle behind it is the isolation of the body from the soul so that the soul is free. In the same way, if you try to concentrate after a heavy meal, your body seems to be enlarged and your soul reduced and your spirit is absent. If you have been on a long fast, you will notice that you feel very light. It is just not physical lightness although you will lose a few pounds. But there is another realm of lightness in which your spirit and soul are related to the body but not so firmly gripped by the body. It's like your spirit and soul are floating above your body. That kind of lightness is necessary in order for a person to move into the spirit world. This explains why it is important for a Christian to live a fasted life.

The Realm Of The Spirit

On the extreme end of the scale, there is also a dimension or level whereby one completely disappears in the realm of the spirit in the same way it was a common experience for Elijah to disappear into the spirit realm and reappear in the natural realm. In this realm, your whole body disappears from the natural world as if it was never there. In other words, you become invisible in the natural world but only those in the spirit world will be able to see you. It must be expressly understood that disappearance did not originate with witches or astral travelling. It originated with God and the devil copied. The fact that the devil is copying does not make it his. It's a pity that whenever people see power being demonstrated to a heightened degree in the natural realm, the human mind has a tendency to conclude that it's the devil yet the devil does not have any power except that he pollutes and counterfeits God's power. The truth is that it's not only witches who are able to move in the dimension of flying in the spirit for that's a counterfeit. They even use tools and equipment to hinge on when they move in that realm but if witches think they can fly, wait until they see you fly higher in this end time season. In this last dispensation of time, many people are going to experience deeper dimensions in the spirit. You will be walking with some brethren to a crusade and all of a sudden you disappear. By the time they are looking for you, you will be preaching the word of God and moving in the power.

I heard of a man whom God wanted to go and preach in a certain country but did not have enough money for transportation. So, God instructed him to carry his luggage and head for the airport where he was given further instructions to enter a certain room and when he did, suddenly he appeared in that country where he was supposed to go and preach. There, he ministered powerfully and held great crusades but when the time came for him to go back home, the Holy Ghost instructed him again to go to the airport and enter the same room he had entered before and all of a sudden, he appeared in his living room carrying his luggage. This is the essence of the realm of divine transportation. Such a realm is going to be popular in this last dispensation as the Holy Ghost wants to accomplish God's work with speed. You might not have entered this realm but wait until the day God wants to use you and you urgently require a plane to go for a crusade in a distant place but it's not available. These testimonies are not chronicled so that you may just know how powerful some men of God are. No! They are for you to be so invigorated such that you may develop a perennial hunger, insatiable appetite and unquenchable thirst to launch deeper into the spirit realm. In this end time season, you just have to develop the quality of your spirit through meditation on the word, praying in tongues, ministering to people so that your spirit is in an upper room position to enter the greater depths of divine transportation in the spirit. The question is: Are you ready to enter these realms?

As we pray we enter into the spirit world. And it's important for us to understand what the spirit world is like. The bible has some principles and guidelines as to what the spirit world is like. However many times we are just left with our experiences with the spirit world. Which is why I dare not being a theologian call something as laws of the spirit world unless I can really know that they are laws and that they are revealed in the Word. If it's a subjective area that the Word is silent upon we can only call it as common experiences. First of all the spirit world has no distance. That we know in principle. But the experience of it can be astounding. And as we began to explore this realm, we understand that the spirit world needs a lot of interpretation. But the realm of the spirit has no distance. That means that as you pray as you enter into the depths of the spirit some of the things you see and experience could be from another place or another land. Or it could be nearby. So geographical distance is never there in the spirit world. When we talk about geographical distance we also want to include the distance between the heavenly realm and the natural realm here.

Let's look at the book of 2 Kings. And we see some statements made by Elisha that give us a clue of the spirit realm. And we not only share those experiences, we also want to share about the how and the what in the spirit world. In the book of 2 Kings. 5 the background is how Naaman has been healed. And Naaman offered some gifts to Elisha who refused the gifts but Gehazi, Elisha's servant was covetous and went after those gifts. 2 Kings. 5:20-27 Gehazi the servant of Elisha the man of God, said, "See, my master has spared this Naaman the Syrian, in not accepting from his hand what he brought. As the Lord lives, I will run after him, and get something from him." So Gehazi followed Naaman. And when Naaman saw someone running after him, he alighted from the chariot to meet him, and said, "Is all well?" And he said, "All is well. My master has sent me to say, "There has just now come to me from the hill country of Ephraim two young men of the sons of the prophets; pray, give them a talent of silver and two festal garments." And Naaman said, "Be pleased to accept two talents." And he urged him, and tied up two talents of silver in two bags, with two festal garments, and laid them upon two of his servants; and they carried them before Gehazi. And when he came to the hill, he took them from their hand, and put them

The Realm Of The Spirit

in the house, and he sent the men away, and they departed. He went in, and stood before his master, and Elisha said to him, "Where have you been Gehazi?" And he said, "Your servant went nowhere." But he said to him, "Did I not go with you in spirit when the man turned from his chariot to meet you? Was it a time to accept money and garments, olive orchards and vineyards, sheep and oxen, menservants and maidservants? Therefore the leprosy of Naaman shall cleave to you, and to your descendants for ever." So he went out from is presence a leper, as white as snow.

Elisha was taken up right at the moment as Gehazi was turning back not as he was going. The moment the man was turning back Elisha was there in the spirit. And he saw the whole thing and heard the whole thing except they cannot see him for he was in the spirit world. In the occult realm, which is a non-Christian realm, they have what you call astral traveling. Those who yield themselves to the occult state of spirit realm seem to be able to travel into that realm. They thought that everything in that realm is good not realizing there are also evil spirits out there. But there is a realm that even the unbelievers who yield themselves utterly to the realm of the spirit seem to be able to move into. They even might have what you would call a word of knowledge. I read some accounts by Christians who researched into both Christians and non-Christians astral traveling. They call it astral from secular definition. And some of these non-Christians who move into that realm talk about areas of walls that they come to meet or demon spirits (they don't call them demons but they call them creatures) that they saw outside. And for the unbelievers and the occult people to do that, they need a certain level of freedom from their body.

There are different levels in which our body is related to our soul and our spirit. Lets say this bible is the body and your human spirit is the hand. Your body can be under the dominion of your mind and your spirit. Or your body can be dominating your soul and your spirit. The spirit, soul and body are in different types of relationship. It's just like a husband and wife relationship. There are some wives who are dominates their husbands. And there are some husbands that dominate over their wives. There are some who have a perfect relationship of equality and consultation. And you could see many couples have different types and degrees of relationship. In a similar comparison there is a relation between our spirit, soul and body. And some people have their body control them so much and their soul control them so much that they are never able to move into the spirit realm whether they are unbelievers or whether they are Christians. Even the unbeliever who wants to move into the realm of the spirit and experience astral traveling has a price to pay. They either go on a vegetarian fast or they try to seclude themselves from worldly activities. They give themselves to concentration of what they call meditation in order to enter that realm. The principle behind it is the isolation of the body from the soul. So that the soul is free. In the same way if you try to concentrate after a heavy meal, your body seems to be enlarged and your soul reduced and your spirit absent.

If you have been on a long fast, you will notice you feel very light. It is just not physical lightness although you will loose a few pounds. But there is another realm of lightness like your spirit and your soul are related to the body but not so firmly gripped by the body. Like your spirit and soul are floating above your body. That kind of lightness is necessary in order for a person to move into the spirit world. Which is why a Christian needs to have a fasted life. Now verse 26 a sentence that has been used by Elisha is did not my heart go out with you. In some of the older translation the translators put did not my spirit go out with you? Elisha's spirit went and saw all the things that took place. In the book of II Cor. 12:3-4 And I know that this man was caught up into Paradise whether in the body or out of the body I do not know, God knows -and he heard things that cannot be told, which man may not utter. Now here Paul says he reached a point, we know he is talking about himself because later on he says because of the abundance of these revelations a thorn in the flesh came into his life. So we know it was him in the end. But here is an experience in the spirit world where Paul was not sure whether he was just there in the spirit or whether his body was also there. That qualifies our statement that transportation in the realm of the spirit has no distance. There is a degree where we move into God where only our spirit is able to transcend geographical distance.

I would classify such transportation in the spirit realm into 3 categories. The first is where those geographical places you see in your visions come to you, like over a phone line or satellite transmission in the natural. When you look into a television and see a satellite transmission let say of a live Olympic games, you are not there but yet you know what is happening there. All those things that are happening there are transmitted through electro magnetic waves and they bounced off the satellite. They come right down to where you are even though you could be on the opposite side of the earth. It could be the picture or the places coming into your living room.

The second degree is where like Elisha where his spirit actually goes to the place itself. Does it come slowly or does it come instantly? Usually such traveling could be quite fast. But there are times where some people have experienced it as a slow motion. If you are new in the spirit world, when you are praying you may have a very interesting sensation of rising up. But when you check your body you find that it is still down there. This is the second realm. And as they are rising up they may get very frightened. The first time where I experienced it was in a Baptist seminary. We did our students' devotion after we come back from our fieldwork and each one of us took turns to lead. It was my turn that night. That night I closed my eyes, which I usually do to lead in prayer before the devotion. As I was praying I felt a floating sensation. Although my voice was still speaking I felt as if my spirit was on the ceiling. It was a very odd and queer sensation. The reason we share this thing is that in case some of you experience the same things you won't think that is queer, peculiar or strange. Sometimes it helps to hear another person's experience. It encourages you not to be frightened.

Then there were a few times when in deep prayer I had a sensation of being lifted into the heavenly. I know it was the second realm where my body didn't go up. That was when we were sharing in a church about the second coming of Jesus. When in prayer it was like I was taken out and I reached a certain distance where I saw the curvature of the earth. Suddenly I was being moved into an area where I could see Europe, India and Asia. That was quite high up. In the spirit realm that was when I saw demon forces that looked like warriors. They look like intelligent looking human beings. A group of them were coming in a South Easterly direction down towards India and South East Asia. This happened before the walls of communism came down. And I saw these warriors coming downwards and the Lord told me that these are warring demons and that they have come to create war. Subsequently after that you read in the papers about things that happened in India. The Lord was speaking about praying against them coming to this direction. It seems that they were being moved out of Eastern Europe to create trouble in India and South East Asia. When demons are cast out from a place they do not become unemployed. They look for work somewhere else. They look for things to do. So they just shift their place of work or create new trouble.

Then there are times I experienced things like what Paul mentioned in Col. 2:5 For though I am absent in body, yet I am with you in spirit rejoicing to see your good order and the firmness of your faith in Christ. So there are times in the spirit that you are transported like Elisha where you are watching in the human level not so high up. Paul was saying here that he could behold the order of the Colossians. There are times when God gave him to know what is happening in the church of Colossae by a supernatural visitation. So there were times when in prayer the Lord has taken me into the homes of people, usually for certain purposes and reasons in order to show something. I have not had the kind that Kenneth Hagin had where one day in the spirit he got into the car with a young girl (whom he was interested in) and a young boy. And he was seated in the car behind them. And he was with them all the way as they drove into the park committed sin and drove back. All the time Kenneth Hagin was sitting there.

When you have the first type you are physically aware of your physical body. Just like you are watching the Olympic games on T.V. You could be conscious of what you are doing physically. Conscious of what is happening in front of you. But when you are having the second category you completely loose consciousness of your physical body. All your consciousness gets into your spirit. And sometimes when you get back into your body you suddenly feel cold. Because your body was cold all the time but you never felt it. Or you feel your knees having those familiar needles sensations for kneeling too long. But you only feel it after you get back into your body. Before you get back into your body all those sensations that you have are not there. You are only conscious of the spirit world. Possibly what Paul experienced in II Cor. 12 is the second type, where he was not aware whether he is in the spirit or in the body. By the time you reached the third category you are physically transported. There is a total awareness that your body has been taken up. You won't be in the zone where you are thinking was it in the spirit or in the body.

The third type of transportation is where even your physical body is transported like Philip who was transported. Your body has yielded to a certain extend. It has to do with our relationship with our spirit, soul and our body. Some of us are not related properly to your physical body. If you are not related properly to your physical body you won't be able to experience all these differences. We have to have a right relationship with our physical body. So when our physical body knows its place and is very yielded to the realm of the spirit it can reach a stage where your spirit carries your body along. The Spirit of God coming upon you carries your body along. And at that time your physical body seems to take on a peculiar quality, which was never there in the natural. For example let's look over to the book Ezek. 3:1-3 In the sixth year, in the sixth month, on the fifth day of the month, as

The Realm Of The Spirit

I sat in my house, with the elders of Judah sitting before me, the hand of the Lord God fell there upon me. Then I beheld, and lo, a form that had the appearance of a man; below what appeared to be his lions it was fire, and above his lions it was like the appearance of brightness, like gleaming bronze. He put forth the form of a hand, and took me by the lock of my head; and the Spirit lifted me up between earth and heaven, and brought me in visions of God to Jerusalem, to the entrance of the gateway of the inner court that faces north, where was the seat of the image of jealousy, which provokes to jealousy.

If you read carefully you will notice that in verse 3 although the word visions is mentioned that there was a physical catching hold of Ezekiel. He was caught by the hair and taken in the midst of the people he was sitting with and transported to Jerusalem. And even though he was physically taken to Jerusalem the people there could not physically see him. The physical body may take on a special quality of invisibility in the third category of transportation that is not naturally there all the time. Even in Acts 8 as Philip was translated physically, his body had to take on a different physical quality in order to break the force of gravity. This is something that is physically not possible. So under the third category the body takes on a very supernatural quality. Which explains why when Moses was with God for 40 days and 40 nights he didn't have to eat. His stomach must have taken on a special quality. Some of you try to fast 7 days on water already knows what it is like. Moses went 40 day and 40 nights without food and water. The bible especially mentioned without food and water. How could he stand that in the natural? Your stomach will be protesting. Your physical body will feel weak.

There is a time during a 40 day fast that your body crosses the line of the spirit. If our body doesn't cross that line our body is just subject to the spirit. But when our body crosses that line and enter into the spirit world the body takes on a different quality. I believe when Moses came down from the 40 days fast he didn't come skinny. Moses walked down and he was so strong that he took the tablets and he broke it. He still got all his strength and he looks the same. Not a single pound lost after 40 days and 40 nights. It was because he was in the depths of God's strong presence. So we need to reach a stage to understand that the spirit realm really over rules the natural. And there are times when God permits you to get into that realm so deep that your natural body is just simply overruled. And the higher laws start working. It doesn't age it doesn't feel hungry it doesn't need any physical sustainer. And it can go through walls even in its natural state if he is suspended under the spirit realm. It can do things which normally only people who are very well trained, skilful, circus actors can do. They tie their hair to a lorry and pull the lorry. When they do it takes great concentration on their part. But for a person like Ezekiel, he was just caught by the hair and pulled like a rocket up. Even when those guys who pull the lorry by the hair do it by slow motion. God just caught Ezekiel up. Under natural circumstances, something you could never do it on your own. Your hair can never carry the body weight. But the spirit realm rules the natural body in this third realm.

We need to have an awareness that is there. Even if some of you have not experienced the first, second and third realm be aware that it's there. And who know that tonight as you are praying you may suddenly experience the first realm. Then the second realm is when you feel floating. As you pray you feel like you are walking on the ceiling. Maybe second realm is opening just be open to that. In the second realm we still need our heart to be in the right attitude for the experience to continue. Do you know that a spiritual experience can be cut short by natural event, especially in the second stage? But the third stage is you are gone already. The second stage is possible where you are just about to take off into the spirit and you are praying and somebody comes to you and say hey, hey, you are sort of wake up from the spirit world and all that you are getting into suddenly is cut short. It is possible in that realm. But there is a stage where you will never be disturbed. But there is a stage in twilight zone where you can be disturbed, can be called back and that is the stage which can be very critical. When we move into this area we may have to put a do not disturb sign.

The second area of experience in the spirit world is what I call spiritual material, spiritual food, spiritual creatures that are there in the spirit world. The spirit world doesn't just have spirits. They also have real spiritual tables, spiritual bread, spiritual food, spiritual books and things out there in the spirit world must not be taken lightly. Each one of those spiritual materials has a quality to impart certain thing. This is what I believe. When God made the tree of life. When you eat it, what do you get? You get life. If God make a tree of wisdom, and you eat it you get wisdom. When God makes a tree of knowledge of good and evil, when you eat it you get a knowledge of good and evil. If God make a tree called holiness, and you eat it you get holiness. Just as in the natural we eat different type of food, and we get different substances from different type of food. There is in the spirit world qualities

The Realm Of The Spirit

that are acquired through partaking. If you would to have an opportunity in the spirit world to see some of the things in the spirit, if you ever partake of it they impart a quality into your spirit and into your soul sometimes into your physical body in ways that we cannot explain in the natural. They have a certain quality of impartation that affect spirit, soul and body.

Charles and Frances Hunter wrote about Roland Buck in Angels on Assignment and his daughter wrote the other book about him in The Man Who Spoke To Angels. He met Gabriel the angel. He met Michael the Archangel and spoke to them. And had visions and conversation with them which are recorded in those books and all of them are very good. But there was one particular thing that happened one night. One of the angels appeared to him with a ladle. In that ladle was a liquid that looks like a golden colored liquid. Then the angel said tonight I have gift from Father God to you. He was a slightly overweight man. After he ate eat that food from heaven, instantly he felt a sound on his physical body. He was wondering what it was. Then he realized that all the fat was burned up. So if after tonight you saw somebody coming here overweight and went back reduced to ordinary weight that may have taken place while they were praying. But of course it was just one special gift the God gave. And he felt stronger and he felt 30 to 40 years younger. All these sound strange to many people.

Once you are aware of the fact that the spirit world is very real, you will find that it is as real as the natural world. There are foods up there. Sometimes God gives you an opportunity to partake of it. And when you partake there is an impartation in spirit, soul and even physical. There is a positive side effect upon your life. I Kings. 19:4-6 But he himself went a day's journey into the wilderness, and came and sat down under a broom tree; and he asked that he might die saying, "It is enough; now, Lord, take away my life; for I am no better than my fathers." And he lay down and slept under a broom tree and behold, an angel touched him and said to him, "Arise and eat." And he looked and behold, there was at his head a cake baked on hot stones and a jar of water. But it was no ordinary cake. This would have been really genuine angel's cake. And there was a jar of water. So he ate and drank and laid down again. Verse 7 the second time the angel said arise and eat because the journey is too great for you. Verse 8 he arose and ate and drank. And he went in the strength of that food for 40 days and 40 nights. These two meals lasted for 40 days and 40 nights. For it scientifically to happen that meal has to have natural and molecular effect on his physical stomach and body. It has to be something physically imparted for him to carry on like that for 40 days and 40 nights. So here are scriptures that tell that there are times God does give us heavenly food. The Israelites tasted manna, which the book of Psalms tells us its angels' food.

Why do they have to eat in the spirit world? The only reason for eating in heaven is impartation as well as pleasure. So that everything we eat impart something into our spirit, soul and body. The pure need for eating in the natural today is mainly to sustain our body, to keep our body in good shape and form. But in the spirit world the spirit food has tremendous impartation value. I heard the testimony of a Christian who went up to heaven and visited some members of her church there. In one home that she visited, she was offered a glass of water to drink, which she found refreshing and soothing. She also ate some fruits offered by her host. Her host in heaven told her that in heaven they eat to remain young looking. The process of eating the heavenly food is part of the system like we have like laying on of hands. Laying on of hands today is besides baptism in the Spirit, healing, deliverance or ordination is also for impartation. We lay hand to impart. In heaven part of the impartation is received through the food itself.

Let's look at the book of Deut. 2:7 For the Lord your God has blessed you in all the work of your hands; he knows you're going through this great wilderness; these forty years the Lord your God has been with you; you have lacked nothing. Then chapter 8:4 your clothing did not wear out upon you, and your foot did not swell, these forty years. The book of Psalms records and tells us that there was not a single weak or sick person in their midst for 40 years. How was that possible? The answer was in verse 3 of chapter 8. And he humbled you and let you hunger and fed you with manna, which you did not know, nor did your fathers know; that he might make you know that man does not live by bread alone, but that man lives by everything that proceeds out of the mouth of the Lord. It is connected to the manna in some way. There is a tremendous impartation in that spirit world and that spirit food. While you are praying the spirit world opens itself to you and suddenly you see the cup filled with liquid in front of you, you rub your eyes and pray and it's still there. Why do you think God shows you a cup? Take it, drink it, something will take place in your life. There will be an impartation. It will not only impart physical changes in your soul, in your physical body. But it will impart sometimes even an actual gift. You could in the spirit world if there is such a tree let say a tree of music. You partake it even though you are a non-musician straight away you can play music. In the spirit world that's how things are imparted. Or if there is a tree call fruit of prophecy. You have never prophesied before, but when you ate it suddenly you prophesy.

In the book of Revelation, John saw this huge angel coming down from the heaven above. Revelations. 10:8-11 then the voice which I had heard from heaven spoke to me again, saying, "Go, and take the scroll which is open in the hand of the angel who is standing on the sea and on the land." So I went to the angel and told him to give me the little scroll; and he said to me, "Take it and eat; it will be biter to your stomach, but sweet as honey in your mouth." And then I took the little scroll from the hand of the angel and ate it; it was sweet as honey in my mouth, but when I had eaten I my stomach was made bitter. And I was told, "You must again prophesy about the many peoples and nations and tongues and kings." That book was an actual impartation of the Spirit of prophecy. It took place through eating in the spirit world. The same thing also happened to Ezekiel in chapter 12:17-19 "Son of man, eat your bread with quaking, and drink water with trembling and with fearfulness; and say of the people of the land. Thus says the Lord God concerning the inhabitants of Jerusalem in the land of Israel; they shall eat their bread with fearfulness, and drink water in dismay because their land will be stripped of all it contains, on account of the violence of all those who dwell in it.

Now there is here an actual eating. But as he was eating in the natural there was something that took place in the natural. He was shaking as he ate it. Now the Spirit of prophecy was working through the natural substance as well. Now the real spiritual one is in chapter 3:1-3 "Son of man, eat what is offered to you; eat this scroll, and go, speak to the house of Israel." So I opened my mouth, and he gave me the scroll to eat. And he said to me, "Son of man, eat this scroll that I give you and fill your stomach with it." Then I ate it; and it was in my mouth as sweet as honey. Same like John the apostle. And after that the Lord says you go and you speak. Now these two experiences of Ezekiel come quite close. One is completely similar to John the apostle. The other is Jesus Christ taking the cup and the bread. And saying this bread is my body and this cup is my blood. Now the partaking was like the turning point. When they partake they were his. But when he partook wrongly like Judas it says after that very moment the devil came into him.

Frequency Revelator

The apostle Paul mention in the book of Cor. 11 it says that the Lord's Supper is partaken wrongly by some and because of it they died. But if partaken correctly it brings tremendous blessings. That is the reason why Christians practice saying grace. Not only as a thanksgiving to God. But by saying it we could experience the anointing of God on the food. Sanctify it by word and prayer and partake it and have some sort of an impartation also in the spirit world as a release of our faith. In the ways spiritual things are imparted up above. As there is a realm there it may happen in your dreams, it may happen in your prayer. I was having a 3 days fast without food and water many years ago. And I was in the third year of seminary. On the second night I had a very peculiar dream. In that dream I was in my old house. And there was this man who came to the house. That man looks very like my father. And the man was carrying many layers of round type of food that looks like pancakes. In that particular dream I was sitting in front of the house like waiting. When he came by the man said eat all of this it's for you. So I took it and I ate it one by one. After I ate it I woke up. When I got up I felt the presence of God. And that night the Lord said I have given to you what you have asked. And that night I realized something was imparted to me. And I knew in my spirit that I have actually eaten something. When I woke up I still felt the thing in my stomach. Remember I have not eaten because it was the second day of my total fast without food and water. I knew that there was something that was imparted. Each time something was imparted it seems that even my personality changed. It seems to affect your soul totally. So that the more you receive this kind of thing in that spirit and it gets into you the more you move into the spirit realm and partake of the spiritual thing. Just like Roland Buck his physical body was changed.

You will not believe in 10 years' time the person you will become. You could be the most introverted person ever. But through a series of partaking certain type of heavenly food, you could be the most explosive personality. This is something which is quite impossible in the natural. For the heavenly food transform our personality, transform our mind, and transform our being. And I know that something that took place inside. Of course I didn't understand it fully in those days. But through time there have been many more things that have been partaken. You ask, "Can dreams be so real?" Yes, what about Solomon. Remember that it was in a dream that the Lord asked him, "Ask of me what you want." He may have slept let say with an I.Q. of 150. And he woke up with an I, Q. of 400. So something does take place in the spirit realm. In your prayer sometimes you see a light. And you want to run from that light. Even the light that shines can transform us.

The Realm Of The Spirit

John G. Lake was fasting for the baptism in the Spirit in his early days. One day as he was praying he felt a ray of light came and shone around him. That one ray of light was what he held to for the rest of his life. The purity of that light has continued to transform his life even onto the late days of his ministry.

In the book Scenes beyond the Grave there was a scene in which they saw Jesus Christ in the children's paradise and all the scene was being reacted. And after that there was a scene of a preacher going out preaching. Then there was this person who did not accept Christ yet. Right at that moment what they saw in all the 5 dimensions including time and the spirit dimension was a ray of light came right down from heaven and came into this man's heart. Something physically was imparted. There was a real light that shone on that person. And there has been many times in my prayers I have seen light sometimes flashes of light. And I have been opened to them. And when I am opened they went out. Not all that we see in the spirit is necessary of God. Satan can also appear as an angel of light. I want to be balanced here not to frighten you but to be balanced. Otherwise people will yield to every funny kind of manifestation without having the Word. If you yield to the spirit realm minus the Word is the most dangerous thing you could ever do. Without the Word there is no protection in the spirit realm. There is no guidance in the spirit realm. It is just like driving a car when everybody has no rules. You can drive on any side of the road and there is no traffic light. It will be a mess. In the spirit world the Word is the protection. As long as you know your conscience is clear, your spirit is right in the sight of God. Usually all those disturbances do not come. And many of those manifestations are from the Lord. And when they are from the Lord we still have to yield to them.

Let me recount an incident from Kenneth Hagin's life. Before Hagin had the vision of the angel. In one of the visions he saw both Jesus and the angel. As he was talking to Jesus he saw the angel next to Jesus. And every time he turned around to look at this angel, the angel opened his mouth like he wanted to talk. But when he looked back at Jesus the angel closed his mouth and did not talk. He did that several times. Then when Jesus had finished talking to him, Jesus said, "The angel here has a message for you." And of course Hagin being like many intellectual said, "Lord if you are here why you don't give me the message. Why must it be him?" So the Lord has to show Hagin all the scriptures that didn't my word say the angel will be ministering to you. Finally Hagin turn to the angel. The moment he turned to the angel. The angel said these words: "I have been wanting to speak to you about your finances." And the angel said, "Some finances are on the way. By the way that man has offered to do all your things here. You are not supposed to give it to him because that is not God's will for you." But there is one funny part. The angel said I have tried to come and tell you before. That means that before the first encounter with the angel, the angel had tried to talk to Hagin. And he mentioned that incident sometime back. And that incident was before this incident when Hagin was living in a trailer. He remember one night that the angel recounted. When he was in his trailer and that night he felt like somebody came into the trailer stood right near to him. You know the feeling like somebody had just entered the room. But this is the statement he gave me. The angel said, "Because you did not open yourself to the spirit world, l could not speak to you." The angel told him, "I have come to talk to you earlier because you didn't open to the spirit I could not speak to you." And between that trailer experience and the time the angel appeared to him next to Jesus, he went into financial difficulty and financial problem. All because he didn't open himself to the ministering spirit who came to minister to him, he ended up with financial problems. Angels are working with us. Jesus is working with us. Holy Spirit is working with us. And we need to be open to all.

I know some Christians are critical spiritually. O we have Jesus why we need Holy Spirit. We have Holy Spirit why we need angels. There are others who say we have Father God. God doesn't want us to play favorites like that. He wants to learn to relate to God the Father, to Jesus the Son, to the Holy Spirit and to the angels. He wants us to learn all these different relationships. But there is a realm in the spirit where unless we open ourselves to it we cannot move in. And they cannot manifest. But through sharing experiences like that in the spirit we become more familiar with them, we become more aware of them and we become more in a state of realization of the possibility when they do happen. So that when God so chooses we could just go into that realm. Sometimes a spiritual manifestation take a choice involved. You choose to yield you choose not to. Sometimes some of you have the experience when you pray, pray it looks like if you just pray a little more and you stay a little longer you are going to break into something but you stopped. And in the end you are the loser and you lose out on what God has for you. And I have learnt that it is not only important when to pray, what to pray and how to pray is important where to pray. God can be quite strict. If God want to appear to you on a mountain and you are not there He is not going to appear to you. Which is why I can understand when God tells Moses to meet Him on the mountain. If Moses were to meet anywhere else He won't appear. Why many times Jesus had to climb all the way up to the mountain? Why didn't God talk to Him down in the valley? Besides being quietness there are reasons behind God's manifestation.

Why Elijah should go all the way to the mountain in I Kings. 19. Is God only there? No God is everywhere. But God has His workings, His requirements to discipline us, to check our hunger for Him, our desire for which all works out to physical areas of where, how, which everything which becomes our total expression of our seeking for God. If God so chooses to manifest to you and say tonight I want you to be in such and such a prayer meeting. And you are not there you may miss out. We need to be open in the spirit realm where God has a peculiar way, a particular way of manifesting in the spirit world. And that is how the spirit world runs and is like. The first area we have said that there is no geographical barrier. And there are 3 realms of moving into that area where you transcend geographical barrier. The second we said that there are spiritual materials. And there is an impartation when we partake of spiritual substances and spiritual materials that have a tremendous effect on our physical bodies and on our souls.

Prophetically speaking, you might have toiled in your Christian walk for years but not had any spectacular spiritual experience but as you take the command from the Holy Ghost and launch into the deep, you will reach levels, depths, degrees and dimensions you have never tapped in your life before such that you are penned as a wonder in this world.. Therefore shake off the shackles of your sleep and get ready to enter into these amazing, spectacular realms in God. The reason why I'm presenting this revelation is that in case some of you experience the same things, you won't think that is queer, peculiar or bizarre but you will just yield and flow along with the experience. Sometimes it helps to hear another man of God relating his own experience in the glory realm. It encourages you not to be frightened but creates in you a hunger and an insatiable appetite to launch further into the depths of the supernatural realm.

THE ANGELIC REALM:

THE REALM OF ANGELIC ENCOUNTERS, VISITATIONS AND CONVERSATIONS

This is a dimension in the realm of the spirit in which a man begins to of walk, live, function and operate at the same level as angelic beings.

Frequency Revelator

Concerning the ministry of angels which God has made available to us, Paul ask a rhetoric question: Are they not ministering spirit sent for those who will inherit salvation. The word serve in in its original context in Greek connotes to attending to or waiting upon a superior in the same manner in which a servant waits for a King. Although angels are more powerful than us, in terms of protocol or rank in the order of creation and inheritance, we are superior to them. Hence, it is our divine legitimate birth right to engage them and seek for their assistance in executing divine tasks and assignments delegated upon us from Heaven. This is to tell you that when God gives you an assignment, don't you dare sweat from brow to bone trying to do it alone, instead, engage His angels and you will experience a smooth sailing.

In the angelic realm, you don't only see angels in the spirit as is the case in the dimension of open vision. Instead, you are catapulted to a level where you literally walk with them, talk to them, interact with them, have conversations with them, to the extent of commanding them to undertake certain divine tasks on your behalf. At this level, you no longer encounter angels in an apparition state or expanded form. Instead, you encounter them in a solid form to the extent that if you were to shake the hand of an angel, it would be as solid as the hand of a man. In this dimension, not only is the realm of the supernatural unveiled to you, but you begin to explore, walk, live and operate in it just like angels. In actual fact, you can make it your second home. If you are not in your living room, you are there in the spirit, if you are not in your dining, you are there interacting with angelic beings as if they are your friends. As you mature in the spirit realm, it becomes a common experience to visit or operate in that realm. Everything that you do or is connected to you, flows from that realm. When you pray, you pray from that realm, when you preach, you preach from that realm and when you minister to the masses, you minister form that realm. There are different types of angels that you can interact with in this realm and each serves a different purpose or assignment. For example, there are, ministering angels, guardian angels, ministry angels, warring angels, messenger angels, glorified angels, territorial angels, arch angels, Seraphims and Cherubims, all different kinds of angels.

As aforementioned, it is in this realm that you don't just see angels as in the case of open vision but you go beyond that level to walk with angels, talk with angels, and fellowship with angels to the extent of even discussing plans touching Heaven and earth. For a normal Christina, just seeing an angel is an experience of a life time but for a mature Christian it is naturally

The Realm Of The Spirit

supernatural to have dinner with angels. It is in this realm that an angel cooked food for Elijah (1 Kings 19:7). Elijah woke up to freshly baked pastry with such a tantalising Heavenly aroma that lasted for days in his body system. In other words, in modern day language, he had dinner with angels. Ironically speaking, when you operate at that level, while other people ceremoniously visit malls for dinner, you join angels for a better one. Talking to someone at this level or realm is like talking to an angel. Those who reach that breakthrough point begin to take on the countenance of an angel. It is for this reason that when Peter appeared amongst the brethren after his arrest and when a young girl by the name of Rhoda told the brethren that she had seen Peter, they insisted it was his angel. It is in this realm that you are constantly walking and moving with angels as if they are your body guards. It is common for angels to wake you up in your sleep and talk to you. That's how close you walk with God in that realm. You can wake up in the morning and find a note by your bed side written with the handwriting of an angel. I am talking about the depths of God and fellowship with the Spirit, where you see angels and talk to God twenty four hours all through the day.

In the case of Jacob's experience in this realm as recorded in Genesis 28:10-22, it says that heavens were opened and he began to see angels ascending and descending. The most striking thing is that he did not end at that level of just seeing the spectacular spiritual performance. As he saw angels, he engaged them, questioned them, talked with them to the extent of wresting with them and finally got a blessing. This is the spectacular angelic dimension which we must push into in this end time season. Owing to lack of faith and revelation, some people's wish is just to see angels but if that is all you are wishing for, you might not see them at all because God does not make you see angels just for the fun of it. God desires that you don't only see them but you interact with the creatures He has made available to assist you in all ways.

Daniel was one of the people who mightily functioned in the angelic realm. In Daniel 7:15-16, he testifies that "I, Daniel was grieved in my spirit within my body, and the visions of my head troubled me. I came near to one of those who stood by, and asked him the truth of all this. So he told me and made known to me the interpretation of these things." Apparently as Daniel was having these visions, he was also aware of these spirit beings standing nearby. It didn't say that he suddenly saw them and came to them. It looked like he interrupted into the Spirit world and the activity that was going on. While he was puzzled with this vision, he saw a few angels. Daniel broke into this realm and saw these angels walking about and standing and talking. He had been to the spirit realm before and God allowed him to hear the angels discussing and talking. In that realm, Daniel must have seen them talking since he approached one of them, and asked, "Can you tell me, what is this that I see," and the angel explained it to him. And this happened several times to show you there are lots of spiritual activities going on and Daniel sort of interrupted into that realm when he came in.

To give another quintessential example, Zechariah was another prophet who constantly broke into this realm and overheard angelic conversations. Sometimes when he didn't understand something that he has heard, he would ask God for the meaning of it. There are many voices going on in the spirit world but we don't hear them. The natural man doesn't hear them but the spiritual man hears them all the time. A lot of spiritual activities are going on all the time. In Zechariah 1: 8, 9, Zechariah testifies that, "I saw by night and behold a man riding on a red horse and it stood among the myrtle trees in the hollow and behind him were horses, red, sorrel and white. Then I said, 'My Lord what are these?' So the angel who talked with me said to me, "I will show you what they are." Now the myrtle trees were real trees in the natural realm but the horses were spiritual. This is to tell you that it was definitely an open vision. Notice that Zechariah testifies, "Then I said, my Lord what are these". However, it doesn't tell when the angel appeared or whether the angel was already there with him all the time. When you walk into that realm, you are constantly aware of your guardian angels. You are aware of all angels that move in and out in your life all the time. You are constantly working together with all the angels to glorify God; you walk with them and they walk with you. I realise that the Lord is also with us and He puts His presence in us, but God has his system of working, so we flow together with His system. Such is the spectacular realm that is available for you to explore in this end time season, to operate so much in the angelic realm as if you are talking to your classmates, colleagues and associates. However, precaution should be taken so that you don't go to the extreme and end up opening yourself to demonic spirits for even the devil masquerades as an angel of light. Whatever encounter you make with angels, whatever conversation you have with them, weigh out everything with the transcending Word of God. If they tell you something that is not consistent or not in line with the Word of God, chances are, you are being tricked into a trap hence you need to be vigilant. Nonetheless, the angelic realm is such a fascinating experience that can change your life forever. The truth is that your angels have been waiting for you to respond and engage them. Now, it's your time, let the games begin. Are you ready?

THE REALM OF GLORY

This is a realm whereby one is catapulted right into higher realms of God's glory to such an extent that one walks with God hand on hand, develops the heartbeat of God, and sees things as God sees, thinks as God thinks, talks as God talks and perceives as God does. In this realm not only are you walking, running, flying in the spirit dimension but you are catapulted to the highest realms of Glory and depths of His presence. It is a realm of catapult action which is far beyond waking, running or even disappearing in the spirit. In this realm, you don't only explore the spirit world but are catapulted right into the presence of God in the Holy of Holies where God lives and you begin to walk with him hand on hand. In the realm of transportation, you can either be transported through walking, running, flying and disappearance into the outer court or Holy place but in the realm of Glory, you are catapulted right into the most Holy place, the Throne Room which is God's house and the centre of the universe. In this realm not only you experience God in measures but in His fullness. Paul earnestly prayed in Ephesians 3:14 that the Ephesians would reach this dimension so that they may know the exceeding greatness of glory.

This is the realm that Jesus tapped into during transfiguration when His countenance was transfigured or changed to dazzling white appearance on Mt Olivet and he was seen talking to Elijah and Moses (Mark 9:2; Luke 9:28). In other words, his body was transformed and took on a different quality of glory. Moses also tapped into that realm of glory on Mount Sinai where he communed with God for 40 days, 40 nights to such an extent that the glory of God permeated his being and soaked through his body such that his face was shining and no one could look at him(Exodus 34:29-35). It is in this realm where God contended that I speak to any man through dreams and prophecy but as for my servant Moses, I speak face to face with Him. The glory of God is so powerful such that when it comes into contact with an object, it transforms it to take a different quality. Hence there is such a dimension in the glory realm called transformation by the glory.

The secret of power is in walking with God in this realm. When you walk with God in this realm and the cry of souls rises up to God, they also echo through your ears. When you look at sinners, you see them with the eyes God uses to see them. In this realm, you become the eyes, hands, ears and mouth of God. This is what the Bible speaks about in Amos 3:7 when it declares that God does nothing unless He reveals it to His servants the prophets. It is in this realm that you can boldly declare it is no longer I that lives but Christ living in me because God would have gotten hold of your spirit such that you no longer have control over your own selfish desires. It is in this realm that you become a very key member of the government of God as you are elevated into the board of Heaven. God can listen to you in the same way He listened to Joshua when he commanded the sun to stop. In this realm, you can influence the activities of Heaven on earth, as you engage God at a higher and personal level and negotiate for souls in the same manner in which Abraham and Moses negotiated with God concerning the destiny of the masses and He listened to them.

This realm is the foundation for the realm of translation. Elijah and Enoch entered that realm before they were caught up or translated to Heaven Enoch walked in this realm and he was catapulted to heaven. I believe that it is possible to walk with God so closely that you get perfected spirit, soul and body. And there is a stage where you reach perhaps higher realms of glory like Enoch where you walk and walk with God and you just walk into the glory of God. There is a stage where you walk with God just like Elijah although you may have your weakness. James says Elijah had passion like each one of us. We know in 2 Kings 19 how he ran away from Jezebel. He displayed all his weaknesses but at the end of the road, he overcame his weaknesses. He changed and became a better person. Enoch did not start walking with God until later when his child was born.

It is possible to walk in different realms in God. I believe that you could be perfectly sanctified spirit, soul and body while on this planet earth. I believe that you could have a perfection of your soul and of your spirit and a certain measure of perfection in your body in terms of divine health but not in a sense of a new body yet or achieving physical immortality. There is a presence of God in the Throne Room that we go in and out in order to perform different duties. We come to the Throne Room of God and then we leave it. One day when we are out of this physical body and according to our Heavenly callings, God may have some of us working closely to His Throne. There are different works according to our developments spiritually in God. There is a realm where you enter into the Throne Room Presence. There is a realm where you enter into the outer court presence. There are also different realms in this dimension, higher realms of glory and lower realms of glory. Walking in the realm of glory leaves a permanent mark in one's life. Elisha's bones still contained the power of the anointing four hundred years after his death because that was where the anointing resided in his life. It was within his very bones. Which explain why when he had to channel the anointing he had to put his whole body on the child who was dead. For a deeper revelation of the glory realm, I would kindly refer you to one of my anointed books titled, "The Realm of Glory".

THE REALM OF VISITATION TO THE THRONE ROOM

This is a realm that we can tap into when we have walked, fellowshipped and communed with God so much to the extent that by His grace, He grants us permission to temporarily visit His Throne in Heaven in order to get a foretaste or glimpse of how things are like at His throne. Prophetically speaking, this is a characteristic feature of the end time dispensation and in this season of Throne Room visitation s, multitudes of believers will be catapulted right into the Throne Room on a study tour to explore the glory of God and the new territories of the glory realm. This is the realm that Paul tapped into in 2 Corinthians 12:2, in what he penned as, "Being caught up to the Third heavens". We also have testimonies of some believers around the world who are still entering that realm as God pleases like the seven Columbian youths whom Jesus took to both Heaven and hell to see what is happening there.

In a view to unfold the mystery of visitation to the Throne Room, Paul spoke about his own experience of Throne Room visitation, although using the third person figure of speech in 2 Corinthians 12:1-4 saying, I know a man in Christ who fourteen years ago was caught up to the third heaven, whether in the body or out of the body I do not know, God knows. And I know that this man was caught up into Paradise, whether in the body or out of the body I do not know, God knows and he heard things that that cannot be told, which man may not utter. Note that Paul was a very educated man and he would not be short of words to describe his experience of visitation to the Throne Room as far as the average man is concerned. So, you could imagine the impact of what he is saying. This is not just an ordinary man who lacks the vocabulary talking here, but an intelligent and well educated man. To provide a background on the man's academic profile, Paul was brought up under the tutelage of Gamaliel, one of the most renowned and highly educated scholars in his days. So, for him to make a statement that he had been in the spirit realm, and that when he came back, he could not describe what it was like, imagine the impact of that! It was just like a Noble prize scientist who is on the top echelon of intellectual ability coming back from the spirit realm and say I could describe atoms, molecules but I can't describe what is there. It would have the same impact. Paul was above the ordinary in everything that he pursued in God. This implies that there is a spirit realm, which is quite hard to comprehend, and there is something in that area that could motivate us deeper into that realm.

To fully comprehend this revelation, let's explore some few details. When Paul says "I know of a man", we know he is talking about himself because later on he says because of the abundance of these revelations a thorn in the flesh came into his life. So, we know it was him in the end. He is of course referring to himself because in verse 7 he wrote that, "Unless I should be exalted above measure by the abundance of revelations". So, we know that he is speaking about himself in the third person and of the abundance of the revelations that has come into his life. You see, if you just grab a slice of a verse and run with it as is the norm in the modern day church, it might cost you a revelation, but it's when you cross reference to other scriptures that all of a sudden you begin to secure a full revelation. Do you also notice that he made use of a phrase, "things that are inexpressible for man to tell". Note that it doesn't mean that Paul heard things and then was told not to tell anybody. No! It means he heard them, however he did not have the vocabulary to punctuate and code them in such a way that he could meaningfully explain or relate them to the natural mind. The explanation is that the spirit world is a realm that doesn't operate on logic as is the case in our natural world. The spirit is a realm where our natural logic breaks down. Do you also notice that Paul twice repeats the phrase, "Whether in the body or out of the body I do not know, God knows". It's not just playing with words as we know him Paul is unveiling the two dimensions of Throne Room visitation which are, inside-the-body experience and outside-the-body experience. An inside-the-body experience is a dimension whereby you are catapulted to the Throne Room of God in Heaven whilst inside your body. In other words, the body tags along with the spirit and appears before the Throne of God. On the other side of the coin, outside-the-body experience is a dimension whereby your spirit vacates the body and rises into the realm of the spirit and enters the Throne Room of Heaven, leaving the body in the natural realm. There is an experience in the spirit world where Paul was not sure whether he was just there in the spirit or whether his body was also there. That qualifies our statement that transportation in the realm of the spirit has no distance. There is a degree where we move into God where only our spirit is able to transcend geographical distance.

The Realm Of The Spirit

How And When Do We Qualify To Visit The Throne Room?

The most important thing about visitations of God is the timing. It is not just in preparations alone, which is important for we need to have a right heart before God. It's not how holy you are, or spiritual or how much good works you have done for God but it's the fullness of the timing of God that determines the visitation of God upon your life. God has a place and time for it. At times, there is some spiritual knowledge which God wants us to be built up first before He could reveal the Throne Room. It is to make the visitation more permanent in our lives. That is what I mean by proper timing. We cannot afford to be anxious about the visitations of God upon our life in any way. We need to tell Him, "Lord, it doesn't matter how you manifest or when you do it, we just want to be in the perfect will of God to receive the right things at the right time." If it is not God's time for your visitation and if it happens the impact and the effect of that visitation would not be permanent.

THE REALM OF TRANSLATION TO HEAVEN

This is the highest level of operation in the realm of God. It is the 7th dimension in the realm of God. This realm is not for everybody, which is why very few people have tapped into it. To provide a quintessential example of this scenario, the Bible testifies in Genesis 5:24 that Enoch walked with God and was caught up to Heaven. Deriving the revelation from this scripture, this tells me that you start by walking with God and when you have matured in that realm, God can translate you straight to the Heavenly realm. The question that you are probably asking yourself is: Why was Enoch translated? It's because when he reached that realm, his whole physical body transformed. He found he was no more breathing in the natural. Instead, he was now breathing in the spiritual just like angels. Colloquially speaking, he no longer needed the polluted oxygen of the natural world to breathe but an atmosphere of glory to sustain him just like spirit beings. In other words, he lived like a spirit being on earth and that was when the translation took place.

Elijah is another man who walked so closely with God and he operated so much in the spirit realm to the extent that he closed and opened Heavens at his own discretion and reached a certain quality of the spirit which qualified him to be catapulted into the Heavenly realm, hence chariots of fire came and took him. Elijah walked so close with God to the extent that angelic visitations were like contact with human beings. Even at the end of his life, in 2 Kings 1 and 2; he seemed to be always with God. Do you remember his popular statement of address: "I am Elijah who stands in the presence of God" This was just not a religious cliché used by prophets in his days. Instead, it was a declaration of authority, an affirmation of identity and power. To stand in the presence means to operate in an office; to constantly attend to God. That was a legal statement which had far reaching spiritual repercussions in the realm of the spirit. It sent signals in the realm of the spirit that power and authority was being exercised. It also notifies spiritual subjects of his constant presence in the spirit world. From that statement flow signs and wonders because he understood who he was on earth in relation to God's eternal plan. Elijah fully understood that the business of Heaven was his own business and God's agenda was his own agenda. Elijah stood in such a high degree of God's presence that earthy mortals could not reach. When he was lonely, God sent His angels because there were not many saints in the Old Testament who had entered that realm. There was a level he reached whereby he walked so close with God that when he was about to complete his ministry, the Lord said: "Elijah Come straight home" and chariots of fire came and whisked him straight to Heaven.

Jesus is another quintessential example of someone who was translated to Heaven after His resurrection and the Bible records that as they looked up, they saw Him enter a cloud until he was no more. This is undoubtedly the highest realm that a man will ever enter in God. It's the 7th dimension in the realm of God. In this realm you don't taste death or decay but you are taken to Heaven straight away. This tells me that, although death has been known to be ravaging humanity since time immemorial, it is possible not to taste death or the grave at all. The truth is that if Old Testament folks walked with God without the regenerate spirit to the extent of being translated straight to Heaven, how much more us the new creation with the indwelling presence of Christ Himself. If only you could catch this revelation, you can be the next wonder in this world to be translated to God's Throne. The difference between the realm of visitation and translation is that visitation is temporary while translation is permanent. In both realms the will of God is paramount for no one can encounter such an experience in his own devise. Paul spoke about the abundance of revelations in the 6th dimension which is the realm of visitation but in this last dispensation, we will talk about the abundance of revelations of the 7th dimension which is the realm of translation.

CHAPTER SIX

THE HEAVENLY REALM OF MUSIC, RYTHM AND MELODY

There is a continuous flow of music and melodies of heaven. Let's refer to Colossians. 3:1 *If then you have been raised with Christ, seek the things that are above, where Christ is seated at the right hand of God.* We need to set our hearts and our minds on things in heaven. That is the reason why we are teaching on this series Wonders of Heaven. Our key verse we have taken is from the book of Hebrews chapter 6:5 and have tasted the goodness of the word of God and the powers of the age to come. God wants us to draw from our inside the things from our spirit to taste of the good word. And the author of Hebrews says of the powers of the age to come. We have talked about the gifts of the Spirit and how the gifts of the Spirit sometimes manifest in our lives. And all the manifestation of the Spirit has to do with the things that are in heaven. So let's just close our eyes and set our hearts and affection on the things of heaven. Think of some of the things that are in heaven and let the longing come upon our hearts and our lives as we draw towards the things of heaven. The reason we have you to sing some songs even though we are going to minister the word is because there is something about music and singing that we are going to talk about.

In heaven there is what we call the power of music or melody. That is another realm that is in heaven. In heaven music flows on continuously. It is non-stop. All the time the music just keeps flowing. And there is not a moment or time when music ceases. Except in the time of revelation where it talked about God was about to show His wrath, and as He was grieving there was silence in heaven for a moment of time. And the music that is in heaven is very powerful. It is something that we only have a foretaste of on this earth. In fact being filled with the Spirit is being linked up to the kind of music that we can receive from God. Turn to Eph. 5:18-19 do not get drunk with wine, for that is debauchery; but be filled with the Spirit, addressing one another in psalms and hymns and spiritual songs. Some times when the Spirit of God move we feel like something in our hearts wants to reach out onto Him. Most of the time we grab a song or a melody that we know and we sing it and it comes out from our life. But as our walk in God increases the heavenly presence is so much in us that the earthly melody cannot contain what we want to express. And we need to reach into something deeper than that. And that is why God gives us a new tongue to worship Him. Like this morning you could sense it in your spirit you feel like there is something in you that just want to reach out to God. And unless we could let that melody flowing out there is something that is just not contacted or something that is just not there. Just close your eyes and lift up your hands for a moment. And just let the melody on your inside worship God. And you sense the atmosphere different. Doesn't something on your inside feel good like something lifting you up? Like something is lifting you up into the heavenly presence. That's what we want to talk about this morning that the words that God gives us and the tune that God gives us in Ephesians. 5:19. making melodies in your heart has a sort of quality you can call it power that seems to take something from inside us and bring us into the heavenly place. We know that He gave us melody in chapter 5:19 of Ephesians. The question we want to deal with is why He gives us the melody.

In the Hebrew language there are many words for the word rejoice which is also translated as gladness some times. In English we have rejoice, cheer, joy, and in the Hebrew they have different words to express that joy in our hearts. There are different degrees of what I call the heavenly music that can fill our lives. How many of you felt that atmosphere different just after you worship in tongues. Why should it be different? That's what we are going to touch on this morning. To gain some understanding of why it is different and what is the process that was taking place. We know it is different but we want to know why it is different.

In Proverbs 17:22 A cheerful heart is a good medicine, but a downcast spirit dries up the bones. There is something about the joy that God gives that has a supernatural quality of being able to transform our life and bring healing to us. The word merry in the Hebrew is the word sameah. And sameah has a bigger meaning than the word merry. When we think about the word merry it just reminds us of merry making. We wish you a merry Christmas. But today we changed the tune to we wish you a blessed Christmas because we want more the blessing than just the merriness. Because merry making reminds us a little bit too much about wining and drinking and that kind of fun that they have in the world. It is not that Christians do not have fun, we have fun but our fun is a different type with no hangovers. The merry is the word sameah, which has a very wide element of joy. Now in Hebrew there is a joy that refers to the joy that is in our spirits, in our hearts. There is a joy that is in our soul. And there is a joy that is in our physical body.

And music is actually just harmonizing vibrations. You could even take a musical instrument and you just simply strike any key but it won't just harmonize. It has to be in a certain tune. When the keys are struck in a certain pattern that is harmonized one to another it carries a different impact on our lives. The bible does say that all that has breath worship and praise God. God has put music in life. Where there is life there is music. Everything in this life flows according to some rhythm. Electricity flows in a rhythm. Even your tap water doesn't just come in one flow. If you observe very carefully it comes in rhythm. And depending on the speed of the rhythm you cannot see it. There is a rhythm to life and that rhythm we call music. The music that God had set in the heart, in the spirit, the music in our soul and the music in our physical body. Even all the atoms and molecules synchronized with one and another.

Do you know that when your body is sick your body is not in rhythm? Most of you know about X-ray. And today they also know about the sonar scan where they use sound waves to scan for example the position of a baby. But they also have another way of scanning call the magneto scan where the cells that are sick show up in a spot because it's not in the pattern. Sick cells, diseased body parts show up in a magnetic scan because they cannot move in rhythm. If there was a cancerous cell on a magneto scan they can see a dark spot where the magnetic lines could not flow through. It has lost its ability to flow in the rhythm. It's based on a simple principle of magnetic rhythm in our body.

The Bible says *a merry heart doth well like a medicine*. It's because the rhythm that is in heaven where health is there where life is there flows upon our spirit, upon our soul and upon our body. And our body began to beat with the rhythm in heaven. And healing is there. There is a process of health and healing that is there. The only reason why your body is in sickness is your body lost that rhythm. I am not talking about tongue rhythm but there is a heavenly rhythm that it has lost. The cells are not able to move in the rhythm of life. Adam and Eve were created with the heavenly nature, and the Garden of Eden was like a heaven. Everything was in harmony. But the moment Adam and Eve fell into sin this was the curse that came in. Genesis 3 verse 17-19 Because you have listened to the voice of your wife, and have eaten of the tree of which I commanded you, "You shall not eat of it," cursed is the ground because of you; in toil you shall eat of it all the days of your life; thorns and thistles it shall bring forth to you; and you shall eat the plants of the field. In the sweat of your face you shall eat bread, till you return to the ground, for out of it you were taken; you are dust, and dust you shall return. To the woman He says in verse 16 I will greatly multiply your pain in childbearing. Sorrow only came in after the fall. Remember the testimony by Sister Sally. She said in heaven she could not see a single sad face because in heaven there is the heavenly music that is joy. It is on earth and since the fall of man that sorrow came. From the time that Adam fell into sin all the trees and all the herbs began to produce things that were not really designed to produce. From that day onwards suddenly there were thorns. The rhythm in the plant was disrupted. And the energy that went to produce beautiful flowers and eternal leaves went to produce thorns. Obviously the rhythm of life is disrupted. It is just like a beautiful plant and you began to take away nutrition from it. That beautiful plant can become crumpled and wrinkled. Just like many of you who have eaten well, you look well. You see people who are undernourished especially in Africa. You see those young children who don't have enough food their facial features look like old man because they didn't have enough nutrition. Now amplify that a million times because when Adam fell into sin it was more than that. It was passing out of spiritual life into darkness. And all the energy of that rhythm of life began to produce noise. The noise of the rhythm of life ended up with thorns.

And so from that day onwards in Romans chapter 8:20-22 For the creation was subjected to futility, not of its own will but by the will of Him who subjected it in hope; because the creation itself will be set free from its bondage to decay and obtain the glorious liberty of the children of God. We know that the whole creation has been groaning in travail together until now. All of creation from the day of the fall lost its music. When we lost the rhythm of life sickness came, sorrow came, and imperfection came. You could in a sense say in this manner that when Adam and Eve fell we lost our music. When Adam and Eve fell mankind lost the heavenly music. And man for thousands of years has tried to lift themselves out of that mighty cave with their own form of music. And music has played a role in all of man's highest moments. Any wedding in any culture in any religion is not complete without music. Then the greatest suffering of mankind when man face death in a funeral. When man wrestle with things that are so difficult to accept they need music.

The Realm Of The Spirit

From that day when man fell man struggled to get back that music. Sometimes he succeeded in a small degree and it lift him up. Sometimes he failed. From time to time mankind has managed to taste some of the heavenly music. People like Beethoven his music has certain majesty involved. And when you hear it, it lifts you up. And some other kind of music that has lifted mankind out of their suffering, out of their sorrow, helped mankind taste the fullness of joy. And all of the highest music of man cannot reach what it takes to reach the musical state before Adam fell into sin. From that day onwards men sought for that music. Which is why in Proverbs 17 it says a merry heart do good like a medicine. When at least a little bit of that rhythm is still there you get divine health.

Just to give you an idea of how powerful the original music that we have lost if you really have that heavenly music you don't just have health you have immortality. If a merry heart does well like a medicine heavenly music brings you immortality. Adam and Eve were once immortal. They could have lived for 10000 years and still have not a single wrinkle. Imagine living 10000 years without sorrows. All of us have lived many years but we could never say that all those years were without sorrows. There have been sorrows there have been joy and all overall if your joy is more than your sorrow you are still going strong. If your sorrow is more than your joy you feel very depressing. Thank God Jesus is your joy. Can you imagine living 10000 years and not knowing sorrow? See that heavenly music that we only have a glimpse of not only have the power of life it has a power of immortality. And that is that kind of music we are talking about the sameah that comes from the Spirit and will affect your soul and your body.

Turn to Acts 2:25-26 For David says concerning him, "I saw the Lord always before me, for He is at my right hand that I may not be shaken; there my heart was glad, and my tongue rejoiced; moreover my flesh will dwell in hope. Now you know why this is a reference to Jesus Christ? The music in Jesus' life and the joy that was in His heart never dies. Hebrews 12 verse 2 tells us that the Lord Jesus Christ when He saw the cross had joy, looking onto Jesus the author and finisher of our faith, who for the joy that was set before Him endured the cross.." Now this is the same Lord Jesus who for the joy that was set before Him, the joy that was in Him, and the music that was in Him his flesh did not see corruption. No germ, no virus could touch that body. Yes He did die for our sins and for our sicknesses. He Himself bore our sickness and diseases and that was a legal transaction.

So then what happened at Gethsemane when He cried? What about Hebrews 5 when Jesus cried and wept? Have you ever experienced where you laugh and laugh until you cried? If you really let go you laugh until you cry. You laugh until the tears come out from your eyes. It is possible to weep because you are happy. Now Jesus Christ had 2 things going on at Gethsemane. In His heart there was joy that He will be raised up again. See Jesus looked to the cross expectantly. Although He told the Father that, "If you desire let this cup pass from Me" but then He goes on and said, "Nevertheless not my will but yours be done." Some of you got the wrong picture in Gethsemane that Jesus was saying to the Father, "I don't like this take it away from me." Jesus never lost His joy. You ask, "How do you know?" Don't you remember the night before He was betrayed what was He talking about? Therefore you now have sorrow; but I will see you again and your heart will rejoice, and your joy no one will take away from you (John 16:22) until now you have asked nothing in My name. Ask, and you will receive, that your joy may be full (John 16: 24)

These things I have spoken to you, that in Me you may have peace. In the world you will have tribulation; but be of good cheer, I have overcome the world (John 16: 33) this is the Lord Jesus speaking on the night when He was betrayed. He was there comforting His disciples and imparting joy into their lives although there was sorrow because of physical separation and the sin of the world. Yet on His spirit of joy for doing God's will is there. That's why on the cross 2 things happened. He took our sorrows but His joy was more powerful than our sorrow that's why He won. The life that was in Him yielded to God and that resurrection life flowed out of Him.

But this reference in Acts 2 Peter was explaining about the tongues they had received. They were speaking in tongues and all the people say they were drunkard. And Peter was explaining that this is the outpouring of the Spirit as prophesied by Joel. And this is what David says in verse 26 therefore my heart rejoiced, and my tongue was glad. Now the word glad is a special Greek word and not the normal word for joy. It is the word, which means leaping with joy. And my tongue was leaping with joy. It is the word translated jumping with joy. He was giving a picture of the Lord filling their lives. The filling of the Spirit is the filling of joy. He anoint us with the oil of gladness, and that ties back to Eph. 5:18-19 it says, "Be filled with the Spirit speaking to yourself in psalms, hymns and spiritual songs, singing and making melody in your heart." When you are baptized in the Holy Spirit God gives you a melodious inspiration on your inside. And it was so full you can't contain it you say praise God, thank you Lord. See that joy that filled your inside is your tongue leaping.

Cross reference to where he took that passage from in the book of Psalms 16:9 Therefore my heart is glad, and my soul rejoices; now the word glad in Hebrew here is the same word found in Proverbs 17:22 A merry heart do good like a medicine. A sameah heart do good like a medicine. My heart is sameah my heart is so happy. And he says my soul (in reference to the tongue) rejoices. The word rejoices here is the word gul or gil, which means to spring about. No wonder when they translated it into the New Testament in Greek they have to choose a special word. Remember that verse in Isaiah 28:11 for with stammering lips and another tongue. And Paul later in Corinthians refers that to speaking in tongues. I point to all these words to show forth that when God filled us with the Holy Spirit in the process He gave us something that He longed to give to mankind the heavenly melody in our life. Which is why some times you go deep into tongues and you pray in tongues and Paul says I will sing with my spirit and I will sing with my understanding. And as he sings with the spirit he touched on the heavenly melody where there is some scene of immortality.

Now there are many Hebrew words for the word rejoice. There are some that are not applicable so much in the spirit but more in the natural realm. There is a word kadar which is found in Exodus 18:4 and it's like Jethro rejoicing over the goodness that was in Moses life. All these are natural joy. Why do the Hebrew have so many words for joy? They discovered all the different types of joy. There is a joy you can have because something good is happening. That is kadar happiness. Then there is a natural joy masos and this is a joy of happy events like for example a wedding. It's a joy that comes because of a happy event. There is another joy tsahal for example Ex. 8:13 and that is the joy that comes when they have just been delivered. Like the Berlin wall came down you should see those East German faces. There is a joy that comes from deliverance. So these are the different examples of natural joy that the Hebrew has a word for it. But there are different degrees of joy that Hebrew talk about. There is a joy you have learnt just now the word gil or gul and that joy is a joy that affects the physical body. It talks about your physical body reacting to that joy. See some people who were born again, tongue talking, demon chasing but their face don't tell you they are Christians. They were supposed to have the peace and joy of our Lord Jesus but it didn't look on their faces. They have sameah joy in their spirit but it never affected into gil or gul joy. A joy that makes you want to celebrate. So gil or gul is a joy that affects your body, and causing you to be leaping and dancing. Some time we forgot that the spiritual natural rhythm the most spontaneous with the Lord would be the most beautiful. That's what joy is about. See joy can never be conformed to rules. You can be trained to smile but if it doesn't come from your heart there is something missing. So it's important for us to understand that there is a sameah joy and a gil or gul joy. From your inside it affects your outside. And that's when healing began to result.

In Isa. 35:1 and 2 the wilderness and the dry land shall be glad, the desert shall rejoice (gil or gul) and blossom like the rose, it shall blossom abundantly and rejoice, even with joy and singing. Now how could a desert blossom, your body could be sick and be like a desert and it needs to blossom in the health and the life of God. You must have gil or gul. And that's the joy from sameah that comes into your body when your tongue moves, your legs moves and you rejoice in the Lord. Even if an untrained person is dancing as the Lord touches he or she there is a beauty to it. Of course when you are trained you can get rid of some discordant movements but don't let that remove that natural rhythm. Do you know what makes a person go from average to genius? They go beyond the boundaries. There are a lot of people who go to art school but not all of them become great artists. Because most people confine themselves to the rules and never look beyond the rules to touch on realms that others dream about. When Beethoven who came after Mozart started his style it was astounding to the people of his time. See genius comes by going beyond the average. Remember what makes people average. They never go beyond their training. They just limit themselves. This is the law. This is the way but they never touch on the beauty of their training. You can learn to play tennis under a great tennis coach but there must be something on your inside that takes those rules and make you a master of some special area.

When golf as a sport was just starting, the golfers were still mastering the rules. In the past, the top golfers were the ones who really could really play the rules well. But then after many years of golf many can play the rules very well. What was considered great 30 years ago becomes average today? Normally when you use a golf club they tell you that the angle must be only at a certain length. So all the masters were teaching that because that was the rule. Then this American came along. He broke every rule. He put it at a stronger angle. His shots were more powerful. And every master was asking how he did it. They analysed his shots and found he increased the angle to

The Realm Of The Spirit

what the masters were saying you should never do. And his shots were so powerful that it goes beyond others.

So what are we talking about? You got to flow with the rhythm. When there is a rule you got to understand why the rules are there. And perhaps there is another way to flow around those rules. Man cannot fly. Man has to discover ways to break the law of gravity. You know what the rules say. Anything that is heavier than air cannot fly. But there are other rules so that a Boeing 747 that weigh about 85 tons still can fly. The aeronautical engineers have figured out a way to get around those things without breaking the natural laws. So it's important for us to let the flow or rhythm comes forth. Remember everything that you earn in life is there and is still in the state of evolution. All the engineering schools are still in a state of evolution. Even the laws continue to change. Everything is in a state of evolution, because things that are seen are subject to a state of change.

How do you control those changes? You don't break the laws of music to create great music. You flow with those laws and you bring it to a higher pattern. You take those things and there is a rhythm because there is a rhythm that is deep in your spirit. Like the first man who built a suspension bridge, all the engineers looked at him and said it cannot be done. But he dreamt and dreamt and said that it can be done. And he conquered that engineering problems and he built a suspension bridge. Today it is nothing to build a suspension bridge. You could be trained in school to do it. But the first man who did it had no school to attend.

There is rhythm in our spirit that we need to flow with the music of our soul so that we are not limited by boundaries. So there is a gil or gul that is there. Notice in Isa. 35:1 the desert shall rejoice and blossom as a rose. That means that if the desert doesn't rejoice it shall not blossom. If the desert doesn't have gil it will not blossom. It shall blossom abundantly and rejoice. Look at verse 3 Strengthen the weak hands, and make firm the feeble knees. Verse 5 Then the eyes of the blind shall be opened and the ears of the deaf shall be unstopped. It all starts with the joy. Every promise of the Holy Spirit is the promise of the heavenly rhythm coming into our lives.

In the book of Joel there is a prophecy on the outpouring of the Spirit. Now Joel chapter 2 starts with fasting and seeking the Lord. And as you seek the Lord there is weeping and mourning. But that is not supposed to be your main condition. That leads to something. There is a fast in verse 15 Blow the trumpet in Zion. Then look at verse 21 now the Lord began to move in their lives. As the Lord moves in their lives what came first. The outpouring came first or the music came first. Let me tell you the music came first. If you want to see visions of heaven, if you want the heavenly experience, let the heavenly music touch you first in your heart. And let it flow out from you, from your spirit to your soul, to your body. Verse 21 Fear not, O land; be glad (the word glad is the word "gil" let that joy touch your body) and (sameah) rejoice. The same word found in Proverbs 17:22 be merry. Verse 23 be glad (gil) O sons of Zion and (sameah) rejoice in the Lord, your God; for He has given the early rain for your vindication. See there is a heavenly music that God gives to us in the New Testament. It is linked to the outpouring of the Spirit.

Every move of God in church history has been accompanied with music. James 5:13 is any one among you suffering? Let him pray. Is any cheerful? Let him sing praise. Why does he ask those who suffering to pray? And those who have joy let the joy fill their life even more. There is a clue given to you in Isaiah 56:7 these I will bring to My holy mountain, and make them (sameah) joyful in My house of prayer. Not you know why those who are sad or sorrowful let them pray. Because when you enter the house of prayer He gives you sameah. It makes your heart merry again. He tells you what happen in His house of prayer. Those who enter His house He gives you sameah which is Proverbs 17:22 a merry heart when you pray through because He wants to keep us in His covenant of blessing in our lives.

There is a word the joy in the soul too. Let turn to Ps. 35:9 then my soul shall rejoice in the Lord, exulting in His deliverance. That word joy is the word sic and that joy is the joy of the soul. So there are many Hebrew words for the word joy. There is a word gil or gul, which refers to the joy that affects the body. There is a word sic that affects the soul. There is a word sameah that is a joy that is in our spirit. So when we talk about rejoice in the Lord and again I say rejoice, there are different degrees of that joy. We must first of all have sameah. Then we need to have our soul rejoicing sic. Then we need to have gil or gul, which is an outward expression of that joy.

And look at what Ps. 35:10 says all my bones shall say. You know your bones can talk. No wonder He says a merry heart do good like a medicine. For when sameah becomes sic and gil in your life, your body began to beat in the rhythm of God. Divine health comes in. There are several Hebrew words with a slight different meaning. The word alas speaks about times when nothing around you seems joyful. You are the only one seem joyful like in Habakkuk. Yet will I rejoice in the Lord though the fig tree does not blossom and the vine doesn't bear fruit yet I will alas before the Lord, which means I will rejoice by faith. The word alas is the word of triumph. I will let joy triumph over my situation. Then there is a word renun, which means to sing out loud to the Lord. All these are related to the joy of sameah, sic and glu.

As we sing and look at heavenly music, we realize that heavenly music begins as a melody in your heart. And every time before God does something you look at the book of Revelation there is always a new song that goes up to God. Today human beings are in sin and them in discord. A lot of the human music is discord. They don't produce health and healing. A lot of the rock music stirs up physical passion. They are in disharmony against God. A lot of the sentimental music gives you a melancholy spirit. It makes you very sad and moody. And so we need to hear the heavenly music that is so different from this earth. You can use any instrument that is there in the natural world but you must play it in the heavenly rhythm. That will produce immortal life. May God give us spiritual ears tune to them? It's the power of music, if you allow this heavenly music to affect you. It starts with your tongue and melody in your heart. You will touch the realm of the heavenly nature.

THE REAM OF MUSIC AND THE SONG OF THE LAMB

The natural world is very real to us, but the natural world is a shadow of the spirit world. And a shadow is something that is a reflection of a solid object or rather a blockage of light prevented by a solid object. As light flows and shines upon an object the area where the light cannot shine through cast a shadow. So the shadows sometimes quite look like the real thing. It depends on the intensity of the light; it depends on the position of the light that affects the shadow. If the light is not intense then the shadow is very faint. Sometimes the position of the light casts a different shadow too. If the light is very close then you have a bigger shadow. If the light is far then you have a small shadow. So in the same way as we describe these things, it depends on the position we are describing from. 3 or 4 people who have gone to heaven can come back and describe the same thing but the description of heaven from each of them will sound different. It depends on the position. It also depends on their own spiritual level that they have come into God.

This series flows forth from the experience of how after for about 48 hours of praying in tongues the spirit world opened. And there were some things that were seen and heard in the spirit world that we are trying to describe in the natural what it is like. We have described about the realm of revelation. We could see into somebody's heart, somebody's eyes and you could have knowledge about their past and everything. Or you could see things almost like the natural scene but actually it is the spiritual realm.

The Realm of the Spirit is a Realm of Music

So the next area we are talking about is the realm of song and music. In the spirit world living things have a song and have music. It seems that there is no living object that doesn't carry a song or carry music. In the spirit realm that God took me in, I was fascinated because I wondered what that sound was. It didn't exactly sound like an organ or a piano or some musical instrument. But there was a constant music at different times in the spirit world. It was a sort of musical vibration that was sounded in the background. Sometimes it sounds like little rivers of water flowing in harmony. Sometimes it sounds like a roar but it's not a roar of discord. It's a roar of harmony. Our natural ears cannot pick up the fullness of heaven's music. In heaven our eyes can see as far as we want to see. But on earth natural eyes can only see to a certain distance. Likewise in heaven our ears will be able to hear as much as we want to. But there is a realm of music, a realm of song that is always there. And every object seems to giving out a sort of music.

Like when there is a heavenly scene, let's say there is a heavenly tree. Each life has a different tune. The tree seems to be giving a sort of music. The heavenly grass seems to be like giving its own music. Then the creatures in heaven or the angels in heaven when they speak their voices have musical quality. Some of you may have images of the angels talking to each other. They talk normally but there is a musical quality to that sound. As they are speaking there is a sparkle of music, which seems to harmonize with all the background. The spirit realm that I entered happened while I was still down here on earth. And here was interesting part. While in the spirit realm, I also found that out of every human being there was also a tune coming out of them. Do you know that to those who had problem with their hearts, the normal heartbeat is music to their ears? I read a story of a Christian who was claiming God's word for a heart problem. And his pulse was fixed to a heart machine. And the sound of the machine goes troup, troup, and every time it goes in rhythm he is very happy. So to him that is music.

Inside each one of us there is music, there is vibration taking place all the time. Your heart is beating so there is music going on all the time. We are not

The Realm Of The Spirit

talking about natural sound. Inside each one of us is a spiritual tune. And in that spirit world you not only see a person but you hear a person. And when someone is in discord, their spiritual music is also in discord. So there is a spiritual tune that flows and it can be detected. The sounds that come forth from those who are out of harmony with God are not music. That's the strange thing. You could tell a Christian by their song. Unbelievers who are not in harmony with God do not give out harmonic sound. There is a discord that flows that is painful to the ear.

Ps.69:34 Let heaven and earth praise him, the seas and everything that moves therein. Let everything worship Him. Let everything praise Him. Let all that have breath praise the Lord. There is a certain voice; there is certain music in all of God's creation. In the birds, in the trees, wherever there is life there is certain music. Now why do we call it music? Music is basically just a harmony of movement and sound and vibrations. When it's all harmoniously put together we have what human defined as music. When the planets move in their order it is music in God's eyes and to God's ears. Music is the synchrony of sounds, of movement. So there is a certain music when there is perfection. Wherever perfection reigns music results. So music is the perfect balance of all of God's creations.

When God first made the world the Garden of Eden and this planet earth in its perfect state, everything vibrated with the harmony and the music of God. In the Garden of Eden before the fall of man all the earth was praising God. Every creature was praising God. The praise was coming forth because everything was in harmony in God's sight. If that is being the case we take our definition further. Where perfection is music results. Since God is perfection personified, God exemplifies music. God Himself is the harmony of harmonies. The rhythm of rhythms. The source of all music. Because from Him flows perfection. God is perfect and there is music in God. And then there is music in everything that God says because God's word is perfect. And there is everything of music in what God does because His works are perfection. For where perfection reigns, music results.

So when say a word it would produce harmony. Now I am going to take a little bit of illustration from the realm of music. Sometimes, let's say you have a choir or a band, when you have a small discord, let says 1 in discord and 99 played in harmony. Do you think it would drown that person? Of course, you could hardly hear the disharmony. However as the statistics increase from 1 to 2, slowly the discordant sound becomes louder. By the time perhaps you reached 10% the discord becomes quite obvious. Do you notice there is something about music? It doesn't quite go by percentage. Let say a person talks about going to heaven being based on good works and bad works. And they say when they stand before the judgment seat of God, God will put all the bad works on one side, good works on one side. If the scale just tilts a little bit on the bad side you go to hell. If it tilts just one little on the good work side, maybe you have given a cup of water to a thirsty man of God, you go to heaven. That's what most religions believe until they come to Christianity they realize that no man can enter heaven by their works.

What we are trying to illustrate is that in some things 50 -50 kind of thing makes a difference. In the realm of music you don't need a 50% thing to weigh equally. Just 10% can destroy the whole orchestra. You don't need half the musicians to be bad to spoil the whole music. If there are 7 musicians 1 bad musician is enough to spoil the music. See music has such a quality that even if a small percentage is discordant, it is very obvious. So we are trying to illustrate here that in the realm of the spirit you don't need a big fat sin to qualify as a sinner. Why is it so? It is because it works in the harmony that flows. There is a discord that begins to drown out all the other things. But in God there is no discord. His word is perfect. His works are perfect. Now what happens is this whenever there is a powerful harmony compared to a small disharmony, that powerful harmony could sometimes affect that disharmony into harmony. It just would be like as you vibrate this tuning fork here the other tuning fork will after sometime vibrate too. So when we are in discord His word can cause harmony into our being once again. The word that is perfection, the word that is harmony, the word that is music when it flows in our lives it causes a harmony to come forth. So in this way every part of our system becomes tuned to the Word. This is what I call a re-tuning that is being done.

Now what are we basing that tuning on. Every tuning has to be based on something. That tuning is based on what a person hears to be harmonies. There are 2 ways to tune a guitar. You could either tune it to the other strings. However if one of those strings was tuned wrongly and the other 4 strings were tuned to that 1 string, you got 5 strings tuned in harmony to that 1 string. You got 1 more to tune and you tuned it exactly to the rest of the 5. They are in harmony but all are tuned to a wrong key. In the same way when God speaks His Word there is full of harmony. There is something in us when God's Word becomes powerful that gets tuned up into God.

The Realm Of The Spirit

Which is why God says in Col. 3:16 when God's words is in abundance not when it is in famine. Col.3:16 Let the word of Christ dwell in you richly, as you teach and admonish one another in all wisdom, and as you sing psalms and hymns and spiritual songs with thankfulness in your hearts to God. When the Word is abundant in us every part of our being the drums in us, the piano in us all get tuned to the Word which is the basic tone that we have to tune to. Then we become in tune with God. See there is always a standard called the key of C. Sometimes when a person tune a guitar they can tune it to D or tune it to E or they tune it to a lower note. And when they press the C cord is not the real C it is an actually lower note.

What's happening here? Let me bring into the realm of human psyche. It is possible for a person to tune their inward being to a certain extent without God through the powers of human concentration, occult, yoga or psychic concentration. They try to think all their inward being into a certain vibration. Let's say the Word of God is middle C. Then you tune everything to middle C. Then it harmonies with the harmony God wants. Without God people are in discord. All their internal parts of their soul are in discord. Sometimes people have bitterness, hurt, childhood experiences, terror, nightmare and all these things. And as they grow up they are in discord. And you wonder why their character is that way. See I am trying to illustrate that life is music itself. Your character is music when it's perfect. Jesus is the perfect symphony. When a person character is irritable and easily angered you know what is coming out. It is a discord. See there is are inner parts of our soul. There are inner parts of our spirit. And there are inner parts of our body. They all flow in harmony together.

What happen with some people especially the occult, the psychic, who try to reach into the spirit realm minus God? You know how they do it. Let's say the word of God is middle C and every part of our being is supposed to be tuned to that. But that person is in discord, don't know God. So they try to tune themselves, they try to reach that realm. Instead of tuning to middle C they end up tuning to D. So their soul, their dead spirit is out of harmony. And everything within them tune to that. What is happening is that there is a tuning to a song but not a song of the Lord. You see the entrance into the spirit realm is that harmony flow. So illegally they try to enter that realm by tuning to the wrong note. And they manage to just touch the surface of the spirit world. Why because the spirit realm contains all the notes. God created all the notes. And they just manage to touch that spirit realm long enough for that evil spirit to contact their soul and manifest. They gain extra strength from the demon spirit where the human spirit that is dead contacts the spirit. Where the human soul contacts the demonic soul and the demonic soul manifests. There is no protection in the spirit realm when you try to enter without God.

But in that spirit realm of God there is a song and a tune. There is an official entrance through Jesus Christ and the word of God that brings us into a continuous flow of the realm of the spirit. It's the song of the Lord. That is why the closer your word resembles the word of the Lord the closer your word contains the heavenly song and the heavenly tune. Let me answer the question that is often asked, why is music linked to prophecy? Everyone can teach that there is a link between music and prophecy, between music and the office of a prophet. But tonight you know why. The reason is because when a prophet or a ministry of prophecy contacts the word of the Lord and speaks it forth, it's perfect, its music. And the reason why music has an entrance into that prophetic realm of uttering God's word is because music is part of your tuning to the perfection of God especially the music of God. At every point in history, in time and in the church, when men and woman of God of old has touched and spoken words that are closed or that are heavenly, it has always been the song of the Lord.

Moses reached a stage of what I will call almost perfection made possible through the grace of God. He still has to be redeemed through the Blood of the Lamb. But Moses had walked like no man has walked. He had known God like no man before him had known God. And at the peak of his ministry as he came to the conclusion and although he died he was resurrected. The book of Jude says God sent Michael to get the body of Moses because Moses was resurrected before the normal resurrection. He had walked too close with God. The song was even in his body. When prophecy reached its greatest height it becomes song and linked with music.

Look at Moses in Deuteronomy 31:19 now therefore write this song, and teach it to the people of Israel; put it in their mouths, that this song may be a witness for me against the people of Israel. But that song also prophesies good blessings. And that word that was uttered forth nearly about 2000 B.C. continues on as the word of God although it was known as the song of Moses. And when God speaks a word it will always come to pass. Whether that word came directly from God, that word came from an angel or that word came through man's lips, that word contains the music of God. Even at the climax of the Jewish age which Moses had looked forward to and

The Realm Of The Spirit

prophesied, we find that they are still singing the Song of Moses. One of the climaxes is in the book of Rev. 15:3 and they sing the song of Moses. That song has not been completed even in the church age. But that prophetic song that was released will be completed in the Jewish dispensation after the rapture.

There have been men and women of God who had moved into that realm. When Paul was writing his epistles, he may not have realized it himself but the music of God was flowing in him. And as he wrote those epistles to persons like Timothy, Titus and to the churches in his time, his words continue on through age after age, through generation upon generation. Until today the 20th century the words of Paul still carry the same weight and authority. And we call it the infallible word. But it came from a humble ordinary pen and through a humble clay vessel. The guitar may be imperfect but when a good guitarist strums a song he will still bring out a song. That explains why whenever there is music the music of God and the praises and worship of God we sense the Thus says of the Lord so much stronger. And why do prophecy comes forth when music comes? It is because music is harmony.

In the book of I Chronicles 25:1-3 David and the chiefs of the service also set apart for the service certain of the sons of Asaph, and of Herman, and of Jeduthun, who should prophesy with lyres, with harps, and with cymbals. The list of those who did the work and of their duties was: Of the sons of Asaph: Zaccur, Joseph, Nehtaniah, and Asharelah, sons of Asaph, under the direction of Asaph, who prophesied under the direction of the king. Of Jeduthun, the sons of Jeduthum: Gedaliah, Zeri, Jeshaiah, Shimel, Hashabiah, and Mattihiah, six, under the direction of their father Jeduthun, who prophesied with lyre in thanksgiving and praise to the Lord.

Have you ever wondered why prophecy and the harp, music, symbols go together? They were tuning to the song of God. Without music mankind cannot reach its highest aspiration. Great nations rise with great anthems. Great disasters are overcome with a great song in the hearts of God people. It is said and it is true that when the Japanese nation was conquered in the Second World War, the entire nation was devastated. They have lost hope in their religion. They have lost hope in anything that they have. But there was a song that came to them. Today Japan is known as the Ninth Symphonies. Japanese call it No. 9. That symphony by Beethoven took the hearts of the Japanese people and gave them back the hope, gave them back the desire to rise. It was performed yearly and the crowds kept getting bigger and bigger. The CD diskette has 74 or 76 minutes. Why such an odd number? Why not 60 or 90 minutes? Because when they did it the Nine was so popular, they said we must modify the CD so that all of the nine symphonies can fit into one CD. That is the history of the 74 or 76 minutes CD. Beethoven's music raised up the people of Japan even though Beethoven himself may never have even met a Japanese. But his music lives on. That nation today has risen.

That's just natural music. Think about the song of the Lamb. Now there is a relationship between natural and spiritual. We humans love and draw towards harmony. People flee disharmony and riots. And people are drawn towards harmony. We draw towards harmonies in the same way there is a drawing towards God and music helps. Which explain why in II Kgs. 3 when Elisha had to prophesy, he says bring me a minstrel. As he hears the minstrel play the Spirit of the Lord came on him. The closer we go to God the more musical you become.

Getting Into The Realm of Harmony

The second area which we want to focus on is when you understand that all of the spirit realm is music, then the entrance into the spirit realm by the correct door is to learn to harmonize into that realm in God. How do we get into that realm? There is an easy way. We all know in Eph. 2 it says that we are seated with Christ in the heavenly places. Why do many don't feel that they are seated up there. They only feel it occasionally. Sometimes as you pray you feel yourself ascending the height of the spirit realm and being seated up there. Sometimes after a prayer meeting, after the presence of God has been experienced in your closet, you walk out with a sense of authority, a sense of harmony, a sense of love. Things can happen and it doesn't affect the peace of God that passes your understanding. Things around you can be in disharmony. But it never causes disharmony in your life. And you have love towards all. You have peace towards all. Because you are experiencing what is like to be seated in the heavenly places. But how do I ascend and remain there? Some people find it hard to ascend into that realm.

Music is the key. And each one of us has a song. If you will listen carefully to your inward man there is a song inside. If that song ever dies you are spiritually dead. Sometimes that song is weak because your spirit is weak. Sometimes that song is strong because your spirit is strong. I am not talking about ordinary song. I am not talking about what many of you experienced of waking up and having a nice tune going on inside like a scripture song, like Morning Has Broken, or Amazing Grace or any of the songs we know. That melody goes deeper than human vocabulary songs or tune. What is happening is that, that song on the inside is flowing forth is the song that speaks of joy which express that song to your understanding and soul. That song touches a song you know in your memory. When that song on your inside is weak you don't feel like singing. You don't feel like worshiping. You don't feel like reading the word. But isn't it different when that song is inside. All you want to do is read the bible. The first time you come back from work you say where is my bible not where is the newspapers. That song is alive in you. Understand I am teaching you a spiritual truth that is powerful. If you could maintain that song throughout your working life 9 to 5 you will get back home still full of the Holy Spirit. You don't have to get back from work and say fill me Lord, fill me.

I am teaching you a key to maintain that hunger. If you understand the spirit world, you would maintain that song in your heart. And if that song is strong and you listen to it all the time, you will maintain a healthy spiritual life. The bible describes it in a special way it calls it making melody. It is not composing songs. The bible didn't say Eph. 5:18-19 be filled with the Holy Spirit, speaking to yourself in Psalms and spiritual songs, composing songs and melody in your heart. No it says making melody in your heart. The result of the spirit realm being filled in your life, the result of the word being full in your life is the song comes out stronger. The result of your devotional life and meditating on the word, the result of the spiritual realm touching your spirit, refreshing you is that the song comes out stronger. Paul even qualifies it as psalms, spiritual songs and hymns. So we need to develop that song.

In Revelation it calls it the song of the Lamb. Rev. 15:3 and they sing the song of Moses, the servant of God, and the song of the Lamb. It is not just a special song. It's the spirit of that song that flows from God. He composed song and all those songs are expression of that real inner song. That is why you could learn a new song and after 6 months be tired of that song. It is not that there is something wrong with your inside. But it is that we need new expression. That song that is in our spirit is so powerful that no earthly song could fully express the extent, the color, the rainbow and the variations of that one song in your heart. It keeps having the need to be expressed differently. You don't get up every morning and have the same song for 60 years. The Joy of the Lord is my strength let's say every Sunday you come here and sing The Joy of the Lord is my strength by the 30th Sunday it's a routine a habit. They can't sing The Joy of The Lord with joy. But it's different if one Sunday you come and sing The Joy of the Lord is my strength. The next Sunday you sing Jesus took my burden and roll them into the sea. It is a different song but the same joy.

Can you understand what we are trying to describe in that spirit world. It is one song but many colours. Because it's the colour white that increase different colours. Red is only one of the colours of white. Blue is only one of the colours of white. You mix it all together it is white like. It contains all the different wavelengths. And every time when God does something new in our life or brings you into a higher realm, it all start changing on your inside. The song goes fast or slow and your life goes fast and slow. In Rev. 5:8-9 And when he had taken the scroll, the four living creatures and the twenty-four elders fell down before the Lamb, each holding a harp, and with golden bowls full of incense, which are the prayers of the saints; and they sang a new song.

That song must never die in our hearts. As long as that song of the Lamb flows strong we will have the presence of God as seated in the heavenly places 24 hours a day. We have just given you the secret of the presence of God for 24 hours, and that is to hold fast to that melody in your life. Sometimes that melody needs different earthly songs to keep it on your natural mind. But it's a song in your inside. As you pray to God tonight, each one of us have the same Lord but we have a different song on our inside. That song on your inside describes your entire life. It was a song written in the book of life about you. And the day you were born again you were given that song. He wrote it in your heart and in your spirit. And since the day you were born again it has started flowing.

But for some of you circumstances have deafened you to that song and you can't hear the melody in your heart. A melody is not an earthly song. A melody is a tune by earthly definition. It is on your inside. Emmanuel God with us is on your inside. When you tune to that song inside, that song will carry you into the heavenly places. If you tune tonight to that song on your inside, that song will carry you into the spirit world where you can live and move constantly in that realm. The earthly sorrows and earthly circumstances will never touch you up in the heavenly places. Sadly people have not learned the secret of living in that realm. Once in a while they catch hold of that song. They attend the church on Sunday. Their spirit caught that song from the preacher. Caught that song from the worship. And they went back with the song. They feel the presence of heaven but they don't know what is happening on their inside. They didn't realize that the song was being stirred up. So after sometime they don't hear that song any more. They feel depressed, they fell down, and they feel lonely. Remember this as long as that song comes strong you will never be sick.

Listen very carefully, whoever can tune 100% to that song, he or she has become perfected and may be translated because that song will change your physical body. That song will prevent your spirit from clinging to your body. That song will resurrect your mortal self into immortality. We all know that there is a small illustration in the natural. Those who are positive, those who are cheerful, they know that even plants respond to song and grow better. Human being that are sick are healed naturally by medicine and by natural circumstances faster with music. How much more that song of the Lord that not only heals but that it immortalizes because the song of the Lamb is immortal.

Tonight if you understands Col. 3:16, Eph. 5:18-19 that the word and the spirit works together like the violin and the piano to produce, to magnify the song of the Lamb in your life. It is God's perfect will that His people live in the perfect world 24 hours. Even when you're doing your business, even when you are out there in the hot sun, as long as you hear that song you are in the spirit. Whenever you cannot hear that song you are no more in the spirit. You are in the natural. May God quicken our spiritual ears? Tonight as you pray in the spirit let your spiritual tongue get hold of that inner spirit on your inside.

Rewards In Heaven

Let's refer to the account when the New Jerusalem was reviewed to the apostle John the city of God from the book of Revelation chapter 21. Verse 9 onwards Then came one of the seven angels who had the seven bowls full of the seven last plagues, and spoke to me, saying, "Come, I will show you the Bride, the wife of the Lamb." And in the Spirit he carried me away to a great, high mountain, and showed me the holy city Jerusalem coming down out of heaven from God, having he glory of God, its radiance like a most rare jewel, like a jasper, clear as crystal. It had a great, high wall, with twelve gates, and at the gates twelve angels, and on the gates the names of the twelve tribes of the sons of Israel were inscribed; on the east three gates, on the north three gates, on the south three gates, and on the west three gates. And on the wall of the city had twelve foundations, and on them the twelve names of the twelve apostles of the Lamb. And he who talked to me had a measuring rod of gold to measure the city and its gates and walls. The city lies foursquare, its length the same as its breadth; and he measured the city with his rod, twelve thousand stadia; its length and breadth and height are equal. He also measured its wall, a hundred and forty-four cubits by a man's measure, that is, an angel's. The wall was built of jasper, while the city was pure gold, clear as glass. The foundations of the wall of the city were adorned with every jewel; the first was jasper, the second sapphire, the third agate, the fourth emerald, the fifth onyx, the sixth carnelian, the seventh chrysolite, the eight beryl, the ninth topaz, the tenth chrysopsrase, the eleventh jacinth, the twelfth amethyst. And the twelve gates were twelve pearls, each of the gates made of a single pearl, and the street of the city was pure gold, transparent as glass.

Remember the sister how she was taken up to heaven earthly time was about one minute but heavenly time was about one hour. And the Lord showed her all the things in heaven. And she saw the streets were made from gold and some of the walls were made from gold. And the gold in heaven was different as it is transparent. We all do know that in Jn. 14 Jesus told His disciples, "Be of good cheer for in my Father's house are many mansions." We all have mansions in heaven given to us free in God because of His love for us. We need to know that our life on earth will affect our condition in heaven and that kind of reward we receive. We know it vaguely and generally that according to our faithfulness here on earth God will reward us in heaven. But we need to know how intricately it does affect that kind of reward that we receive and the place and the glory where we stay in.

I like to read a little passage from a book by H. A. Baker, Beyond the Veil. He wrote the book based on the children's experiences of Adulam's Cave, an orphanage in China. And the children had a revival and God started taking some of the children to heaven and showing them the things and the glory in heaven. He also came out with one book on angels and one book on heaven and the angels. When he was seeing these things taking place among the children he did a research in all the Christian writings to see what other Christians speak about heaven and the angels. And so here are some of those he had researched and quoted from.

CHAPTER SEVEN

PROPHETIC INSTRUCTIONS ON HOW TO EFFECTIVELY OPERATE IN THE REALM OF THE SPIRIT

There is a physical world and there is a spiritual world. In the spiritual world there are spiritual things and substances, otherwise the bible wouldn't call them things. These spiritual substances are made of things that are not visible or perceptible to our five senses. On the other hand, the physical things in this world are visible and perceptible to our senses. For us we need to understand that every physical thing starts from the spiritual thing first. The physical world came from the spirit world. Every natural substance is derived from a spiritual substance. The chair you are sitting in, the desk you are working at, all came from a spiritual place before it became tangible. Therefore the physical world is influenced by the spiritual world. The physical world is subjected to the spiritual world. Many Christians want to change the physical world around them without changing the spiritual world around them. And it is not possible to change the physical world until we change the spiritual world. This is because the physical world is subject to the laws that govern the spirit world. Many times the laws of the spirit transcend and prevail over and above the physical laws. That is why sometimes a person who has been given up to die may get healed by a miracle of God instantly. There is a higher law in the spiritual realm operating over a lower law in the physical realm. This physical world that we have is built from the spiritual world. Recently, the Lord gave me a next level understanding of the fact that we must operate from the spirit realm to the natural realm on a daily basis. We have been taught for a long time that we must do something in the natural before we can receive form the spirit; which is wrong. We must operate from the spirit realm to the natural realm to see what we desire come to pass. God is spirit and He created the world in the spirit before manifesting it in the natural (tangible, visible). In order to be truly effective in the spiritual realm, you must see in done and complete; whole lacking nothing in order to see it manifest in the natural realm. It is important that you learn how to change things from the spirit realm. Changes in government, whether by military coup or election, often change nothing. The reason is that nothing has changed in the spiritual realms. Influences from the spiritual realms explain why economic crises occur, when economist's thing the situation is improving.

Let me read a few more scriptures that we could use to expound on this understanding. In 2 Corinthians 4: 16-18 Paul knew this principle and he operated this same principle.

Therefore we do not loose heart for though our outward man is perishing yet the inward man is being renewed day by day. For our light affliction, which is but for a moment, is working for us a far more exceeding and eternal weight of glory, while we do not look at the things which are seen. For the things which are seen are temporary but the things which are not seen are eternal.

That is amazing for although he is living in the physical realm, he was constantly conscious of living in another realm. He says we are not looking at the things that are seen but at the things which are not seen. The things that we can see is temporary and is subject to change. It is changeable, moveable and removable. But the things which are not seen is eternal. It controls the physical realm.

LEARN THE ART OF WALKING IN THE SPIRIT

In learning the art of how to walk in the spirit, it is important that we strike a balance between spirit, soul and body. This is because you cannot live life in just one of these dimensions. Allow each of these areas in your life to expand and grow. Physical exercise, soul and social activities should not be neglected in the pursuit of spiritual activities. Paul says in Galatians 5:16-19;

But I say, walk by the Spirit, and do not gratify the desires of the flesh. For the desires of the flesh are against the Spirit, and the desires of the Spirit are against the flesh; for these are opposed to each other to prevent you from doing what you would. But if you are led by the Spirit you are not under the law. Verse 25 if we live by the Spirit, let us also walk by the Spirit.

There are different levels of being in the Spirit. A person can call him or herself Spirit filled but yet lives in the flesh. There are different levels of being in the Spirit and there are also things to do in order to keep being in the Spirit. The vast majority of the church of Jesus Christ is not in the Spirit. If the whole church of Jesus Christ is moving in the Spirit today, the

The Realm Of The Spirit

whole world today will be shaken by what God is doing. I would rather say it this way. Most of the churches are in the Spirit some of the time. But only some in the church are in the Spirit all the time. And there is a certain realm in the Spirit that, that is there. We got to learn to flow with the Spirit. We got to maintain in order to qualify in a way God will look down and say that's being in the Spirit. Jesus Christ as He moved on this earth was always in the Spirit.

Let me just give you a few tips here. If you ever worry about anything on this earth, you have just moved out of the Spirit. Do you know that Jesus never worries? He himself said in Matt. 6 look at the birds of the air and the grass in the field. They put their trust entirely in the hands of the heavenly Father. Jesus rebuked, exhorted and told the disciples they must not worry. Most of us know Matt. 6:33 which says, "Seek ye first the kingdom of God, And all these things shall be added onto you." The condition to receive all the blessings of God is to seek first the kingdom of God. But that is only one of the conditions. The other conditions are mentioned prior to verse 33. You have to read first from verse 25 -33. And those are the other conditions. If for a moment you worry about your needs you have just stepped out from the realm of the Spirit to the realm of the flesh. This is Jesus himself speaking in Matt. 6.

So that's just one of the small points I am talking about. It looks like major point but that's only a small point. Being in the Spirit, living in the Spirit and maintaining in the realm of the Spirit is not as easy as people make it. A lot of people go in and out of the kingdom all the time. They say I am abiding in the vine. But most of the time they are pulling away from the vine and then coming on again. Then they ask Jesus, Jesus why do I not have fruit. You say that if I abide in the vine I will bear much fruit. Jesus says you are abiding some of the time. Most of the time you are running around. Those little time that you have with Jesus, He would quickly channel all the nutrition to you so that you could bear fruit. And just as you got a few droplets you pulled off and you went aside again. No wonder it takes a long time to bear fruit.

Once in the Old Testament God expressed His desire for all His people. When He brought them out of Egypt and before they did anything wrong, before they fell into transgression in Exodus 19:6 God spoke to the Israelites led by Moses. Aaron hasn't become the priest yet. The priestly revelation was not given yet. Moses had just led them out and they were fresh and new. You shall be a kingdom of priests. It was His will that Adam and Eve walk with Him. God has grieved ever since Adam and Eve fell. Our Father's heart in heaven was grieved. It was almost like having a child that you can never hug. Think about having children born to you that you can never hold and embrace.

Man is a special creation. God had His angels before He made man. God has His other beings before He made man. But when He made man, He wanted this creature called man to be close to Him. When Adam and Eve fell, He couldn't draw them close any more. His heart grieved. Man was in sin and yet God loves man. And He taught man the blood covenant. He loves them so much even though they fell that before He sent them out of the Garden of Eden He took one of His animals, (remember all His animals could talk at that time) and He killed one of those animals. Think about that -God killed because of sin. And He took the skin of the animal while it was dripping with blood and He covered Adam and Eve as a way of saying that they can only come to Him through the blood covenant. Yet, man could not come through the blood covenant to the closeness that He had wanted. The blood of this animal was only a shadow of what was really necessary. It was just enough so that God could at least bless them. The heart of God does not desire to bless us only. The heart of God desires to take us into His bosom and embrace us. When God revealed Himself to Abraham, to Isaac, to Jacob, to Joseph, to Moses, and He brought them out of the land of Egypt, He bared His heart to them by saying, *"I want you to be a kingdom of priests. I want you to be able to come into the Holy of holies. I want every one of you to be able to approach Me."* All God wanted was for them to love Him, to obey Him, to do all that He wanted them to. That was what He expressed in Exodus 19 that He wants them to be special treasure so that He could bring them close to Him. And that He could draw close to them.

But we know what happened in that story in Exodus. God was revealing to Moses on Mount Sinai all the beautiful plans He had to teach His people and how to come to the Holy of holies. While God had such great plans for every tribe -from the tribe of Judah to the tribe of Benjamin -all the tribes except the tribe of Levites fell into sin. Once again, God's heart was grieved. He couldn't have all the twelve tribes. He could only have one tribe. Since the tribe of Levi didn't transgress and worship the golden calf, God made Aaron a priest and all the Levites to serve under him. Again you can see that God's perfect plan was set back a little bit by His people. He has to re-organize the whole system. Time passes and we enter into the New

Testament. God has a special plan for the church. Jesus said that He has redeemed the church and He wants the church to come close to Him, to draw near to Him, to discover the place.

ACTIVATE YOUR SPIRITUAL SENSES THROUGH IMPARTATION

This present physical world focuses on mental acquisition and outward results but in the spiritual world they focus on the inner cause and source of the results. For it is a spiritual law that when an individual is inwardly transformed by receiving the impartation of God's life and light, the results would be automatically secured. Thus the spiritual world focuses on individuals absorbing the truth of God into their very substance and not just mental knowledge of a truth. The reason why it takes time for the outward manifestation of an inward reception and impartation is because the inward transformation is incomplete. Even though sometimes individuals think (mentally), and convince themselves that they already have it, in their true selves they haven't got it fully yet until it is an automatic, subconscious and habitual part of their daily lives. When one first receives a truth or a new impartation and understanding of life, they do not have it until it is within their subconscious, in their actions and is a part of their daily habit of life.

It is not just when we think and believe about something that we have it, but it is when we are practising the truth that we truly have it. It is when we are not thinking about it and yet it forms part of our substance of life-consciousness that we truly have absorbed it into us. In the spirit world all truth is simultaneously a substance of life and not just mere knowledge (John 14:6). Whoever abides in Him does not sin; whoever sins has neither seen Him nor known Him (1 John 3:6). Whoever is born of God does not sin, for His seed remains (abides as a part of the life-substance and principle of the individual and not mere mental knowledge) in him; and he cannot sin because he has been born of God (1 John 3:9). Don't just believe in love; practice love until it is a part of your life, until your very nature becomes the love nature of God.

Another thing I've learned about God's power and gifts is that although they flow out of His grace and are activated by faith, personal preparation in the areas of character, integrity and holiness enable us to sustain a constant flow of His power through our lives. However, we must always remember that He is the source, and it is by His grace that we are qualified to be partakers of His heavenly glory. It has nothing to do with our efforts or works. If it did, we could take some of the credit. Since it doesn't, God gets all the glory. He wants to develop our character so we will be grounded in Christ and will properly steward the power He pours through us. But you don't have to wait until you are a mature Christian to allow God to use you. You can begin to operate in the Spirit the moment Christ enters your heart. On the following pages are eight secrets to operating in the creative, miracle-power of God. This is by no means a simple three-step process, but I do believe if you apply these principles to your life, you'll see signs and wonders released through you on a daily basis.

1. Cultivate God's presence in your life. The more you can cultivate an environment that's conducive to the Holy Spirit, the more of God's presence you will carry. The more of His presence you carry, the more power you will have. You cultivate this environment by spending time doing whatever it takes to have the person and presence of the Holy Spirit hanging out with you. Quickly confess and repent of the slightest leaning toward sin or spiritual darkness. Pray in tongues often. Cover yourself under the blood of Jesus. Meditate in the Word. Express worship to the Lord through song and prayer. Constantly invite the Holy Spirit to be with you in evident ways as often as possible. Avoid anything that would grieve Him. You'll find that as your life is filled with the atmosphere of the Holy Spirit, miracles, signs and wonders will be a natural overflow.

2. Cultivate God's faith in your heart. True supernatural faith flows out of the spirit and affects the mind—not the other way around. Faith defies logic and natural reality for a higher spiritual reality. It causes natural things to line up with what God has already accomplished spiritually. We must live in the Word and constantly renew our minds. Faith is born from revelation in the heart. When truth is revealed to your mind and heart by the Holy Spirit through the Word, faith comes alive on the inside of you. John 8:32 says, "And you shall know the truth, and the truth shall make you free" (NKJV). Soak your mind and spirit in God's Word by constantly setting your thoughts on it, and the revelation of truth will produce supernatural faith in your heart. Heart-faith produced by the revelation of truth is the ultimate key to operating in God's power, and the Bible tells us it comes from Jesus: "Looking away [from all that will distract] to Jesus, Who is the Leader and the Source of our faith [giving the first incentive for our belief] and is also its Finisher [bringing it to maturity and perfection]" (Heb. 12:2, The Amplified Bible).

3. Add action to your faith. The power anointing comes for a reason and has an intended purpose. Isaiah 61:1 says, "The Spirit of the Lord God is upon Me, because the Lord has anointed Me to preach good tidings to the poor; He has sent Me to heal the broken-hearted, to proclaim liberty to the captives, and the opening of the prison to those who are bound" (NKJV). The power anointing for healing and miracles will manifest only if you're praying for sick people to be healed. You must be intentional in looking for opportunities in which this anointing will be needed. The Bible tells us, "Faith without works is dead" (James 2:20). The power anointing is given to help other people in a supernatural way and in the process reveal God's heart and nature to them. Don't allow yourself to get discouraged. Stay focused and tenacious. No matter what you see, set your vision higher, know and understand God's will and truth, and allow His faith to move you to action. This action will release the power of God and produce the miraculous.

4. Passionately pursue spiritual gifts. First Corinthians 14:1 tells us to earnestly desire spiritual gifts. I often lay my hands on my own belly during times of prayer and ask the Holy Spirit to stir up and manifest the gifts of the Spirit that are within me. Spiritual gifts of healing, working of miracles, words of knowledge and faith are all invaluable manifestations for the ministry of the miraculous. As you ask God to stir them up, He will. The Greek word for the gifts of the Spirit is charisma, which Strong's Concordance defines as "gifts of grace; a favour which one receives without any merit of his own." You can't work for or earn them. They are given freely by the Holy Spirit just as salvation is. You can have all of them—and the more you pursue them, the more you will have!

5. Practice prayer and fasting. Matthew 17:14-21 gives an account of the healing of an epileptic boy. The disciples couldn't cure him, but Jesus did. When Jesus was asked why the disciples had no success, He said it was because of their unbelief. It wasn't a question of God's will. Nor did Jesus focus on the boy's faith. It was the level of faith in the disciples' hearts. Yet He also pointed out that "this kind does not go out except by prayer and fasting" (v. 21). Prayer and fasting help to release God's faith within us. It's the faith that produces the miracle, not the fasting. Fasting and prayer in this instance serve as the passageway into the fullness of faith that exists in God's heart. Again, it isn't by our works, but by His faith and grace extended toward us.

6. Learn to hear God's voice. To operate in the supernatural we must develop a keen sensitivity to the person of the Holy Spirit. God doesn't work the same way all the time, and we need to hear His direction for each situation. Consider Jesus. He saw signs and wonders on a consistent basis in His daily life, but He never prayed the same way twice. Sometimes He laid hands on people; sometimes He instructed them to take a specific action; sometimes He did unusual things Himself such as spit in mud and put it into a person's eyes. He was unconventional but completely Spirit-led. The key is He did only what He saw His Father doing (see John 5:19). His ability to hear and see the actions of His heavenly Father came out of the time He spent with Him in prayer and communion. If you want to sensitize your spiritual eyes and ears, you must put yourself in a place where you can see and hear God. This will often require you to pull away into a "deserted place" so you can place all your heart and mind on Him. When you exercise your spiritual senses by learning to listen and not just talk, you will be led by the Spirit to see wonderful manifestations of His power.

7. Pursue the anointing. A major key for me in being brought to a new level of God's power was learning that it was OK to go where God was moving. Some people think: If God wants to give me something, He can come right here into my room. I don't need to go anywhere. Of course God can meet us in our own rooms, and many times He does. However, that doesn't negate the fact that you can literally "catch" the anointing by putting yourself in a place where God is moving. Find people and ministries that are carrying God and get around them. We learn from one another and receive impartation of power through association. These corporate encounters with God do not replace your hidden devotion expressed in the place of private prayer. They simply add to and enhance your relationship with God. I've been blessed to have been able to associate with some of the most anointed people on the earth today. My fellowship with them has not only stirred my faith but also released a transference of wisdom, revelation and power into my own life and ministry. Anointed fellowship, whether from meeting with another person or from listening to anointed teaching CDs and videos, is crucial to cultivating the anointing in your life. Associate with God's power by hanging out where He is.

8. Be motivated by love. Love must be the foundation for everything you do. Without it, power can lead to pride and self-inflation. Love is the greatest manifestation of God's power. It was because of love that Jesus walked in total obedience. It was because of love that the power of sin and

The Realm Of The Spirit

Satan were defeated. Love is what motivates our faith (see Gal. 5:6). Love is what causes us to live in the Spirit. Love is the greatest virtue of all. Without faith you can't please God. But without love you can't know Him at all. Love filled with truth is the ultimate spiritual weapon against sin, temptation, offense, disunity, sickness, oppression and spiritual corruption, and death. Love conquers all. As you apply these principles to your life with God, expect to see His glorious power and anointing released in you and through you. There is someone out there who is waiting for a miracle. They need God's touch. Your life and obedience to God may be the missing ingredient!

THE AUTHOR'S PROFILE

Frequency Revelator is an apostle, called by God through His grace to minister the Gospel of the Lord Jesus Christ to all the nations of the world. He is a television minister, lecturer and gifted author, whose writings are Holy Ghost breathings that unveil consistent streams of fresh revelations straight from the Throne Room of Heaven. He is the president, founder and vision bearer of Frequency Revelator Ministries (FRM), a worldwide multiracial ministry that encompasses a myriad of movements with divine visions such as Resurrection Embassy (*The Global Church*), Christ Resurrection Movement (CRM) (*a Global movement for raising the dead*), the Global Apostolic & Prophetic Network (GAP) (a *Network of apostles, prophets and fivefold ministers across the globe*), Revival For Southern Africa (REFOSA) (*a Regional power-packed vision for Southern Africa*) and the Global Destiny Publishing House (GDP) (*the Ministry's publishing company*). The primary vision of this global ministry is to propagate the resurrection power of Christ from the Throne Room of Heaven to the extreme ends of the world and to launch the world into the greater depths of the miraculous. It is for this reason that Frequency Revelator Ministries (FRM) drives divergent apostolic and prophetic ministry visions and spiritual programmes such as the Global School of Resurrection (GSR), Global Resurrection Centre (GRC), the Global Healing Centre (GHC), Global School of Miracles, Signs and Wonders (SMSW), Global School of Kingdom Millionaires (SKM), Global Campus Ministry as well as Resurrection Conferences, Seminars and Training Centers. To fulfil its global mandate of soul winning, the ministry spearheads the Heavens' Broadcasting Commission (HBC) on television, a strategic ministerial initiative that broadcasts ministry programmes via the Dead Raising Channel *(a.k.a Resurrection TV)* and other Christian Television networks around the world.

Presiding over a global network of apostolic and prophetic visions, Apostle Frequency Revelator considers universities, colleges, high schools and other centers of learning as critical in fulfilling God's purpose and reaching the world for Christ, especially in this end-time season. As a Signs and Wonders Movement, the ministry hosts training sessions at the Global School of Resurrection (GSR) which includes but not limited to,

The Realm Of The Spirit

impartation and activation of the gifts of the Spirit, prophetic declaration and ministration, invocations of open visions, angelic encounters and Throne Room visitations, revelation teachings, coaching and mentorship as well as Holy Ghost ministerial training sessions on how to practically raise the dead. This global ministry is therefore characterized by a deep revelation of God's word accompanied by a practical demonstration of God's power through miracles, signs and wonders manifested in raising cripples from wheel chairs, opening the eyes of the blind, unlocking the speech of the dumb, blasting off the ears of the deaf and raising the dead, as a manifestation of the finished works of the cross by the Lord Jesus Christ. The ministry is also punctuated with a plethora of manifestations of the wealth of Heaven through miracle money, coupled with the golden rain of gold dust, silver stones, supernatural oil and a torrent of creative miracles such as the development of the original blue print of body parts on bodily territories where they previously did not exist, germination of hair on bald heads, weight loss and gain, as well as instantaneous healings from HIV/AIDS, cancer, diabetes and every manner of sickness and disease which doctors have declared as incurable.

The author has written a collection of 21 anointed books, which include *The Realm of Power to Raise the Dead, How to become a Kingdom Millionaire, Deeper Revelations of The Anointing, Practical Demonstrations of The Anointing, How to Operate in the Realm of the Miraculous, The Realm of Glory, Unveiling the Mystery of Miracle Money, New Revelations of Faith, A Divine Revelation of the Supernatural Realm, The Prophetic Move of the Holy Spirit in the Contemporary Global Arena, The Ministry of Angels in the World Today, Kingdom Spiritual Laws and Principles, Divine Rights and Privileges of a Believer, Keys to Unlocking the Supernatural, The Prophetic Dimension, The Dynamics of God's Word, The Practice of God's Presence, Times of Refreshing and Restoration, The Power of Praying in the Throne Room, The End Time Revelations of Jesus Christ and Rain of Revelations,* which is a daily devotional concordance comprising a yearly record of 365 fresh revelations straight from the Throne Room of God.

Apostle Frequency Revelator resides in South Africa and he is a graduate of Fort Hare University, where his ministry took off. However, as a global minister, his ministry incorporates prophecy, deliverance and miracle healing crusades in the United Kingdom (UK), Southern Africa, India, Australia, USA, Canada and a dense network of ministry visions that covers the rest of the world. As a custodian of God's resurrection power, the apostle has been given a divine mandate from Heaven to raise a new breed of

Frequency Revelator

Apostles, Prophets, Pastors, Evangelists, Teachers, Kingdom Millionaires and Miracle Workers *(Dead raisers)* who shall propagate the world with the gospel of the Lord Jesus Christ and practically demonstrate His resurrection power through miracles, signs and wonders manifested in raising people from the dead, thereby launching the world in to the greater depths of the miraculous. To that effect, a conducive platform is therefore enacted for global impartation, mentorship, training and equipping ministers of the gospel for the work of ministry. Notable is the realization that the ministry ushers a new wave of signs and wonders that catapults the Body of Christ into higher realms of glory in which raising the dead is a common occurrence and demonstrating the viscosity of the glory of God in a visible and tangible manner is the order of the day. Having been mightily used by God to raise the dead, in this book, Apostle Frequency Revelator presents a practical model of how one can tap into the realm of God's resurrection power to raise the dead, impact the nations of the world and usher an unprecedented avalanche of billions of souls into the Kingdom, Glory to Jesus! May His Name be gloried, praised and honored forever more!

AUTHOR'S CONTACT INFORMATION

To know more about the ministry of Apostle Frequency Revelator, his publications, revelation teachings, global seminars, ministry schools, ministry products and Global missions, contact:

Apostle Frequency Revelator

@ Resurrection Embassy

(The Global Church)

Powered by Christ Resurrection Movement (CRM)

(Contact us in South Africa, United Kingdom, USA, Germany, Canada, Australia, India, Holland & Other nations of the world).

As a Global Vision, The Ministry of Apostle Frequency Revelator is present in all the continents of the World. You may contact us from any part of the world so that we can refer you to the Resident Ministry Pastors and Associates in respective nations.

Our offices and those of the ministry's publishing company (Global Destiny Publishing House (GDP House), are ready to dispatch any books requested from any part of the world.

Email:

frequency.revelator@gmail.com

Cell phone:

+27622436745

+27797921646/ +27785416006

Website:

www.globaldestinypublishers.co.za

Frequency Revelator

Social Media Contacts:

The Author is also accessible on Social media via Facebook, twitter, instagram, YouTube, and other latest forms of social networks, as Apostle Frequency Revelator. For direct communication with the Apostle, you may invite him on Facebook and read his daily posts. You may also watch Apostle Frequency Revelator on the Dead Raising Channel a.k.a Resurrection TV and other Christian Television channels in your area.

Christian products:

You may also purchase DVDs, CDs, and MP3s and possibly order all of the 21 anointed books published by Apostle Frequency Revelator, either as hard cover books or e-books. E-books are available on amazon.com, Baines & Nobles, create space, Kalahari.net and other e-book sites. You may also buy them directly from the author@ www.gdphouse.co.za. You may also request a collection of all powerful, revelation teachings by Apostle Frequency Revelator and we will promptly deliver them to you.

Ministry Networks & Partnerships:

If you want to partner with Apostle Frequency Revelator in executing this Global vision, partnership is available through divergent apostolic and prophetic ministry visions and spiritual programmes such as the Global School of Resurrection (GSR), Christ Resurrection Movement (CRM), Resurrection TV (a.k.a The Dead Raising Channel), the Global Apostolic & Prophetic Network (GAP), Global Resurrection Centre (GRC), the Global Healing Centre (GHC), Global School of Miracles, Signs and Wonders (SMSW), School of Kingdom Millionaires (SKM), Global Campus Ministry and other avenues. By partnering with Apostle Frequency Revelator, you are in a way joining hands with God's vision and thus setting yourself up for a life of increase, acceleration and superabundance.

ABOUT THE AUTHOR GLOBAL MISSIONS, PARTNERSHIPS & COLLABORATIONS:

If it happens that you are catapulted into a higher realm of prophetic accuracy following the reading of this book, please share your testimony with Apostle Frequency Revelator at the contacts above, so that you can strengthen other believers' faith in God all around the world. Your testimony will also be included in the next edition of this book.

If you want to invite Apostle Frequency Revelator to your church, city or community to come and spearhead Resurrection Seminars, Conferences, Dead Raising Training Sessions or conduct a Global School of Resurrection (GSR), whether in (Europe, Australia, Canada, USA, South America, Asia or Africa), you are welcome to do so.

If you want to start a Resurrection Centre or establish the Global School of Resurrection (GSR) in your church, city or community under this movement, you are also welcome to do so. We will be more than willing to send Copies of this book to whichever continent you live.

If you want your church or ministry to be part of the Christ Resurrection Movement (CRM) and join the bandwagon of raising the dead all around the world, you are welcome to be part of this Heaven-ordained commission.

If you want more copies of this book so that you can use them in your church for seminars, teachings, conferences, cell groups and global distribution, please don't hesitate to contact Apostle Frequency Revelator so that he can send the copies to whichever continent you are. Upon completion of this book, you may also visit www.amazon.com and under the "Book Review Section," write a brief review, commenting on how this book has impacted your life. This is meant to encourage readership by other believers all around the world.

Frequency Revelator

If you want to donate or give freely to advance this global vision, you may also do so via our ministry website (www.globaldestinypublishers.com) or contact us at the details provided above. If you need a spiritual covering, impartation or mentorship for your Church or ministry as led by the Holy Spirit, you are welcome to contact us and join the league of dead-raising pastors that we are already mentoring in all continents of the world.

If you have a burning message that you would like to share with the whole world and you would want Apostle Frequency Revelator to help you turn your divine ideas and revelations into script and publish your first book, don't hesitate to contact us and submit a draft of your manuscript at the Global Destiny Publishing House (www.globaldestinypublishers.com). We will thoroughly polish your script and turn it into an amazing book filled with Throne Room revelations that will impact millions across the globe, glory to Jesus!

The Lord Jesus Christ is coming back soon!

Made in the USA
Middletown, DE
03 June 2024